Flash™ 5 For Dummies®

Cheat Sheet

Drawing Toolbox

Arrow tool (for selection) — Subselection tool
Line tool — Lasso tool (for selection)
Pen tool — Text tool
Oval tool — Rectangle tool
Pencil tool — Brush tool
Ink Bottle tool (for strokes) — Paint Bucket tool (for fills)
Eye Dropper tool (copies strokes & fills) — Eraser tool

Pan — Zoom

— Stroke Color
Fill Color — Swap Stroke & Fill Colors
Default Stroke & Fill — No Color

Snap (to objects) modifier
Smooth modifier — Straighten modifier
Rotate modifier — Scale modifier

Common Keyboard Shortcuts

File Menu Commands

Command	Windows	Mac
New	Ctrl+N	⌘+N
Open	Ctrl+O	⌘+O
Open as Library	Ctrl+Shift+O	⌘+Shift+O
Close	Ctrl+W	⌘+W
Save	Ctrl+S	⌘+S
Import	Ctrl+R	⌘+R
Quit	Ctrl+Q	⌘+Q

Edit Menu Commands

Command	Windows	Mac
Undo	Ctrl+Z	⌘+Z
Redo	Ctrl+Y	⌘+Y
Cut	Ctrl+X	⌘+X
Copy	Ctrl+C	⌘+C
Paste	Ctrl+V	⌘+V
Paste in Place	Ctrl+Shift+V	⌘+Shift+V
Clear	Delete/Backspace	Delete/Clear
Duplicate	Ctrl+D	⌘+D
Select All	Ctrl+A	⌘+A
Deselect All	Ctrl+Shift+A	⌘+Shift+A
Copy Frames	Ctrl+Alt+C	⌘+Option+C
Paste Frames	Ctrl+Alt+V	⌘+Option+V

For Dummies®: Bestselling Book Series for Beginners

Flash™ 5 For Dummies®

Cheat Sheet

Common Keyboard Shortcuts

(Continued)

View Menu Commands

Command	Windows	Mac
Timeline	Ctrl+Alt+T	⌘+Option+T
Snap	Ctrl+Shift+/	⌘+Shift+/
Show Shape	Ctrl+Alt+H	⌘+Option+H Hints
Hide Panels	Tab	Tab

Modify Menu Commands

Command	Windows	Mac
Instance	Ctrl+I	⌘+I
Frame	Ctrl+F	⌘+F
Movie	Ctrl+M	⌘+M
Transform⇨ Add Shape Hint	Ctrl+Shift+H	⌘+Shift+H
Group	Ctrl+G	⌘+G
Ungroup	Ctrl+Shift+G	⌘+Shift+G
Break Apart	Ctrl+B	⌘+B

Control Menu Commands

Command	Windows	Mac
Play	Enter	Return
Rewind	Ctrl+Alt+R	⌘+Option+R
Step Forward	. (period)	. (period)
Step Backward	, (comma)	, (comma)
Test Movie	Ctrl+Enter	⌘+Return
Enable Simple Buttons	Ctrl+Alt+B	⌘+Option+B

Insert Menu Commands

Command	Windows	Mac
Convert to Symbol	F8	F8
New Symbol	Ctrl+F8	⌘+F8
Frame	F5	F5
Remove Frames	Shift+F5	Shift+F5
Keyframe	F6	F6
Blank Keyframe	F7	F7
Clear Keyframe	Shift+F6	Shift+F6

Window Menu Commands

Command	Windows	Mac
Panels⇨Info	Ctrl+Alt+I	⌘+Option+I
Panels⇨Align	Ctrl+K	⌘+K
Panels⇨ Character	Ctrl+T	⌘+T
Panels⇨ Paragraph	Ctrl+Shift+T	⌘+Shift+T
Panels⇨ Instance	Ctrl+I	⌘+I
Panels⇨Frame	Ctrl+F	⌘+F
Actions	Ctrl+Alt+A	⌘+Option+A
Movie Explorer	Ctrl+Alt+M	⌘+Option+M

IDG BOOKS WORLDWIDE®

For Dummies®: Bestselling Book Series for Beginners

TM

...For Dummies

References for the Rest of Us! ®

BESTSELLING BOOK SERIES

Are you intimidated and confused by computers? Do you find that traditional manuals are overloaded with technical details you'll never use? Do your friends and family always call you to fix simple problems on their PCs? Then the *...For Dummies*® computer book series from IDG Books Worldwide is for you.

...For Dummies books are written for those frustrated computer users who know they aren't really dumb but find that PC hardware, software, and indeed the unique vocabulary of computing make them feel helpless. *...For Dummies* books use a lighthearted approach, a down-to-earth style, and even cartoons and humorous icons to dispel computer novices' fears and build their confidence. Lighthearted but not lightweight, these books are a perfect survival guide for anyone forced to use a computer.

"I like my copy so much I told friends; now they bought copies."

— Irene C., Orwell, Ohio

"Quick, concise, nontechnical, and humorous."

— Jay A., Elburn, Illinois

"Thanks, I needed this book. Now I can sleep at night."

— Robin F., British Columbia, Canada

Already, millions of satisfied readers agree. They have made *...For Dummies* books the #1 introductory level computer book series and have written asking for more. So, if you're looking for the most fun and easy way to learn about computers, look to *...For Dummies* books to give you a helping hand.

IDG BOOKS WORLDWIDE ®

Flash™ 5

FOR

DUMMIES®

Flash™ 5 FOR DUMMIES®

by Gurdy Leete
and Ellen Finkelstein

IDG Books Worldwide, Inc.
An International Data Group Company

Foster City, CA ◆ Chicago, IL ◆ Indianapolis, IN ◆ New York, NY

Flash™ 5 For Dummies®

Published by
IDG Books Worldwide, Inc.
An International Data Group Company
919 E. Hillsdale Blvd.
Suite 300
Foster City, CA 94404
www.idgbooks.com (IDG Books Worldwide Web Site)
www.dummies.com (Dummies Press Web Site)

Library of Congress Control Number: 00-101541

ISBN: 0-7645-0736-2

Printed in the United States of America

10 9 8 7 6 5 4 3

1O/RX/RR/QQ/IN

Distributed in the United States by IDG Books Worldwide, Inc.

Distributed by CDG Books Canada Inc. for Canada; by Transworld Publishers Limited in the United Kingdom; by IDG Norge Books for Norway; by IDG Sweden Books for Sweden; by IDG Books Australia Publishing Corporation Pty. Ltd. for Australia and New Zealand; by TransQuest Publishers Pte Ltd. for Singapore, Malaysia, Thailand, Indonesia, and Hong Kong; by Gotop Information Inc. for Taiwan; by ICG Muse, Inc. for Japan; by Intersoft for South Africa; by Eyrolles for France; by International Thomson Publishing for Germany, Austria and Switzerland; by Distribuidora Cuspide for Argentina; by LR International for Brazil; by Galileo Libros for Chile; by Ediciones ZETA S.C.R. Ltda. for Peru; by WS Computer Publishing Corporation, Inc., for the Philippines; by Contemporanea de Ediciones for Venezuela; by Express Computer Distributors for the Caribbean and West Indies; by Micronesia Media Distributor, Inc. for Micronesia; by Chips Computadoras S.A. de C.V. for Mexico; by Editorial Norma de Panama S.A. for Panama; by American Bookshops for Finland.

For general information on IDG Books Worldwide's books in the U.S., please call our Consumer Customer Service department at 800-762-2974. For reseller information, including discounts and premium sales, please call our Reseller Customer Service department at 800-434-3422.

For information on where to purchase IDG Books Worldwide's books outside the U.S., please contact our International Sales department at 317-572-3993 or fax 317-572-4002.

For consumer information on foreign language translations, please contact our Customer Service department at 1-800-434-3422, fax 317-572-4002, or e-mail rights@idgbooks.com.

For information on licensing foreign or domestic rights, please phone +1-650-653-7098.

For sales inquiries and special prices for bulk quantities, please contact our Order Services department at 800-434-3422 or write to the address above.

For information on using IDG Books Worldwide's books in the classroom or for ordering examination copies, please contact our Educational Sales department at 800-434-2086 or fax 317-572-4005.

For press review copies, author interviews, or other publicity information, please contact our Public Relations department at 650-653-7000 or fax 650-653-7500.

For authorization to photocopy items for corporate, personal, or educational use, please contact Copyright Clearance Center, 222 Rosewood Drive, Danvers, MA 01923, or fax 978-750-4470.

About the Authors

Gurdy Leete has been working as a computer animator, computer animation software engineer, and teacher of computer animation since 1981. He has been teaching Flash and other computer animation programs for seven years at Maharishi University of Management, where he is assistant professor of digital media. There he runs the coolest lab on campus, filled with Linux, SGI, and Mac G4 computers because he craves raw power and speed.

Ellen Finkelstein has written numerous best-selling computer books on AutoCAD, Word, and PowerPoint. She also provides training in these programs and others. The two editions of her *AutoCAD Bible* have sold over 40,000 copies. Her first book, *AutoCAD For Dummies Quick Reference,* is now in its third edition. She writes at home so she can take the bread out of the oven on time.

ABOUT IDG BOOKS WORLDWIDE

Welcome to the world of IDG Books Worldwide.

IDG Books Worldwide, Inc., is a subsidiary of International Data Group, the world's largest publisher of computer-related information and the leading global provider of information services on information technology. IDG was founded more than 30 years ago by Patrick J. McGovern and now employs more than 9,000 people worldwide. IDG publishes more than 290 computer publications in over 75 countries. More than 90 million people read one or more IDG publications each month.

Launched in 1990, IDG Books Worldwide is today the #1 publisher of best-selling computer books in the United States. We are proud to have received eight awards from the Computer Press Association in recognition of editorial excellence and three from Computer Currents' First Annual Readers' Choice Awards. Our best-selling *...For Dummies*® series has more than 50 million copies in print with translations in 31 languages. IDG Books Worldwide, through a joint venture with IDG's Hi-Tech Beijing, became the first U.S. publisher to publish a computer book in the People's Republic of China. In record time, IDG Books Worldwide has become the first choice for millions of readers around the world who want to learn how to better manage their businesses.

Our mission is simple: Every one of our books is designed to bring extra value and skill-building instructions to the reader. Our books are written by experts who understand and care about our readers. The knowledge base of our editorial staff comes from years of experience in publishing, education, and journalism — experience we use to produce books to carry us into the new millennium. In short, we care about books, so we attract the best people. We devote special attention to details such as audience, interior design, use of icons, and illustrations. And because we use an efficient process of authoring, editing, and desktop publishing our books electronically, we can spend more time ensuring superior content and less time on the technicalities of making books.

You can count on our commitment to deliver high-quality books at competitive prices on topics you want to read about. At IDG Books Worldwide, we continue in the IDG tradition of delivering quality for more than 30 years. You'll find no better book on a subject than one from IDG Books Worldwide.

John J. Kilcullen

John Kilcullen
Chairman and CEO
IDG Books Worldwide, Inc.

Eighth Annual
Computer Press
Awards ≥1992

Ninth Annual
Computer Press
Awards ≥1993

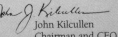

Tenth Annual
Computer Press
Awards ≥1994

Eleventh Annual
Computer Press
Awards ≥1995

IDG is the world's leading IT media, research and exposition company. Founded in 1964, IDG had 1997 revenues of $2.05 billion and has more than 9,000 employees worldwide. IDG offers the widest range of media options that reach IT buyers in 75 countries representing 95% of worldwide IT spending. IDG's diverse product and services portfolio spans six key areas including print publishing, online publishing, expositions and conferences, market research, education and training, and global marketing services. More than 90 million people read one or more of IDG's 290 magazines and newspapers, including IDG's leading global brands — Computerworld, PC World, Network World, Macworld and the Channel World family of publications. IDG Books Worldwide is one of the fastest-growing computer book publishers in the world, with more than 700 titles in 36 languages. The "...For Dummies®" series alone has more than 50 million copies in print. IDG offers online users the largest network of technology-specific Web sites around the world through IDG.net (http://www.idg.net), which comprises more than 225 targeted Web sites in 55 countries worldwide. International Data Corporation (IDC) is the world's largest provider of information technology data, analysis and consulting, with research centers in over 41 countries and more than 400 research analysts worldwide. IDG World Expo is a leading producer of more than 168 globally branded conferences and expositions in 35 countries including E3 (Electronic Entertainment Expo), Macworld Expo, ComNet, Windows World Expo, ICE (Internet Commerce Expo), Agenda, DEMO, and Spotlight. IDG's training subsidiary, ExecuTrain, is the world's largest computer training company, with more than 230 locations worldwide and 785 training courses. IDG Marketing Services helps industry-leading IT companies build international brand recognition by developing global integrated marketing programs via IDG's print, online and exposition products worldwide. Further information about the company can be found at www.idg.com.   1/26/00

Dedication

To MMY for explaining that life is meant to be lived in happiness and teaching us how to realize that reality in daily life.

Authors' Acknowledgments

A few words from Ellen:

This book was very much a group effort. First, I'd like to thank my coauthor, Gurdy Leete, without whom I could not have completed this book, or even thought of writing it. Gurdy was always a pleasure to work with, always in a good mood and helpful. He's a brilliant artist and something of a programmer, too, while I am neither. I've been quite impressed.

At IDG Books, I'd like to thank Mike Roney, our acquisitions editor, for trusting us with this book. Great kudos go to Jodi Jensen, our project editor. I don't know how she does it, but she kept together more details in a few months than I could handle in a few years. She was always helpful, supportive, and responsive. A treasure! In addition, a small army of very capable copy editors paid attention to every detail of the text; thanks to Christine Berman, Jeremy Zucker, and Nicole Laux.

Our great technical editor, Sam Lieb, carefully checked every statement on both the Mac *and* the PC. He brought to our attention details we had never thought of and taught us even more about Flash.

Personally, I'd like to thank my husband, Evan, and my kids, Yeshayah and Eliyah, who helped out and managed without me as I wrote every day, evening, and weekend for months. I love you all.

Thanks to Macromedia for creating Flash and supporting Flash authors. They were very helpful during the beta period while we were learning the new features of Flash 5, testing Flash, and writing — all at the same time.

Finally, I'd like to thank the Flash community — specifically all the Flash designers who contributed Flash movies to make this book and its CD-ROM more valuable. Most computer books use dummy files, and we made up a few of our own to illustrate certain points. But the real-world files we received for this book will help open up new vistas for our readers.

And now, a few comments from Gurdy:

I'd like to echo all of Ellen's words and thank her for being such a great collaborator. She has such a talent for explaining things with the simplicity, precision, and humor that is so characteristic of the deeper workings of the cosmos. I'd also like to thank my intrepid research assistants, Radim Schreiber of the Czech Republic, Burcu Cenberci of Turkey, and Praveen Mishra of Nepal, whose research activities on the Internet were so helpful in the writing of this book. Thanks to my omnitalented MA in Animation student, Mike Zak, for the wonderful collection of clip-art drawings he created for the CD-ROM. And thanks to my adorable wife, Mary, and my children, Porter and Jackie, for being so supportive during the many hours I spent working on this book.

Special Acknowledgments

The design of this book didn't allow for long acknowledgments in the text, so our publisher let us have this space instead to add some special acknowledgments to the people who kindly provided us with Flash movies for the CD-ROM. It's a great advantage to have professionally made Flash movies when you're starting out. You can pick up some great techniques and see the infinite possibilities. Here then, in alphabetical order, are our thanks to our contributors.

Leslie Allen-Kickham gave us a Flash Player file based on the Dennis Interactive Web site at www.dennisinteractive.com. Dennis Interactive is a leader in multimedia design and interactive applications. The company's products include Internet/intranet applications, CD-ROMs, DVDs, and interactive kiosks. Thanks also to **Jason Pearson** (Copy Writer and Creative Direction) and **Jason Crawford** (Art Director and Flash Animation). Look in the Ch06 folder for di.swf.

George Andres of Acro Media Inc., creators of the www.weldersmall.com Web site, gave us weldersmall.fla, which you can find in the Ch09 folder of the CD-ROM. Acro Media is "committed to pushing media development to the next level, incorporating the finest aspects of artistic creation and technology to revolutionize the expectations of an audience." Check out their site at www.acromediainc.com.

Stefano Gramantieri provided us with the Flash movie he created for Time Ltd. at www.timeonline.it. Time Ltd.'s products include Web design, multimedia, CD-ROMs, global communications, and direct marketing. Look in the Ch05 folder of the CD-ROM for time.fla. We used it as an example of great text animation.

Jay M. Johnson sent us his cool YE2k.fla for the CD-ROM. Look in the Ch10 folder of the CD-ROM and check it out for yourself. Jay is a video arts student at Maharishi University of Management.

Thanks to **Phil Marinucci**, Project Manager/Web Marketing Specialist & Webmaster, of Xerox.ca and **Julie Raymond,** Manager, Training and Web-Enabled Selling, of Xerox Canada for several Flash files from the Xerox Web site. They are responsible for the creation of the Virtual Demo prototype, Virtual Demo Project Management, and training and development for Xerox Corporation Worldwide. Online, look for http://download.xerox.com/downloads/demos/657L.swf. You can find two movies, Xerox 657e.fla and dc12_e_2.fla in the Ch03 folder of the CD-ROM.

Stephan Oppliger provided us with a Flash movie, `invent.fla`, based on the site at `www.omm.ch`. You can find it in the Ch07 folder of the CD-ROM. OMM Oppliger Multimedia is a professional Web design company in Bern, Switzerland. You can contact them at `mail@omm.ch`. Stephan offers the following tip for creating symbols: "Try to edit the single symbols making up animation sequences — and look at the results. Many of the effects you see in this sample were originally coincidental. Just keep experimenting a lot and dive into the many possibilities. It's how a child plays: take a toy and try different versions of the same game. Besides, it's fun and you learn a lot!"

Jiri Rydl, PR manager of SorcererWare Ltd. sent us the Flash movie, `showreel.fla`. To see the full show, go to `www.sorcererware.com`. SorcererWare "builds complete solutions for building and maintaining an online business from defining the strategy to application development."

Jesse Spaulding created `picturetour.fla` for part of The Raj's site at `www.theraj.com`. Look in the Ch09 folder of the CD-ROM for this movie, a nice example of a Flash movie divided into scenes. Thanks to Jesse and **Lindsay Oliver** of The Raj for this Flash movie.

Craig Swann of Crash!Media contributed `draganddrop_ex.fla` for the Ch14 folder of the CD-ROM. This movie is a great example of using drag and drop along with complex parameters. Crash!Media, at `www.crashmedia.com`, helps clients define Internet strategies, architecture, and design, and also develops and implements applicable solutions.

Jennie Sweo is a fine artist who uses Flash for her Web site as well as for Director presentations. She does freelance graphics and teaches computer graphics at the University of Maryland, University College. Check out her Web site at `http://sweo.tripod.com`. You can find her movie, `opening movie.fla`, in the Ch03 and Ch09 folders of the CD-ROM.

Luke Turner gave us part of the opening scene for thevoid's Web site, which is at `www.thevoid.co.uk`. Luke says, "The Void's philosophy has always been that it is the ideas behind the animation, rather than use of 'flashy' effects, that count the most toward making the biggest impression on the viewer. Indeed, content without clutter as we like to feel. The 'paper sucks, get connected' campaign has perhaps been our most effective to date, partly because of the slick, fast-paced action, but primarily because it makes a bold, witty, and memorable statement. This, we believe, is the secret to effective high-impact animation. People often forget that Flash is simply the tool with which to put their concepts into practice — the new medium. A comprehensive knowledge and understanding of the software is a definite advantage, but it is vital to remember that Flash for Flash's sake makes bad design." You can find this Flash movie, `thevoid.fla`, in the Ch09 folder of the CD-ROM.

Jeremy Wachtel, Vice President of Project Management at Macquarium Intelligent Communications, sent us some beautiful files from the Macquarium site at www.macquarium.com. You can find these files on the CD-ROM in the Ch08 folder (nav_button.fla) and the Ch10 folder (bounce.fla). "Macquarium designs Web sites that push Web technology to its limits."

Dan Zajic contributed a Flash movie he created for the Maharishi University of Management's Youth Evolution 2000 conference in May 2000. Dan is a computer science and math major at Maharishi University of Management, exploring Web design as a hobby. We think he has a possible career in the field. You can find flashsite_big.fla in the Ch09 folder of the CD-ROM.

Publisher's Acknowledgments

We're proud of this book; please send us your comments through our IDG Books Worldwide Online Registration Form located at www.dummies.com.

Some of the people who helped bring this book to market include the following:

Acquisitions, Editorial, and Media Development

Senior Project Editor: Jodi Jensen

Senior Acquisitions Editor: Michael L. Roney

Copy Editors: Christine Berman, Nicole A. Laux, Jeremy Zucker

Proof Editors: Teresa Artman, Sarah Shupert

Technical Editor: Sam Lieb

Media Development Specialist: Angela Denny

Media Development Coordinator: Marisa E. Pearman

Media Development Supervisor: Richard Graves

Senior Permissions Editor: Carmen Krikorian

Editorial Manager: Kyle Looper

Editorial Assistant: Jean Rogers

Production

Project Coordinator: Maridee Ennis

Layout and Graphics: Amy Adrian, LeAndra Johnson, Jill Piscitelli, Heather Pope, Jacque Schneider, Rashell Smith, Brian Torwelle, Jeremey Unger

Proofreaders: John Bitter, Joel K. Draper, Andy Hollandbeck

Indexer: Sharon Hilgenberg

General and Administrative

IDG Books Worldwide, Inc.: John Kilcullen, CEO; Bill Barry, President and COO; John Ball, Executive VP, Operations & Administration; John Harris, CFO

IDG Books Technology Publishing Group: Richard Swadley, Senior Vice President and Publisher; Mary Bednarek, Vice President and Publisher; Walter R. Bruce III, Vice President and Publisher; Joseph Wikert, Vice President and Publisher; Mary C. Corder, Editorial Director; Andy Cummings, Publishing Director, General User Group; Barry Pruett, Publishing Director

IDG Books Manufacturing: Ivor Parker, Vice President, Manufacturing

IDG Books Marketing: John Helmus, Assistant Vice President, Director of Marketing

IDG Books Online Management: Brenda McLaughlin, Executive Vice President, Chief Internet Officer; Gary Millrood, Executive Vice President of Business Development, Sales and Marketing

IDG Books Packaging: Marc J. Mikulich, Vice President, Brand Strategy and Research

IDG Books Production for Branded Press: Debbie Stailey, Production Director

IDG Books Sales: Roland Elgey, Senior Vice President, Sales and Marketing; Michael Violano, Vice President, International Sales and Sub Rights

◆

The publisher would like to give special thanks to Patrick J. McGovern, without whom this book would not have been possible.

◆

Contents at a Glance

Cartoons at a Glance

By Rich Tennant

"Well, it's not quite done. I've animated the gurgling spit sink and the rotating Novocaine earrings, but I still have to add the high-speed whining drill audio track."

page 279

"I can't really explain it, but everytime I animate someone swinging a golf club, a little divot of code comes up missing on the home page."

page 211

"Is this really the best use of Flash 5 animation on our e-commerce Web site? A bad wheel on the shopping cart icon that squeaks, wobbles, and pulls to the left?"

page 43

"See? I created a little felon figure that runs around our Web site hiding behind banner ads. On the last page, our logo puts him in a nonlethal choke hold and brings him back to the home page."

page 9

"Look into my Web site, Ms. Carruthers. Look deep into its rotating, nicely animated spiral, spinning, spinning, pulling you in, deeper... deeper..."

page 125

"Evidently he died of natural causes following a marathon session animating everything on his personal Web site. And no, Morganstern - the irony isn't lost on me."

page 155

"Well shoot - I know the animation's moving a might too fast, but dang if I can find a 'mosey' function anywhere in the toolbox!"

page 313

Fax: 978-546-7747
E-mail: richtennant@the5thwave.com
World Wide Web: www.the5thwave.com

Table of Contents

Introduction

. . . .

*W*elcome to *Flash 5 For Dummies*, your friendly Web animation companion. In this book, we explain in plain English how to make the most of Flash to create stunning Web site animations. *Flash 5 For Dummies* aims to give you all the information you need to start using Flash right away — with no hassle.

About This Book

As if you hadn't guessed, *Flash 5 For Dummies* covers Macromedia's powerful animation product, Flash 5. Flash 5 is Macromedia's latest version of the popular software used on some of the coolest Web sites on the Internet. We comprehensively explain Flash's features, including

- ✔ Working with the Flash screen, toolbars, and menus
- ✔ Understanding what Flash can do
- ✔ Creating graphics and text in Flash
- ✔ Using layers to organize your animation
- ✔ Creating symbols — objects that you save for repeated use
- ✔ Creating Web page buttons
- ✔ Animating your graphics (the key to Flash)
- ✔ Creating interactive Web sites
- ✔ Adding sound
- ✔ Publishing your Flash movies to your Web site

The material in this book gives you the tools you need to create Web site animation yourself. It's lots of fun, so read on.

How to Use This Book

You don't have to read this book from cover to cover. *Flash 5 For Dummies* provides just the information you need, when you need it. If you've never used Flash before, start with the first three chapters. Then play around with graphics until you create what you need for your Web site. You may want to check out Chapter 6 on layers to help you organize it all. Then feel free to jump right to Chapter 9 on animation to create your first real Flash movie. Chapter 13 tells you how to get your movie on your Web site. Then fire up your browser, sit back, and marvel.

Of course, you'll want to refer to other chapters as you need them so that you can create text and buttons, add sound, and create an interactive Web site. Chapter 12 provides some ideas for putting all of the Flash features together for your best Web site ever.

If you're already using Flash but need some assistance, you can probably skip Chapter 1 and skim Chapter 2. Then refer to the chapters that provide the information you need in the nick of time.

Keep *Flash 5 For Dummies* by your computer as you work. You'll find it to be a loyal helper.

Foolish Assumptions

We assume that you're not already a master Flash developer. If you want to use Flash to create high-quality Web sites and you're not an expert animator already, you'll find this book to be a great reference. *Flash 5 For Dummies* is ideal for beginners who are just starting to use Flash or for current Flash users who want to further hone their skills.

Because Flash is generally added to Web sites, we also assume that you know some of the basics of Web site creation. You should know what HTML is and understand the process of creating and structuring HTML pages as well as uploading them to a Web site.

If you need some help on the topic of Web sites, you may want to refer to *Building a Web Site For Dummies* by David and Rhonda Crowder, also published by IDG Books Worldwide, Inc.

Conventions Used in This Book

Sometimes it helps to know why some text is bold and other is italic, so you can figure out what we're talking about. A typographic convention is not a convention of typographers meeting to discuss the latest typography techniques.

New terms are in *italics* to let you know that they're new. In the unusual situation where we suggest that you type something, what you are to type is shown in **bold.** Messages and other text that come from Flash are in a special typeface, like this. Programming code, which you may see very occasionally, is also shown in the same way.

When we say something like "Choose File⇨Save As," it means to click the File menu at the top of your screen and then choose Save As from the menu that opens. To distinguish between choosing a menu item or toolbar button from choosing an object, we always say, "Select the circle" or something similar, to refer to the object. So you *choose* menu items or toolbar buttons but *select* objects on your screen. When we want you to use a toolbar or toolbox button (or tool), we tell you to click it. So now you know the difference between choose, select, and click.

How This Book Is Organized

We've tried to organize *Flash 5 For Dummies* logically. We start by presenting an overview of the Flash universe and then continue in the general order you would use to create a Flash animation. More basic material is at the beginning of the book, while more advanced material (but not too advanced!) comes later on. You may never use all the material in this book for one Flash movie.

To be more specific, this book is divided into seven parts (to represent the seven states of consciousness — okay, we don't have to get too cosmic here). Each part contains two or more chapters that relate to that part. Each chapter thoroughly covers one topic so that you don't have to go searching all over creation to get the information you need.

Part I: A Blast of Flash

Part I contains important introductory information about Flash. In Chapter 1, we tell you what Flash is all about, show you what the Flash screen looks like, and explain how to get help when you need it most. You can also find instructions for starting Flash, starting a new movie, and opening an existing movie. We end Chapter 1 with a few steps to guide you in creating a short Flash movie so that you can get a feel for the entire program and have some fun at the same time.

Chapter 2 explains in more detail the steps for creating a Flash movie. Here you get a good idea of what Flash can accomplish. We also explain some of the basic concepts that all Flashers need to know. Hopefully, this chapter will start your creative juices flowing and give you some ideas for your own movies.

Part II: 1000 Pictures and 1000 Words

Part II explains all the tools available for creating graphics in Flash. Chapter 3 explains the unique drawing tools included in Flash. And you'll find that the Flash graphics have some unusual characteristics but offer some great opportunities. Of course, we also explain how to import graphics if you don't feel like creating your own. Chapter 4 shows you how to edit and manipulate graphic objects, and Chapter 5 is all about creating text as graphic objects.

Chapter 6 explains layers, which help you organize your graphics so that they don't interfere with each other. Layers are an important feature of any good animation, so don't skip over this chapter.

Part III: Getting Symbolic

Symbols are graphic objects that you save to use again and again. Any time you may want to place an object on a Web page more than once, you can save it as a symbol. By using symbols, you can also group many individual objects together, making them useful when you want to manipulate, edit, or animate them all at once. Chapter 7 explains all about creating and editing symbols.

Chapter 8 explains how to create Web page buttons — not the kind you sew, but the kind you click with your mouse. Buttons are a kind of symbol, but they execute an action when clicked. Flash can create cool buttons that *morph,* or otherwise change, when you use them.

Part IV: Total Flash-O-Rama

Part IV explains how to animate your graphics into movies and how to create Web sites that react to users' actions. Here you get to put all your graphics together and make them move.

Chapter 9 covers animation in detail — from frame-by-frame animation to *tweening,* where Flash calculates the animation between your first and last frames. You can tween movement to make your objects move and also to make your objects morph into new shapes. Flash can also tween color and transparency for a full range of exciting options.

Chapter 10 shows you how to create Web sites that react to your viewers. For example, if your viewer clicks a certain button, Flash can jump to a different part of a movie, stop all sounds, or go to a different Web page entirely. To create interactivity, you use *ActionScript,* the JavaScript-like programming language available in Flash. But don't worry, you don't have to write code from scratch. We tell you how to put ActionScript to work — even if you're a complete programming newbie.

Chapter 11 is about adding sound and music to your Flash movies. Sound and music add an element of excitement to a Web site, and you can add sound to both animated movies and to buttons.

Part V: The Movie and the Web

This part helps you put all your animated graphics and cool buttons together and publish your work on the Web. Chapter 12 outlines the various techniques you can use to create a great Web site using only Flash.

Chapter 13 explains how to test your animation for speed and suitability for all browsers and systems. Then we cover all the details of publishing movies as well as the other formats available, such as HTML, GIF, and so on. You can also create projectors — movies that play themselves.

Chapter 14 answers some frequently asked questions about Flash and introduces you to some fun techniques, such as creating drag-and-drop objects and simulating 3-D effects. Other topics include rescaling a movie, synchronizing sound with animation, and the new ActionScript features available in Flash 5.

Part VI: The Part of Tens

What's a *For Dummies* book without the Part of Tens? Chapter 15 offers you the top ten Web design tips, knowing that your Flash work must fit into the context of an entire Web site. Chapter 16 provides you with the ten best resources for learning about Flash (besides this book, of course). Chapter 17 lists our winners for ten great Flash Web sites, although new ones pop up every day. You'll find lots of helpful information in this part.

Part VII: Appendixes

Last, but not least, we come to the appendixes. They add some very valuable information to the end of the book, including setting preferences and options, illustrations of all the tools and panels in Flash 5, what those obscure terms really mean, and what's on the CD-ROM.

About the CD-ROM

Don't forget to check out our CD-ROM. It's stuffed with Flash movies that you can play with, a library of graphics, samples of some great Web sites, and trial versions of Flash and other cool Macromedia products. We've also added some demos and trial versions of programs that you can use to enhance Flash.

Icons Used in This Book

As you flip through this book, you'll notice little pictures in the margin. They're called *icons,* and they help point out special information in the text. Sometimes, they help you know quickly that you don't care about this information and can skip over it without fear.

Look for this icon to quickly find new features of Flash 5. Those of you who have been using Flash 4 may want to skim through the book for this icon to help you quickly get up to speed on the new version.

Occasionally we refer you to other books on Flash or related topics, and we use this icon to point them out.

Look for this icon to find all the goodies on the CD included with this book.

This icon alerts you to information that you need to keep in mind to avoid wasting time or falling on your face.

Flash has some advanced features that you may want to know about — or skip over entirely. This icon lets you know when we throw the heavy stuff at you.

Tips help you finish your work more easily, quickly, or effectively. Don't miss out on these.

Uh oh! "Watch out here!" is what this icon is telling you, or else you never know what may happen.

Where to Go From Here

If you don't already have Flash installed, use the 30-day trial version of Flash on this book's CD-ROM and install the program. Complete instructions for installing Flash are in Appendix A. Then open Flash, open this book, and plunge in.

Contacting the Authors

We would love to hear your comments about this book. You can contact Gurdy Leete at gleete@mum.edu and Ellen Finkelstein at ellenfinkl@ bigfoot.com. Please note that we can't provide technical support on Flash. (If you need technical support, check out the resources listed in Chapter 16.)

Flash Time!

Enough of all this talk. Let's move into the real part of the book and start creating cool movies!

Enjoy!

Part I
A Blast of Flash

"See? I created a little felon figure that runs around our Web site hiding behind banner ads. On the last page, our logo puts him in a nonlethal choke hold and brings him back to the home page."

In this part . . .

In this part, you discover what Flash can and can't do and start to make your way around the Flash world. In Chapter 1, we explain the basic procedure for getting a Flash movie ready for a Web site. We introduce you to Flash, what it looks like and how to use its toolbars and menus. You find out about the Stage and the Timeline, two of Flash's central concepts. Play your way through your first animation to get a firsthand experience of the power of Flash.

In Chapter 2, you get an overview of the entire process of creating a Flash animated movie, from developing your concept to publishing your movie in the format a browser can display. We explain how to set properties that affect your movie as a whole and how Flash works with various kinds of graphics. We close with the steps for printing your movie on paper. This part provides the foundation for future success.

Chapter 1

Getting Acquainted with Flash 5

- -

In This Chapter

▶ Introducing Flash

▶ Figuring out what you can create with Flash 5

▶ Deciding when not to use Flash 5

▶ Perusing the screen

▶ Using Help

▶ Creating your first animation

▶ Closing out of Flash

- -

*O*nce upon a time in a galaxy that seems far, far away by now, there was the Internet, which contained only plain, unformatted text. Then came the Web and we gained text formatting and graphics. Then the Web grew up a little, and Web page graphics got fancier with things like small animations in banner ads. But people, being used to movies and TV, wanted an even more animated and interactive Web experience. Along came Flash.

Flash, created by Macromedia, Inc., is the software that runs some of the coolest Web sites around. When you surf the Web and see sites that contain animation across the entire page or buttons that do spectacular stunts when you click them, you're probably seeing some of Flash's magic. If you create a Web site, you can use Flash to rev up the basics so that your viewers will say, "Wow!"

In this chapter, you find out what Flash is all about, what the screen looks like, and how to use Help. Then you create your first, simple animation so that all the rest of the book makes sense.

Discovering Flash

Flash offers a powerful system for creating animation on the Web. In a nutshell, here's an overview of what you can do with the system:

- ✔ Create a Flash movie by creating graphics and animating them over the duration of the movie.

- ✔ Use the Publish command within Flash to publish the movie into a Flash player file. At the same time, Flash creates HTML code that you need for your Web page.

- ✔ Insert HTML code into your HTML document that creates the Web page to reference the Flash player file. It's similar to adding a graphic to a Web page. Or, you can use the HTML code alone as a new Web page.

- ✔ Upload the new or edited HTML document and the Flash player file to the location where you keep other files for your Web pages.

- ✔ Open your browser, navigate to your Web page, and presto! There's your cool animation on your Web page.

You need a Flash viewer to see the effects that Flash creates. These days, Flash viewers come installed in most computer systems and browsers so most people can view Flash-driven Web sites immediately without any special download or preparation. When you display a Web site that contains Flash effects, your system uses the Flash viewer to play the animation. Users who don't have a Flash viewer can download it for free from Macromedia at www.macromedia.com.

Web sites are getting more and more sophisticated. By using animation and special effects, you can distinguish your Web site from the also-rans. Using animation isn't hard, and you don't have to be a professional graphic artist, either. Anyone can create simple animations to enhance a Web site; it just takes a little time.

To find the most up-to-date Web sites that use Flash, check out the Macromedia site at www.macromedia.com/flash and go to the Gallery. Don't get discouraged by seeing some of the truly professional results at these sites. You can start with a simple, animated site and go from there. (Chapter 17 lists the ten best Web sites that use Flash.)

Understanding What You Can Create with Flash 5

You can use Flash 5 to create simple animation to add to your Web page. Or, you can create an entire Web page or site and incorporate text, graphics, interactive buttons, or animation.

This book helps you use Flash to create a simple or complex Web site. The following list describes some of the ways you can manipulate text, graphics, and sound by using Flash 5:

- **Create simple or fancy text that remains still or appears animated on your Web page.** You can choose to stop the animation after a few seconds or repeat it while your viewers view the page.

- **Use Flash tools to create your own graphics for your Web page, or import graphics.** You can lay out a Web page graphically or add graphics to only a part of a Web page.

- **Animate graphics and make objects appear and disappear by using the transparency feature.** Objects can move, get bigger or smaller, or rotate. Flash also lets you *morph* — that is, transform — shapes into new shapes.

- **Fill shapes and text with *gradients,* which are colors that gradually change into new colors.** You can even fill shapes and text with bitmap images that you import into Flash. For example, you could fill the letters of your name with dozens of flowers. (You aren't a flower child anymore?)

- **Create Web page buttons that not only lead your viewers wherever you want them to go but change shape or color at the same time.** You can make buttons change as you pass your mouse over them. People who view your page can click a button to display a movie (animation). In other words, your viewers can decide which movies they want to see.

- **Add sounds or music to your movie.** You can control how long the sound or music plays and whether it loops to play continuously.

- **Create pop-up menus that viewers can use to navigate your site.**

As you can see, you can go far with Flash if you want to. And why not? It's great fun!

Determining When Not to Use Flash 5

If Flash 5 is so wonderful, why doesn't every Web site designer use it? Why aren't most Web sites created completely with Flash?

Here's the other side of the story.

Although the vector graphics and animation of Flash load quickly, they don't load as quickly as plain text and simple graphics. Adding a movie to your Web page creates some overhead. There's no point in using Flash if you want simple pages consisting of mostly text and a few graphics that you want to stay put and not move.

You can create certain graphic effects much more easily by using *bitmap* graphics. Painted brushstroke and textured effects are examples. Graphic artists create these types of graphics by using graphic editing software, and the results are bitmaps. Similarly, to add photographs to your Web page, you need to scan the photographs as bitmaps. Flash creates *vector* graphics (defined mathematically), which are different from bitmap graphics (defined by lots of dots). (You can find out more about both bitmap and vector graphics in Chapter 2.)

If you want simple animation, such as a few blinking dots or a marquee effect, animated GIFs (the animated bitmap graphics you often see on the Web) are smaller than Flash movies, so they load faster. You can create animated GIFs by using animated GIF editing software.

Flash provides little in the way of 3-D graphics or animation. For those, you need to go to more sophisticated software such as Poser or 3D Studio Max. (See Chapter 14 for more 3-D possibilities in Flash.)

Getting the Right Start

Well begun is half done, as the saying goes. The easiest way to begin using Flash 5 is with a shortcut or alias right on your desktop. Double-click the Flash icon and you're on your way. (See Appendix A for information on installing Flash.)

Starting Flash on a PC

Whether you installed Flash from the CD or by downloading from the Macromedia Web site onto your PC, you may or may not have a shortcut on your desktop. To create one, open Windows Explorer and find `Flash.exe`. By default, it's in `C:\Program Files\Macromedia\Flash 5`. Right-click the file and choose Create Shortcut. Explorer creates the shortcut in the same folder, called `Shortcut to Flash.exe`. Now drag that shortcut to your desktop.

If you press Shift as you drag, Explorer moves the shortcut instead of copying it. (You don't need the extra shortcut in your Flash 5 folder.)

Click the shortcut on your desktop. Then click the text beneath the icon. Type **Flash 5** and press Enter. Just double-click the icon to open Flash.

Starting Flash on a Mac

Whether you installed Flash from the CD or by downloading from the Macromedia Web site onto your Mac, you may or may not have an alias on your desktop. To create one, open your drive and find the file named Flash 5 in the Macromedia Flash 5 folder. Click the file to select it. Then choose File⇨Make Alias. This creates the alias in the same folder, called Flash 5 Alias. Now drag that alias to the Desktop.

Click the alias on your desktop. Then click the text beneath the icon. Type **Flash 5** and press Enter. Now you can just double-click the icon to open Flash.

Creating a new movie

Files that you create by using Flash are commonly called *movies*. When you start Flash, you're immediately ready to create a new movie. You usually start by creating or importing some graphics. (To find out more about working with graphics, see Chapter 3.)

Opening an existing movie

If you want to work on a movie that you've already created, press Ctrl+O (Windows) or ⌘+O (Mac) or choose File⇨Open; then double-click the movie to open it. The first frame appears on your screen, and you can edit the movie any way you want.

Windows users can click Open on the Standard toolbar. If the Standard toolbar isn't displayed, choose Window⇨Toolbars⇨Main.

Taking a Look Around

If you've never created animation, the Flash screen is different from the screens in other programs that you may be used to, so take the time to get to know it. You can also customize the Flash screen. Figure 1-1 shows one possible display.

If your screen opens with several rectangular panels strewn about the screen, press Tab to close them. We explain how to open and use these panels throughout this book, but you don't need them for this chapter.

Drawing toolbox   Layer list   Menus   Timeline

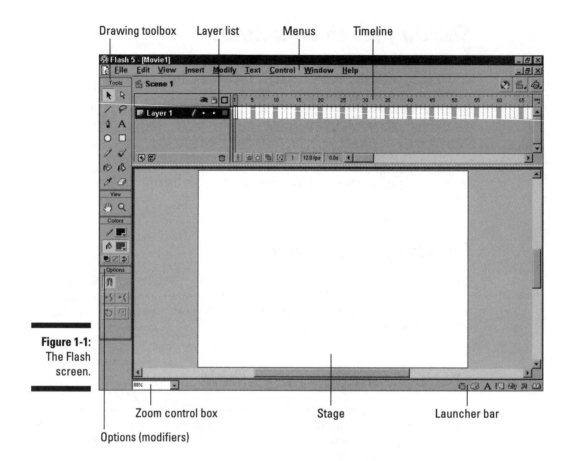

Figure 1-1:
The Flash
screen.

Zoom control box   Stage   Launcher bar

Options (modifiers)

Tooling around the toolbars

Flash contains two toolbars in the Mac version: the Drawing toolbox and the Controller. To display or hide these toolbars, choose Window➪Tools or Window➪Controller. In Windows, Flash offers the four toolbars described in the following list. To display or hide the first three listed here, choose Window➪Toolbars and click the toolbar that you want to display or hide. Here is a description of the toolbars:

   ✔ The Standard toolbar (Windows only), called the main toolbar, contains commonly used commands. Many of these are familiar from other Windows programs. By default, Flash does *not* display the Standard toolbar.

✔ The Status toolbar (Windows only) contains a brief description of tool-bar buttons and tells you when the Caps Lock and Num Lock buttons are on. By not displaying this mostly useless toolbar, you can reclaim some real estate on your screen. By default, Flash does not display the Status toolbar.

✔ The Controller lets you control the playback of movies. For more infor-mation, see Chapter 9.

✔ The Drawing toolbox contains all the tools you need to draw and edit objects. At the bottom of the Drawing toolbox are Options that modify how the tools function. (See Chapters 3 and 4 for a complete description of the features of the Drawing toolbox.)

In addition, at the bottom-right corner of the screen you see the Launcher bar. The seven buttons on this bar open various panels and windows that are discussed throughout the book. Although not technically a toolbar, the Launcher bar functions just like a toolbar.

Discovering the Flash menus

Most drawing functions are available only on the Drawing toolbox. Similarly, you often use the Timeline, discussed in "Following a timeline" later in this chapter, for creating animation. Almost every other function in Flash is on a menu somewhere. You just need to find it. In general, we discuss the specific menu functions as appropriate throughout the book. Table 1-1 offers you a brief overview of the menus.

Table 1-1	Flash Menus
Menu	*Function*
File	Enables you to open and close files; save files; import and export files; print; publish movies for the Web; send a movie as an e-mail attachment (Windows only); and quit Flash.
Edit	Provides commands that let you undo and redo actions; cut, copy, and paste to and from the Clipboard; delete, duplicate, select, and deselect objects; copy and paste entire frames; edit symbols (see Chapter 7 for the whole story on symbols); set preferences; and create keyboard shortcuts for commands.
View	Helps you get a better view by letting you zoom in and out; show or hide various parts of the screen; and view a grid for easy layout.

(continued)

Table 1-1 *(continued)*

Menu	Function
Insert	Enables you to insert symbols or create symbols from objects on your screen (Chapter 7 explains this); insert and delete frames and keyframes (see Chapter 9 for more); insert layers (covered in Chapter 6); and create motion tweens (see Chapter 9).
Modify	Helps you modify symbols, frames, scenes, or the entire movie. Offers tools for transforming, aligning, grouping, ungrouping, and breaking objects apart.
Text	Enables you to format text.
Control	Provides options that let you control the playing of movies; test movies and scenes; engage certain interactive functions; and mute sounds.
Window	Enables you to open lots of things, including a new window; panels that help you control objects; the library (more on libraries in Chapter 2); windows for creating interactive controls (explained in Chapter 10); and the Movie Explorer (to help manage your movie).
Help	Comes to the rescue when you need help.

Many of the menu commands offer keyboard shortcuts. A new feature of Flash 5 lets you create your own keyboard shortcuts. (See Appendix A for instructions.)

If you're using a Windows version of Flash 5, you can display the Standard toolbar to display some of the most commonly used commands. Choose Window⇨Toolbars⇨Main.

The shortcuts are displayed on the menus, next to the command name. Here are some of the most commonly used keyboard shortcuts. (For more short-cuts, see the tear-out Cheat Sheet at the front of the book.)

✔ **Ctrl+N (Windows) or ⌘+N (Mac):** Start a new movie.

✔ **Ctrl+O (Windows) or ⌘+O (Mac):** Open an existing movie.

✔ **Ctrl+S (Windows) or ⌘+S (Mac):** Save your movie. Don't forget to use this often!

✔ **Ctrl+X (Windows) or ⌘+X (Mac):** Cut to Clipboard. Chapter 4 explains more about using the Clipboard.

✔ **Ctrl+C (Windows) or ⌘+C (Mac):** Copy to Clipboard.

✔ **Ctrl+V (Windows) or ⌘+V (Mac):** Paste from Clipboard.

- **Ctrl+Z (Windows) or ⌘+Z (Mac):** Undo. Would you believe that by default Flash remembers your last 100 actions and can undo them? What a relief! The only problem is that Flash doesn't provide a drop-down list of each action, so you're somewhat in the dark about what the next undo is going to undo. Think of it as a journey into the long forgotten past. (See Appendix A for details on customizing the number of Undos that Flash remembers.)

- **Ctrl+Y (Windows) or ⌘+Y (Mac):** Redo redoes actions that you undid by using the Undo button. (Got that?) This button remembers just as many actions as the Undo button. So if you undo more actions than you want, click Redo (or press Ctrl+Y) until you're back where you want to be. Using the Undo and Redo buttons is like traveling through Flash time — and it gives you lots of slack while you're working.

- **Ctrl+Q (Windows) or ⌘+Q (Mac):** Exit Flash.

We mention other keyboard shortcuts throughout this book as we discuss their corresponding commands.

Although it's not a shortcut, it's worth noting that you can find the Zoom Control box at the bottom-left corner of your screen. Click the arrow and choose a zoom factor to zoom in and out.

You aren't limited to the choices in the Zoom drop-down list. Type a number in the Zoom Control box and press Enter to set your own zoom factor. For example, type **85** to set the zoom factor to 85 percent.

Staging your movies

The white box in the center of your screen is the *Stage*. Think of the Stage as a movie screen where you place objects. Each screen is called a *frame,* just like the frames of a movie. You make an animated movie by creating a number of frames that play quickly, one after the other. Flash also plays back movies on the Stage.

Following a timeline

The Timeline window divides your movie into frames. Each frame represents a tiny stretch of time, such as $\frac{1}{12}$ of a second. Creating a movie is simply a matter of assembling frames, which are then quickly played in order.

Chapter 9 explains in detail how to make using the Timeline completely painless. For now, you should just understand the basics. See Figure 1-2 for an example of a Timeline.

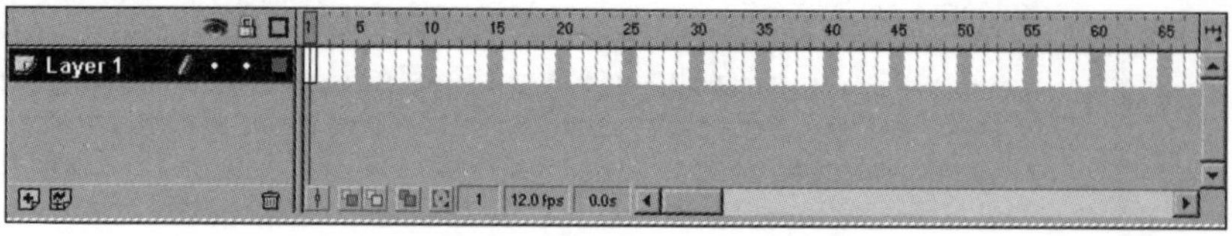

Figure 1-2:
The Timeline is your key to managing animation.

On the left of the Timeline is the layer list. When you open a new movie, you see only one layer, unimaginatively called Layer 1. A *layer* is like a sheet of transparent acetate on which you draw objects. Layers help you keep objects from running into each other, causing unfortunate, messy results. You organize your entire movie by using layers. For example, if you want to keep some text constant throughout the movie but animate a bouncing dot, you would give the dot its own layer and animate it on that layer. The layer list has room for more layers, and you can add as many layers as you want. (Chapter 6 gives you the lowdown on layers.)

You can move the bottom edge of the Timeline to make room for more layers. Hover the mouse cursor over the bottom line until you see the two-headed arrow. Drag downward to add room for more layers.

To the right of Layer 1 you see a bunch of rectangles, each representing a frame. (Actually, before you start using the Timeline, they're just potential frames, like unexposed frames on a roll of film.) By default, each frame lasts $\frac{1}{12}$ of a second. Each layer has its own row of frames because you can have different animations or objects on each layer.

A *keyframe* is a frame that defines some change in your animation. In some animations, every frame is a keyframe. Other animations need keyframes only for the first and last frames.

You don't use the Timeline until you're ready to animate. As you work, however, you should organize your objects onto separate layers. Don't worry, you can always move an object from one layer to another.

Getting Help in a Flash

This book is all you need to start creating great animations, but we'd be remiss if we didn't tell you about the Flash Help system. The Flash manual (you already have it if you didn't purchase Flash by downloading) is exactly the same as online Help. Even the index is the same. Online Help simply adds a search engine. All online Help files are in HTML format, so your computer opens them in your browser.

To use Flash Help, choose Help➪Using Flash or press F1 (Windows only). You see a screen like the one shown in Figure 1-3.

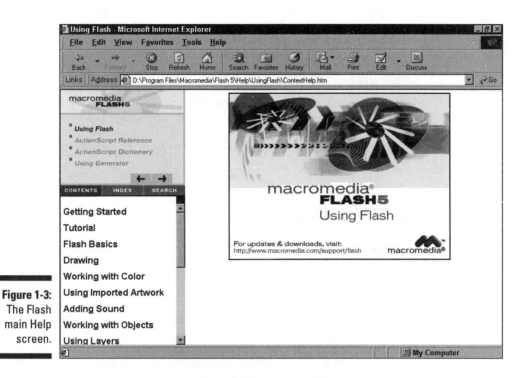

Figure 1-3:
The Flash
main Help
screen.

Four Help manuals

Flash contains four Help manuals. Using Flash is the main Help manual, and another manual covers ActionScript, the programming language that you use to create complex interactive movies. (See Chapter 10 to find out more about ActionScript.) The Flash online Help manual is separated into the Reference Guide and the Dictionary. Finally, Flash provides the Using Generator manual, which you may or may not have online, depending on the type of installation you performed. Generator is another Macromedia product that you can use along with Flash. In this section, we concentrate on the Using Flash Help manual.

Contents, index, and search

The main Help screen has three tabs in the left panel. Click the tab that you think may help you find an answer quickly. The following list describes how to use the tabs:

✔ **Contents:** Click a topic and look at a list of subtopics. Click again and helpful text appears on the right side of the screen.

✔ **Index:** Click a letter of the alphabet or click A-Z to peruse the entire list. Click any topic to display it on the right side of the screen.

✔ **Search:** Type a search word or words to open the Flash search facility. If you search by typing multiple words, put a plus sign (+) between them. Uncheck Case Sensitive for more flexibility. Click List Topics to show the results in the Search box. Double-click the topic to display it on the right side of the screen.

Using the tutorial

Flash contains a set of lessons plus a tutorial to help get you started. We recommend starting with the lessons by opening Flash and choosing Help⇨Lessons⇨Introduction. Follow the on-screen instructions to move from lesson to lesson.

After you finish the lessons, try the tutorial. If you have the printed manual, you can find the tutorial in Chapter 1. Otherwise, choose Help⇨Using Flash. On the left of the main Help screen under Contents, click Tutorial. You may want to print out the pages so that you don't have to switch back and forth between Flash and the tutorial page.

Finding more help on the Web

Macromedia offers some support on its Web site. To access it, choose Help⇨Flash Support Center. The Macromedia Flash Web site, which you can find at `www.macromedia.com\flash`, also has a gallery of Web sites that use Flash — a great place to see what Flash can do.

You can also click the link to `www.macromedia.com/support/flash` at the bottom-left corner of the boxed graphic on the first Help page for updates and downloads.

Choose Help⇨Macromedia Dashboard to access more Flash resources from Macromedia. You need to be online to download the initial Dashboard movie. You can then click links for more information.

Try It, You'll Like It

Perhaps by now you're getting impatient to try out Flash. Getting started is easy. You collect a few ideas, put together some art, add animation, save your movie, and publish it. Then you view it in a browser either online or offline. That's the gratifying part. In the following sections, you get to give Flash a try by working through a basic animation.

Conceiving your first animation

Suppose that you want to add an animated logo to a home page that you have already set up. You want the animation to run when the page loads and then stop. Figure 1-4 shows the Rainbow Resouces company logo — unanimated, of course — that you can find on the CD.

Figure 1-4:
A company logo that could stand some animation.

Suppose that you want the word *Rainbow* to fly into your page from the right and the word *Resources* to fly in from the left. At the same time, you want the graphic to rotate 180 degrees. You find out how to make this happen in the following section.

Flashy drawings

You can use Flash to create a company logo, but importing one from this book's CD-ROM is simpler. Often, you import existing graphics (such as a company logo) from a file rather than create them from scratch. (Chapter 3 explains how to import and manipulate graphics.)

If you're going through the steps and make a mistake, choose Edit⇨Undo (or press Ctrl+Z) and try again. You can use Undo repeatedly to undo several steps, if necessary.

To import the Rainbow Resources logo into Flash, follow these steps (the steps may vary if you're importing some other graphic in a different format):

1. **Start Flash.**

   See the instructions in "Starting Flash on a PC" or "Starting Flash on a Mac" earlier in this chapter, if you need help.

   You see a spanking new movie on your screen.

2. **Choose File⇨Import.**

   The Import dialog box opens.

3. **Browse the dialog box until you find** `rainbow.gif` **in the ch01 folder of the CD-ROM.**

4. **Click to select** `rainbow.gif` **and then click Open.**

   You see the logo on your screen. You need to break the logo into pieces and make it a vector graphic so that you can animate it.

5. **Choose Modify⇨Trace Bitmap and click OK in the Trace Bitmap dialog box.**

   Flash creates a vector graphic and breaks up the graphic into individual components. The entire graphic, however, is selected.

6. **Click anywhere outside the graphic to deselect it.**

7. **Delete the invisible square around the graphic (which is unnecessary) by clicking near, but not on, the logo.**

   You see the square selected.

8. **Press Delete.**

   The square goes away but the rest of the logo stays behind.

You've got your logo! Now you need to set it up for animation.

Grouping your objects

In the logo that you imported in the previous section, each letter is a separate object, which can get pretty confusing. Each line in the logo's design is also separate. But you want your words to stay together and the little design, too. So grouping the letters into words and the lines into one grouped design is a good idea.

To group the words and the logo, follow these steps:

1. **Click the Zoom Control drop-down box and choose 200%.**

   If you don't like that percentage, try 400%. Increasing the zoom helps you select the letters of each word. Use the scroll bar to scroll the words of the logo into view, if necessary.

2. **Click the arrow tool on the Drawing toolbox if it's not already selected.**

3. **Click the upper-right corner of the word *Rainbow* (just above and to the right of the *w*) and drag to the bottom-left corner of the *R*.**

   Dragging from right to left makes it easier to avoid selecting the logo at the same time. You should see the entire word selected. If not, click outside the word and try again.

4. **Choose Modify⇨Group.**

   Flash places a box around the word so that you can see that it's one object.

5. **Repeat the procedure outlined in Step 2 with the word *Resources*.**

   In this case, you may want to start clicking and dragging from the top left; then choose Modify⇨Group again. Now, all the letters of the word *Resources* are a single object.

6. **Click the Magnification drop-down box and choose 100% so that you can see the entire logo.**

7. **Click the top left of the logo and drag to the bottom right to select the entire logo.**

8. **Hold down the Shift key and click each word to remove both words from the selection. Choose Modify⇨Group.**

   Flash creates a group from the lines of the logo's design.

See Chapter 4 to find out more about grouping and editing graphics.

Putting your graphics on layers

Placing different components on different layers is a good idea when you're animating. You can use layers to organize your movie and keep shapes separate so that they don't bump into each other. (See Chapter 6 for the complete story on layers.)

To split your three components onto three separate layers, follow these steps:

1. **Click the word *Resources* to select it.**

   You don't have to select *Rainbow* because it can stay on its original layer.

2. **Choose Edit⇨Cut.**

   Resources disappears.

3. **Choose Insert⇨Layer.**

   Flash creates a new layer, creatively named Layer 2.

4. **Choose Edit⇨Paste in Place.**

   The word *Resources* reappears, seemingly unchanged, but now on a different layer.

5. **Click the logo to select it and repeat Steps 2 through 4 with the logo to put it on Layer 3.**

6. **Click outside the Stage to deselect any objects.**

The pieces of your graphic have now been separated and placed in different layers, so you're ready for the animation process.

Making graphics move

We explained earlier that the goal is to have the word *Rainbow* fly in from the right and the word *Resources* to fly in from the left. You also want the graphic to rotate 180 degrees at the same time. What you see now is how the animation will end — the last frame of the movie — so you need to move the components to their starting positions (see Figure 1-4). This strategy is useful in this particular instance because you have been given the logo in its final state.

Follow these steps to create the last frame of the movie:

1. **In the top row (Layer 2), click frame 30 of the Timeline and choose Insert⇨Keyframe.**

   You can find out more about keyframes in Chapter 9.

2. **In the middle row (Layer 3), click frame 30 and choose Insert⇨Keyframe.**

3. **In the third row (Layer 1), click frame 30 and press F6 (the shortcut for creating a keyframe).**

4. **Choose File⇨Save and pick a location where you save other documents that you create.**

   We don't recommend saving the file in the Flash folder — it may get lost among your Flash program files.

5. **Give your movie a name, such as** Movie of the Year, **and click Save.**

   Flash creates a file named Movie of the Year.fla.

Go back and create the beginning of your movie. Flash can fill in all the blanks in between. Follow these steps to create the beginning of the movie and the animation:

1. **If the Frame panel is not already open, choose Window⇨Panels⇨ Frame to open it.**

   The Frame panel is now open.

2. **Click the first frame of the Timeline in the Layer 2 row.**

3. **In the Tweening drop-down list of the Frame panel, choose Motion.**

4. **Repeat Steps 2 and 3 for the other two layers.**

5. **Click the Close box in the Frame panel.**

6. **Select the word *Rainbow;* then press and hold down the Shift key while you drag the word to the right, off the Stage and into the gray area.**

   You may need to use the horizontal scroll bar to see the gray area. Pressing Shift keeps the object from moving up or down as you drag to the right.

7. **Select *Resources;* then press the Shift key while you drag the word to the left, off the Stage.**

8. **Select the logo design (the only thing left on the Stage) and choose Modify⇨Transform⇨Rotate 90° CW to rotate it 90° clockwise.**

9. **Repeat the Modify⇨Transform⇨Rotate 90° CW command to rotate the design 180 degrees.**

   Your screen should look like the one shown in Figure 1-5.

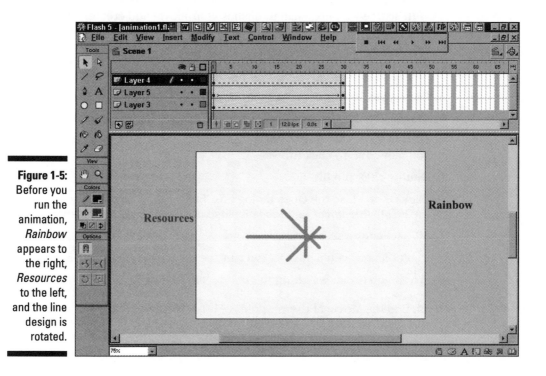

Figure 1-5:
Before you
run the
animation,
Rainbow
appears to
the right,
Resources
to the left,
and the line
design is
rotated.

10. **Drag the horizontal scroll box until the Stage is in the center of your screen.**

    Otherwise, you won't be able to see the entire animation — and you don't want to miss this one!

11. **Press Enter (Return) and watch the animation. (Start writing your Academy Award acceptance speech.)**

12. **Save your movie again by choosing File⇨Save.**

Publishing your first animation for posterity

You can't watch the animation on a Web page until you publish it and insert it into an HTML document. To do so, follow these steps:

1. **Choose File⇨Publish Settings and click the HTML tab.**

2. **Click the Loop check box in the Playback section to uncheck it.**

3. **Click Publish and then click OK to close the dialog box.**

    With scarcely a blip, Flash publishes your movie and creates two files, one named Movie of the Year.swf (assuming you used that name) and Movie of the Year.html. They're in the same folder as your .fla movie file. Movie of the Year.html contains the HTML code required to display your movie on a Web page.

4. **Open your Web browser and work offline.**

5. **Choose File⇨Open and find Movie of the Year.html (or whatever you named your movie file).**

    You may need to click Browse.

6. **Double-click the file.**

    Click OK to close the Open dialog box if necessary. Your browser opens the HTML document and reads its instructions to play the Flash movie.

7. **Sit back and watch it roll.**

    Don't blink or you'll miss it. You can see the movie in Figure 1-6.

8. **When you finish watching the movie, close your browser.**

You can find the Movie of the Year files (FLA, HTML, and SWF) in the Ch01 folder of the CD-ROM.

Exiting Flash

When you finish creating something in Flash, choose File⇨Exit (Windows) or choose File⇨Quit (Mac).

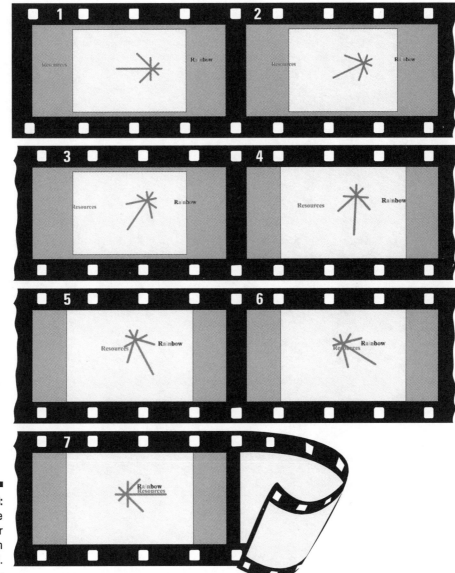

Figure 1-6:
The Movie
of the Year
animation in
detail.

Chapter 2

Your Basic Flash

*T*his chapter starts with an overview of the process of creating animation in Flash. We then discuss some tools and features that are fundamental to using Flash efficiently.

As you find out in this chapter, you use movie properties to set the screen size and color, frame rate, and measurement units for the Flash movie as a whole. We also discuss the Library and how it's a storehouse for images, symbols, and sound. Finally, near the end of the chapter, we explain how you can print a Flash movie.

Looking at the Big Picture

When you use Flash to create animation for your Web site, you generally go through several steps of construction. The steps may vary in their order, but in each case, the skills you use are about the same. After you know the basics, you can start getting creative and make your Web site rock. Here's a typical path to add animation to an existing Web page:

1. **Think about it.** Noodle around, maybe make some doodles on a napkin, collect a few ideas, and choose one or all of them.

2. **Set up your movie.** Flash lets you choose the size and color of the Stage, the speed of animation (number of frames per second), and other general parameters that affect the entire Flash movie. See the next section of this chapter for details.

3. **Add some graphics.** You have to decide whether you want to create graphics in Flash, create them in another graphics software package, or import existing graphics. Your choice partly depends on how artistic you are, whether you have other software available to you, and whether you can find the right graphics elsewhere. You can also use a combination of sources, which is a common practice. (See Chapter 3 for some suggestions on great places to get graphics.)

4. **Lay out your graphics the way you want your animation to start.** Here's where you may want to scale, rotate, or otherwise fiddle with your graphics. (Chapter 4 has more on transforming your graphics.)

5. **Add some text.** Using Flash is a great way to get terrific text onto your Web site. Add text (also called type); then reshape it, make it transparent (if you don't want to be too obvious), add other effects, and place it where you want it. (Check out Chapter 5 for typography tips.)

6. **Organize your text and graphics by using layers.** Layers help you keep track of what each graphic and text object does while you organize everything into a powerful, coherent statement. Layers keep your animations from going bump in the night and getting entangled. So create as many layers as you need and transfer your existing graphics and text to those layers. (See Chapter 6 for further details on layers.)

7. **Turn a graphic into a symbol and multiply it all over the Stage.** Making objects into symbols is also a way to keep them from merging with other objects as they merrily animate. You also use symbols to keep your file size down, to enable animation, and for interactivity, especially buttons. (Turn to Chapter 7 for more info on symbols.)

8. **Design some buttons.** You know those buttons that you click on Web sites all the time? The coolest ones are made in Flash. You can even use movie clips to create animated buttons. (Chapter 8 has more on buttons.)

9. **Animate!** You can create your animation frame by frame or let Flash fill in the animation between your first and last frames, which is called *tweening*. Flash can tween motion, shapes, colors, and transparency, which means that you can create some real magic. (See Chapter 9 for more on animation.)

10. **Get interactive.** You want to start a relationship with your Web viewers, so you can create buttons, frames, and symbols that respond to your viewers' actions. This is probably the most complex functionality of Flash, but we'll make most of it seem easy. (Turn to Chapter 10 for additional info on interactivity.)

11. **Make it louder!** Who wants a quiet Web site? Add sound to your movies or your buttons. (Check out Chapter 11 for more on sound.)

12. **Publish your magnum opus.** Flash makes it easy to get your movie onto your Web site by creating both the Flash Player (SWF) file and the HTML code for your Web page. Flash has other options, too, so you can publish to other formats if you want. (Chapter 12 explains how to put it all together, and Chapter 13 is all about publishing your animation.)

Congratulations! You've completed your first Flash Web animation — in fantasy at least. The following sections cover some details about how to get started.

Setting the Stage

Before you create graphics and animate them — all that fun stuff — you need to make some decisions about the structure of your entire movie. It's best to make these decisions before you start because changing midway can create problems.

The first step is to decide on the size and color of your Stage and other fundamental settings. Choose Modify➪Movie to open the Movie Properties dialog box, as shown in Figure 2-1.

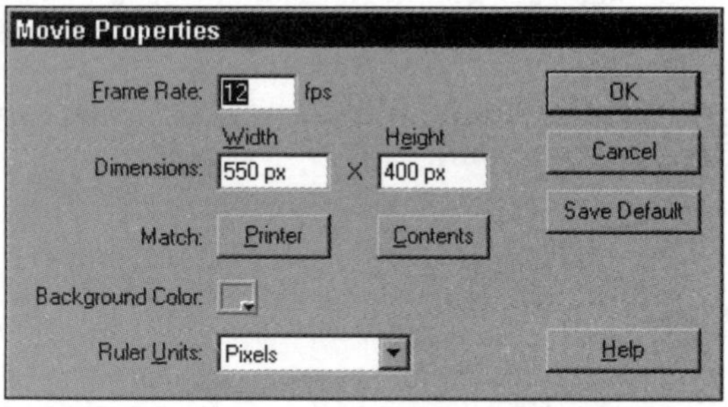

Figure 2-1:
The Movie
Properties
dialog box
sets the
movie's
overall
parameters.

In the Frame Rate text box, you specify how many frames a Flash movie plays each second. A faster rate allows for smoother animation but increases file size, and therefore download time, on your Web page. Chapter 9 explains more about this setting. Flash's default is 12 frames per second, which is a good starting point. But changing the frame rate mid-stream changes the rate of all the animation in your movie, which may not give you the results you want.

Use the Dimensions settings to set the size of the Stage. By default, Flash uses a Stage size of 550 pixels wide by 400 pixels high. To determine the proper setting, you need to know how your Flash movie will fit into your Web page or site. The default fits on almost everyone's browser screen. You may, however, want to fit your movie into a small corner of a Web page: for example, placing an animated logo in a top corner of a page. In that case, make the Stage smaller.

You can type the dimensions you want in the Width and Height text boxes. But Flash offers two shortcuts:

✔ Click Match Printer to set the Stage size according to the paper size set in the Page Setup dialog box (choose File⇨Page Setup). (For the Mac, the Print Margins dialog box, which you access by choosing File⇨Print Margins, also affects the paper size.) Flash sets the size of the Stage to the maximum possible area of the paper, minus the margins. Later in this chapter, in the section "Printing Your Movie," we cover this dialog box in more detail.

✔ Click Match Contents to set the Stage size to the contents of the Stage. Of course, for this to work you need some objects on the Stage. Flash creates a Stage size by placing equal space around all sides of the entire contents of the Stage. If you want to create the smallest possible Stage, place your objects at the top-left corner and then click Match Contents.

You can also set the color of the Stage to create a colored background for your entire Movie. As with other settings, you need to consider the context of the Web page that will contain the Flash movie. For example, you may want to match the color of your Web page's background. If your Flash movie will constitute the entire Web page, set the Stage color to set the Web page background. You can also color the Stage to create a mood for your animation.

To set the Stage color, click the Background Color swatch. Flash opens the Color palette. Click the color you want.

Grabbing a Graphic

The first step in creating animation for your Web site is to create or import graphics. First, you should understand a little about the different kinds of graphics that you can use in a Flash movie.

Understanding vectors and bitmaps

You may know enough about graphics to understand the difference between bitmap and vector graphics. If you do, feel free to skip this section.

Bitmaps are created with lots of dots. Put them all together and you get a picture. As you can imagine, it can take a large file to store the information about all the dots in a bitmap. Another problem with bitmaps is that they don't scale up well. If you try to enlarge a bitmap, it starts to look grainy because you see all those dots (see the bitmap example in Figure 2-2).

Vector graphics are defined with equations that specify lines, shapes, and locations. Blank space doesn't have to be recorded and the equations are particularly efficient in storing information. As a result, file sizes are usually smaller.

Vector graphics are infinitely scalable, either up or down. No matter how big you make your graphic, it always looks perfect, as shown in the vector example in Figure 2-2. In fact, your graphic may even look better when it's larger because the curves are smoother.

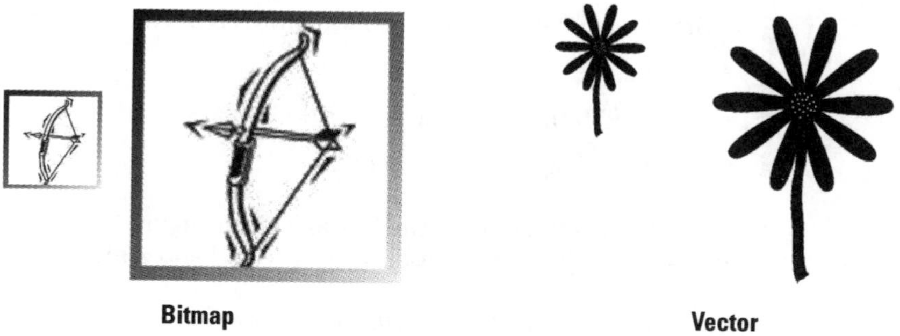

Figure 2-2:
Bitmaps
lose focus
when
enlarged;
vector
graphics
remain
sharp and
clear.

Bitmap

Vector

Flash creates vector-based graphics. The small size of the files means that Flash player files load and play super fast on a Web page. As you undoubtedly know, fast file loading means that your Web page viewers don't have to wait a long time to see your effects. That's the advantage of Flash. (In Chapters 3 and 15, we discuss why you need to know about both bitmaps and vectors.)

Finding graphics

Okay, so you've doodled and played around with some ideas for your Flash animation and perhaps jotted down a few notes or maybe even made a few sketches. You're ready to start building your Flash animation. A logical place to start is to collect some of the graphics that will serve as building blocks in this process.

Where do you get them? You have lots of choices:

- ✔ Use the library of graphics that comes with Flash. You can use these graphics as is or as a springboard for your own, more customized, creations.

- ✔ Create your graphics from scratch (if you feel artistic) by using the Flash drawing tools described later (and in more detail in Chapter 3).

- ✔ Create graphics in another graphics software package such as Fireworks or FreeHand (find demo versions on the CD-ROM accompanying this book).

- ✔ Import graphics from archives of art available on CD-ROM or the Web.

- ✔ Combine any or all of these approaches.

Going to the Library

Every graphic you create in Flash is precious and deserves to be archived in style. Each movie file that you create has a Library. The Library saves the following types of objects so they never get lost:

- ✔ Graphic, movie clip, Smart Clip, and Web button symbols
- ✔ Sounds
- ✔ Imported bitmap graphics
- ✔ Imported QuickTime movies

You'll find yourself going to the Library often. Figure 2-3 shows a library containing several types of symbols plus a sound and a bitmap.

To go to the Library, choose Window➪Library. You can also click the Library button in the Launcher bar or press Ctrl+L (Windows) or ⌘+L (Mac). When you open the Library, Flash creates a new window that you can resize and place anywhere on your screen.

To use any object in the Library, follow these steps:

1. **Select the layer on which you want to put the object or create a new layer for the object.**

2. **Click the point in the Timeline where you want the object to start or appear.**

3. **Click and drag the object from its listing in the Library.**

   You can also select an object from the listing and drag its image from the preview box.

The point on the Timeline that you click (in Step 2) must be a keyframe. Chapter 9 explains keyframes in detail.

Using folders

A Flash movie can contain dozens or even hundreds of symbols, so you need to keep them organized. Flash provides several features to keep you from tearing your hair out.

You can, and should, organize your symbols into folders if you have more than a few. To create a new folder, click the New Folder button at the bottom of the Library window. Flash creates a new folder. Type a name that describes the type of symbols you want to put into the folder and press Enter/Return. For example, you could create a folder called Intro and another called Conclusion.

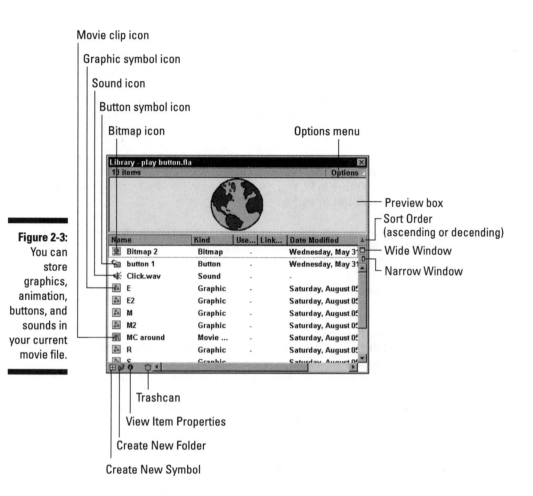

Movie clip icon

Graphic symbol icon

Sound icon

Button symbol icon

Bitmap icon

Options menu

Preview box

Sort Order
(ascending or decending)

Wide Window

Narrow Window

Figure 2-3:
You can
store
graphics,
animation,
buttons, and
sounds in
your current
movie file.

Trashcan

View Item Properties

Create New Folder

Create New Symbol

To put symbols into a folder, drag them onto the folder. You can also move symbols from one folder to another — just drag them.

To keep your symbol list from getting unwieldy, you can collapse folders. A collapsed folder doesn't display its contents. As soon as you need to see what's inside, you can expand the folder. Double-click a folder to either collapse or expand it.

To quickly see the structure of your folders, choose Options from the Library's Options menu. Choose Collapse All Folders. You can also choose Expand All Folders to see everything in the Library.

More Library housekeeping

By default, Flash alphabetizes items in the Library by name. You may, however, have different ideas. You can sort from A to Z (ascending) or from Z to A (descending). You can also sort by any of the columns in the Library. To change the direction of sorting (for any column in the Library), click the Sort Order button in the upper-right corner of the list. To sort, click the heading of the column you want to sort by.

You can resize the Library window by dragging its lower-right corner. Or you can click the Wide Window or Narrow Window button to grow or shrink its width (refer to Figure 2-3). You can resize any column by dragging the column heading's divider left or right.

To rename any Library item, double-click the item's name, type the new name, and press Enter/Return. Don't worry — the original filenames of imported files remain unchanged.

To delete an item, select the item and click the Trashcan.

If you want to find out which items in the Library you aren't currently using, look in the third column (Use Count) for items with a Use Count of zero. To make sure that the Use Count is accurate, choose Options⇨Keep Use Counts Updated or Update Use Counts Now. After you know which items you aren't using, you should delete them to reduce the file size of your Flash movie.

You can keep imported bitmaps and sounds updated if the original files have changed. Select the file and choose Update from the Options menu of the Library window.

Using the Library of other movies

After you place objects in a file's Library, you can use those objects in any other Flash movie you create. In your current movie, choose File⇨Open as Library, choose the movie file containing the symbols you want, and then click Open. If necessary, move the new Library window so it doesn't cover up the old one.

Exploring the Flash stock Library

Flash comes with a Library that contains a basic assortment of stock sounds as well as graphic, button, and movie clip symbols. There are dozens of them, and they're mostly well done, so they're worth looking through. Choose Window⇨Common Libraries to find the library.

Sharing libraries

A shared library is a new concept for Flash 5 and is a library in a movie that has been posted to a Web site and is used by another Flash player file (SWF). The movie using the shared library object doesn't contain the object but just uses it from the shared library. Shared libraries can help make your movies smaller. For example, you can share bandwidth-hogging elements such as sounds and fonts.

Creating a shared library

You create a shared library when you want to make an element in your movie available to other SWF player files. You do this by defining linked objects in a movie's library.

To create a shared library, follow these steps:

1. **With the Library open, select an object, right-click (Windows) or Control+click (Mac), and choose Linkage.**

   The Symbol Linkage Properties dialog box appears.

2. **Choose Export This Symbol.**

3. **In the Symbol Linkage Properties dialog box, type a name (no spaces allowed) for the symbol in the Identifier text box.**

4. **Click OK.**

5. **Save the file.**

6. **Publish the file as an SWF player file (see Chapter 13 for instructions on publishing files).**

7. **Upload the file to your Web site.**

   Remember the URL (location) of the file.

Using a shared library

After you create a shared library, you can open the file and use the library from within a different movie.

To use a shared library, follow these steps:

1. **From your current movie, choose File⇨Open As Shared Library.**

   The Open As Shared Library dialog box appears.

2. **In the Open As Shared Library dialog box, choose the movie file whose shared library you want to use, and click Open.**

   Flash opens the shared library as a library window.

3. **Drag the linked object onto the Stage.**

   If you have the current movie's Library open as well, you can also drag directly from the shared library to the current library.

   Flash automatically sets the linkage property as Import and links to the SWF file of the movie that the linked object came from. To check the link, right-click (Windows) or Control+click (Mac) the object in your current movie and choose Linkage.

4. **Save the file.**

5. **Publish the file (see Chapter 13 for instructions).**

6. **Upload the SWF file to your Web site in the same location as the original movie containing the shared library (so your movie can access it).**

Working with shared libraries requires that all the pieces be in the proper place at the same time. We suggest checking a movie that contains an object from a shared library to verify that the object displays properly. You can do so by going online and viewing it in your browser.

Printing Your Movie

Usually you don't print your movies, you publish them on the Web. But you may want to collaborate on a movie with others who don't have Flash (how unenlightened of them!). Or you may just want to analyze a movie on paper, tack your animation frames on the wall and rearrange their sequence, and so on. In such a situation, you can print out your animation frame by frame.

To print a movie, follow these steps:

1. **To set page margins, choose File⇨Page Setup (Windows) or File⇨Print Margins (Mac).**

   The Page Setup (Windows) or Print Margins (Mac) dialog box appears (see Figure 2-4).

2. **In the Margins section, set the margins.**

   You can probably keep the default margins.

3. **Click the Center check boxes to center the printing horizontally (L–R) and vertically (T–B) on the page.**

4. **In the Layout section, click the Frames drop-down list and decide whether to print only the first frame or all frames.**

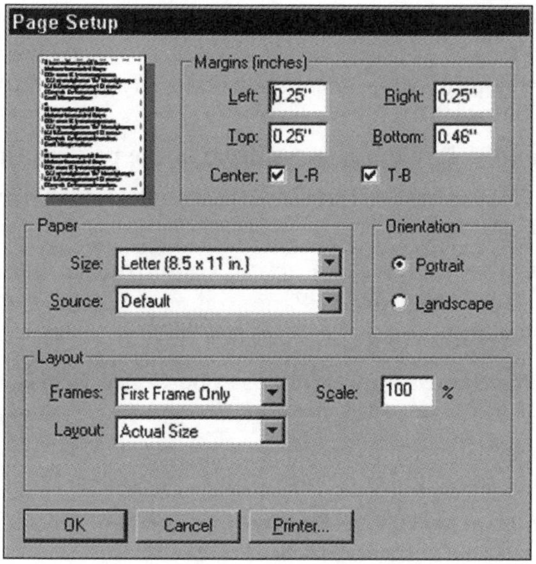

Figure 2-4:
Use the
Page Setup
dialog box
to specify
how you
print your
Flash movie.

5. **Click the Layout drop-down list in the Layout section to choose from the following options:**

   - **Actual size:** Lets you choose a scale. This option prints one frame to a page.

   - **Fit On One Page:** Fits one frame on a page, scaling it to fit the paper.

   - **Storyboard – Boxes:** Places several thumbnail sketches of your movie on a page. You can specify how many frames you want in a row in the Frames Across box. You may need to experiment to get the right result. In the Frame Margin text box, enter the space between the boxes in pixels. The Boxes option places each frame in a box.

   - **Storyboard – Grid:** Creates a grid of lines for your storyboard instead of individual boxes around the frames. This is just a matter of aesthetics — don't get too hung up over these choices.

   - **Storyboard – Blank:** Leaves out the boxes or grid and just prints all your frames in the storyboard. You have the same Frames Across and Frame Margin settings as for the other storyboard options.

6. **If you chose a Storyboard option, click Label frames (Windows) or Label (Mac) to give each frame a number.**

7. **On a Mac, when you finish setting your options, click OK; then choose File⇨Page Setup.**

   In Windows, you skip this step because you already opened the Page Setup dialog box in Step 1.

8. **Select the size and define the paper source in the paper section.**

   Usually, you can leave this section as is because it's based on your printer's default settings.

9. **In the Orientation section, select Portrait (taller rather than wider) or Landscape (wider rather than taller).**

10. **When you finish setting your options, click OK.**

11. **If you chose a storyboard option, choose File⇨Print Preview to preview your movie to ensure that you like the setup.**

12. **Click Print to print directly from the Print Preview screen or click Close to return to the regular display and then choose File⇨Print.**

    Alternatively, you can press Ctrl+P (Windows) or ⌘+P (Mac).

Figure 2-5 shows an example of the storyboard with the grid option and labeling. The storyboard shows four frames across with a landscape orientation.

You can find out more about the Flash viewer's special printing capabilities in Chapter 13.

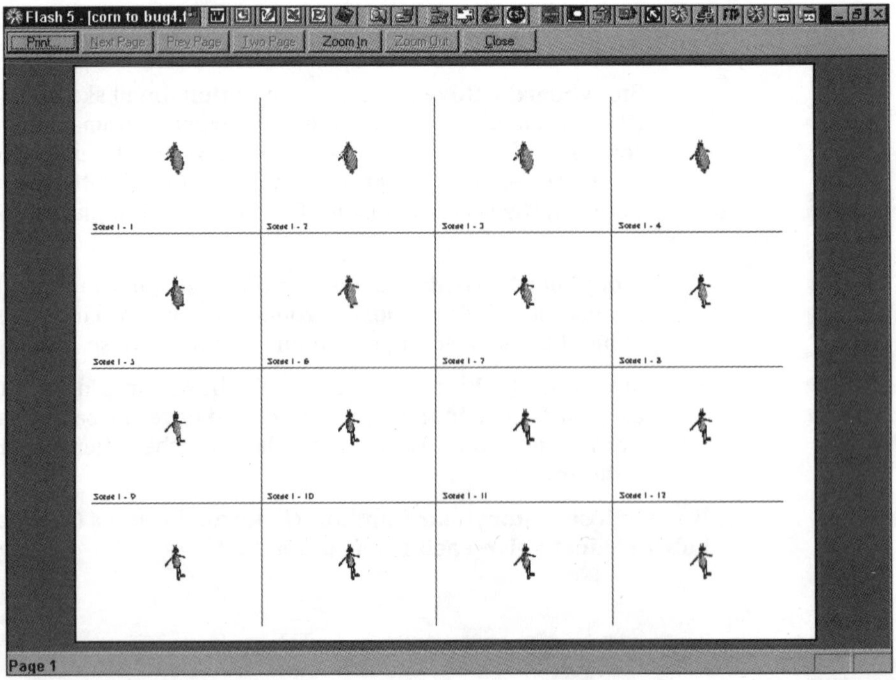

Figure 2-5:
You can print a storyboard of your movie that displays a thumbnail sketch of each frame.

Part II
1000 Pictures and 1000 Words

The 5th Wave   By Rich Tennant

"Is this really the best use of Flash 5 animation on our e-commerce Web site? A bad wheel on the shopping cart icon that squeaks, wobbles, and pulls to the left?"

In this part . . .

Graphics are the basis of animation. Before you can make anything move, you need to create the graphics that form the building blocks of your animation. This part describes all the types of graphics you can use, from basic shapes created in Flash to sophisticated imported bitmap graphics. The Flash tools are quite capable, including the new Pen tool, and you can create exciting effects with gradient fills, softened edges, and transparency. The Flash editing features offer more opportunities to create great-looking graphics — including skewing objects and manipulating fills every which way.

You'll find great ways to say great things with flexible type options and formatting. You can even break up text and animate it, letter by letter. To keep all the pieces of your animation from going completely out of control, you'll see how to use layers to organize your movie animation. You can use special layers to guide animation along a path and hide objects behind a *mask*.

Chapter 3

Getting Graphic

*I*n this chapter, you get down to the details of creating your own graphics in Flash. The Flash graphics tools offer you the capability to easily create interesting and professional-looking shapes. Of course, you can also import graphics created in other programs.

After you master all the techniques for drawing and editing, you can create some very cool graphics. If you're new to Flash, take the time to try out all the tools and techniques until you feel comfortable with them.

For a handy reference to the Drawing toolbox that we refer to throughout the entire chapter, see the Cheat Sheet at the front of this book.

Sharpen Your Pencil

The Flash Pencil tool is designed to be used like a real pencil to create freehand shapes. Whenever you want to create a shape not available from other Flash tools (such as the circle and square), you can use the Pencil. But the Pencil tool goes beyond a regular pencil's capabilities by incorporating several cool features that smooth or straighten what you draw. In addition to those features, the Pencil also includes the *shape recognition* feature (perfect for those who are less artistic). Draw something that approximates a triangle and Flash forgivingly perfects it for you. Here we explain exactly how to use this tool.

To start, click the Pencil tool on the Drawing toolbox. To draw without changing the Pencil modifier, move the cursor onto the Stage, click and draw. After you release the mouse button, Flash modifies the shape according to the active modifier setting.

Setting the Pencil modifier

When you choose the Pencil tool, the Options area below the Drawing toolbox changes to display the drawing mode modifier for the Pencil tool.

The Pencil modifier has three drawing modes:

- ✔ **Straighten:** Straightens lines and converts sloppy squares, rectangles, circles, ellipses, and triangles to perfect ones.
- ✔ **Smooth:** Smoothes out curved lines, eliminating unsightly bumps and lumps.
- ✔ **Ink:** Slightly smoothes and straightens your curves and lines, but leaves them mostly the way you drew them.

In Figure 3-1, you see a right-pointing arrow. You have already drawn the horizontal line and now want to create the arrow's point. See how the point looks before and after Flash modified it by using the Straighten drawing mode to create perfectly straight lines.

Figure 3-1:
Use the Straighten mode of the Pencil tool to draw straight lines.

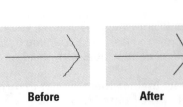

Before   **After**

Suppose, for example, that you want to animate some waves on your Web site. You start to draw the outline of the waves. Figure 3-2 shows how the waves look as drawn and after Flash smoothes them out using the Smooth mode.

Figure 3-2:
The Smooth
mode
makes you
look like
a real
smoothie
when it
comes to
drawing
curves.

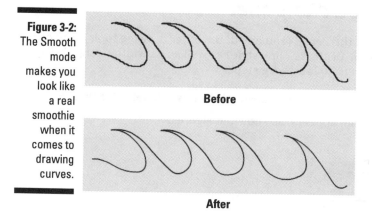

Before

After

For more complex shapes, the Ink mode helps you look good without taking away too much of your own authorship.

How to set smoothing and shape-recognition preferences

You can tell Flash just how much you want it to smooth or straighten curved lines when you draw with the Pencil tool. Choose Edit⇨ Preferences and click the Editing tab. From the Smooth Curves drop-down list, choose one of the following options:

✓ **Off:** Flash doesn't smooth or straighten at all.

✓ **Rough:** Flash only smooths or straightens slightly, honoring your own work as much as possible.

✓ **Normal:** Flash smooths or straightens a medium amount. Normal is the default setting.

✓ **Smooth:** Flash smooths and straightens more so you get fewer bumps and jolts.

In the same way, you can tell Flash how picky you want it to be when recognizing lines, circles, ovals, squares, rectangles, and arcs (90° and 180°). For lines, choose Off, Strict, Normal, or Tolerant from the Recognize Lines drop-down list. Normal is the default. Use Tolerant if you're a klutz; use Strict (or even Off) if you don't want Flash fiddling too much (or at all) with your work.

For other shapes and arcs, choose an option from the Recognize Shapes drop-down list. You have the same Off, Strict, Normal, and Tolerant options.

Using the Stroke panel

While drawing with the Pencil (and any of the other drawing tools), you can also control the type of stroke (line style) as well as its width (weight). To modify stroke settings, follow these steps:

1. **Open the Stroke panel by choosing Window⇨Panels⇨Stroke.**

   The Stroke panel appears, as shown in Figure 3-3.

Figure 3-3:
Use the
Stroke panel
to control
line type
and width.

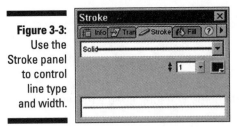

2. **Click the drop-down list to display the available line styles and choose a new line style from the list.**

3. **To change the line weight, type a new weight in the text box and press Enter (Return) or drag the slider bar to the value you want.**

The first available stroke weight in the Stroke panel drop-down list is Hairline, which creates a hairline-width line. Flash measures *weights* (widths) of other line types in *points*. Any line that you create by using a tool will have the properties you specify in the Stroke panel.

A point equals $\frac{1}{72}$ of an inch.

To create a custom weight, type a width in the Stroke panel text box and press Enter (Return). You can type any width, but note that custom line weights increase the size of your Flash movie file.

You can create custom line styles as well. Click the little right-pointing arrow at the top of the Stroke panel and choose Custom. In the Line Style dialog box that opens, you can create your own designer line styles.

Setting the color

When using the Pencil, you can set the color in the Colors section of the Drawing toolbox. In the Stroke Color section, click the Stroke color box to open the Color palette and choose a color. You can also choose a color in the Stroke panel by clicking the Stroke color box to open the Color palette.

We explain more about using colors in the section, "A Rainbow of Colors," later in this chapter.

Creating Shapely Shapes

In the preceding section, we explain that you can draw shapes by using the Pencil tool. You can also draw lines, rectangles, squares, ovals, and circles by using the shape tools. Use these tools when you want more control over your shapes — for example, when you want to draw perfect circles, perfect squares, and horizontal or vertical lines.

Line up

To draw a line, choose the Line tool from the Drawing toolbox. Click the Stage at the desired starting point of the line and drag to the ending point. Then release the mouse button. To keep your lines at multiples of 45 degrees, press Shift while dragging. Flash creates the line at the angle closest to your drag line.

When you use the Line tool, you can modify the line weight, style, and color in the same way as for the Pencil tool, discussed in the preceding section.

Be square

To draw a rectangle, choose the Rectangle tool from the Drawing toolbox. Click the Stage at one corner of the rectangle and drag to the opposite corner. Then release the mouse button. To create a square, press Shift as you drag.

When you click the Rectangle tool, you can modify the line weight, style, and color of the rectangle in the same way that you can modify a line when you use the Pencil tool. With rectangles, however, Flash actually creates two objects: the stroke (the outline of the rectangle) and the fill (the area inside the stroke).

Flash provides the following tools for adjusting the settings for rectangles:

✔ **Fill Color:** Determines the color that fills the inside of the rectangle. You can click the Fill Color box and choose one of the colors from the palette that opens. You can also choose from the gradients displayed at the bottom of the palette. (See the section, "A Rainbow of Colors," later in this chapter, for details about customizing colors and gradients.)

✔ **Stroke Color:** Determines the color of the stroke (outline) of the rectangle. Click the Stroke Color box and choose a color from the palette.

✔ **Default Colors:** Sets the stroke color to black and the fill color to white.

✔ **No Color:** Sets either the stroke color or the fill color (whichever tool is pressed) to no color. You have to click either the Stroke Color box or the Fill Color box before you click the No Color box.

✔ **Swap Colors:** Switches the stroke and fill colors.

✔ **Round Rectangle Radius modifier:** Creates a rectangle with rounded corners (it's located in the Options section of the toolbox). Click this tool to open the Rectangle Settings dialog box, where you can set the radius of corners in points; then click OK to close the dialog box. The rectangle you draw will have nicely rounded corners.

If you want to create a rectangle with no fill, choose the Rectangle tool, open the Fill Color box, and click the box with the diagonal line at the top-right of the Color palette. To create a rectangle without an outline, choose the Rectangle tool, click the Stroke Color tool, and choose the box with the diagonal line at the top of the palette.

Be an egg

To draw an oval, choose the Oval tool from the Drawing toolbox. Click the Stage at one corner of the oval and drag to the opposite corner. (Ovals don't really have corners, but you'll get the idea after you try one or two.) Then release the mouse. To create a perfect circle, press and hold Shift as you drag.

After you click the Oval tool, you can change the line color, type, and weight in the same way as described in the "Using the Stroke panel" section for the Pencil tool. You can set the color for the fill as described in the preceding section on drawing rectangles.

Mixing and Matching Shapes

After you create shapes on the Stage, you need to understand what happens when two objects touch. It's a little weird, but you'll soon see how flexible the Flash drawing tools are. Two basic rules exist about objects that touch. We cover those rules in the following sections.

Cutting up shapes

The first rule is that when you use the Pencil or Line tool to draw a line that intersects any other shape or line, the line acts like a knife to cut the other shape or line. The line you draw is also cut up into segments. You don't see the effect until you try to select or move one of the objects. Suppose, for example, that you want to draw a broken heart. You can draw the breaking line by using the Pencil tool. You now have several objects, and you can easily move apart the two halves of the heart. In the second heart (see Figure 3-4), the line has been erased.

Figure 3-4:
Intersect any shape with a line, and the line splits the shape and is itself segmented.

Placing objects on top of each other

The second rule about objects that touch is that when you place one shape on top of another, the top shape replaces whatever is beneath it. Again, you can only see the results when you try to select or move the shapes. But now it gets a little complicated:

- ✔ If the two shapes are the same color, they merge together into one combined shape.
- ✔ If the two shapes are different colors, they remain separate.

Figure 3-5 shows two circles and a triangle on the left. They are the same color. On the right, you can see the result after moving the triangle up over the bottom of the circles. If you try to select the heart, it's now one object.

Figure 3-5:
Build
complex
shapes by
putting
together
basic
shapes of
the same
color.

When you combine shapes of different colors, you create cutouts. Instead of adding the shapes together, the top shape just replaces the area beneath it. Figure 3-6 shows how you can create a heart cutout. You can't tell in this black-and-white representation of the figure, but the heart is red and the background shape is blue; the heart cutout is white, the color of the Stage background.

Figure 3-6:
By placing
differently
colored
shapes on
top of each
other and
then moving
the top
shape, you
can create
cutouts.

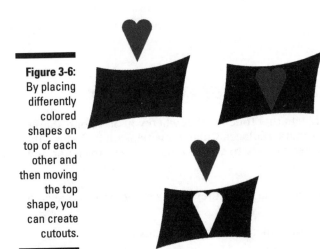

To create a cutout effect, follow these steps:

1. **Create two separate shapes of different colors.**

2. **Move one shape on top of another shape.**

3. **Deselect the shape you moved.**

4. **Select the shape again and move it away from the bottom shape to create the cutout.**

See Chapter 4 for details on selecting and moving objects.

Creating Curves with the Pen

A new tool for Flash 5, the Pen, lets you draw *Bezier* curves, also called splines. Bezier curves are named after the French mathematician, Pierre Bezier, who first described them. Using the Pen tool, you can create smooth curves that flow into each other. You can also create straight lines.

You can set preferences for the Pen tool by choosing Edit⇨Preferences and clicking the Editing tab. We suggest checking Show Pen Preview to display a preview of the line or curve as you draw. This helps you get a better idea of what the result will be. Click OK when you finish setting your preferences.

To create a line or curve, choose the Pen tool from the Drawing toolbox. What you do next depends on whether you want to draw a straight line or a curve. The following sections show you how to draw both.

Drawing straight lines

To draw a straight line with the Pen tool, click the start point and then click the end point. You can continue to add line segments by clicking additional points. Double-click to complete the process. You can also Ctrl+click (Windows) or ⌘+click (Mac) anywhere off the line. Flash previews segments in blue. When you choose another tool (or press Esc on the keyboard), Flash displays Beziers in the current stroke color.

Close a figure by pointing near the start point. You see a small circle. Click the start point and Flash closes the figure. Flash fills in the shape with the current fill color.

Drawing curves

Drawing curves with the Pen tool is a three-step process. To draw a curve with the Pen tool, follow these steps:

1. **Click the start point and move the mouse the desired direction and distance.**

   If you set preferences to show a preview of the curve (as explained in the section, "Creating Curves with the Pen"), you see a stretchy line attached to your mouse cursor.

2. **When the mouse cursor is where you want it to be, click and drag the mouse button to create the curve.**

   You see a *tangent line,* as shown in Figure 3-7. A tangent line defines both direction and length, both of which affect the shape of the curve.

3. **Double-click at the desired end point.**

To continue to draw continuous curves, start in the same way but drag in a new direction at the second point. You can continue to draw curves this way until you double-click to end the curve.

Figure 3-7:
Drawing a
curve with
the Pen tool
is a
three-step
process.

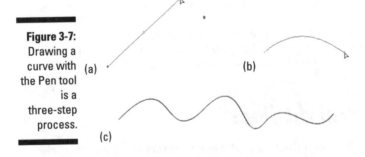

For both lines and curves, you can press and hold Shift to constrain the lines or curves (actually the tangent lines) to 45 degree angles.

Drawing curves with the Pen tool takes practice, but you'll soon get the hang of it.

Getting Artistic with the Brush

The Brush tool lets you create artistic effects that look like painting. You can adjust the size and shape of the brush, and if you have a pressure-sensitive pen and tablet, you can adjust the width of the stroke by changing the pressure on the pen.

 To paint with the Brush tool, click the tool on the Drawing toolbox. Press and hold Shift as you brush to keep your strokes either horizontal or vertical. Set the fill color just as you do for rectangles and ovals, as explained earlier in this chapter, or use the Fill panel. The brush doesn't have a stroke (line) color. Flash creates only fills with the brush.

The Fill panel

You can specify fill properties by choosing Window⇨Panels⇨Fill to open the Fill panel, as shown in Figure 3-8.

Figure 3-8:
Use the Fill panel to tell Flash what type and color you want for fills.

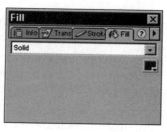

Use the drop-down list in the Fill panel to choose a type of fill. You can choose None to create a closed figure with no fill, or you can choose Solid to fill the figure with a solid color. Click the Color button to open the Color palette and choose a color for the fill. Gradient and bitmap fills are discussed later in this chapter in the "A Rainbow of Colors" section.

The Brush modifiers

When you choose the Brush tool, the Brush modifiers appear in the Options section of the Drawing toolbox, as shown in Figure 3-9.

Figure 3-9:
The Brush
modifiers
control the
size and
shape of the
brush, as
well as how
the brush
relates to
existing
images.

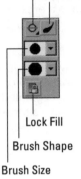

Brush Mode

Pressure

Lock Fill

Brush Shape

Brush Size

Brush Mode

The Brush Mode modifier determines how the brush relates to existing objects on the Stage. Here are your choices for the Brush mode (Figure 3-10 shows some examples):

- ✔ **Paint Normal:** Enables you to just paint away, oblivious to anything else. Use this setting when you don't need to worry about other objects.

- ✔ **Paint Fills:** Enables you to paint fills and empty areas of the Stage. The paint doesn't cover lines. Note that your lines seem to be covered as you paint, but when you release the mouse button, they re-appear.

- ✔ **Paint Behind:** Enables you to paint behind existing objects, but only blank areas of the Stage. As you paint, the brush seems to cover everything, but when you release the mouse button, your existing objects re-appear. You can messily paint over your objects, knowing they won't be affected.

- ✔ **Paint Selection:** Lets you paint only a filled-in area that you previously selected. As you paint, your existing objects are covered but they re-appear when you release the mouse button. You don't need to worry about painting within the lines because Flash only fills the selected area.

- ✔ **Paint Inside:** Lets you paint inside lines. Only the fill where you start brushing is painted. Paint inside also paints an empty area on the Stage if that's where you start brushing. Again, at first the paint seems to cover up everything, but when you release the mouse button, Flash keeps your paint nice and neat, inside the lines—like you learned in kindergarten.

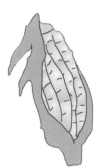

Original corn

**Corn with worms —
Paint Normal**

**Corn with bad kernels —
Paint Fills**

Figure 3-10:
Set the paint
mode when
using the
Brush tool
to get the
effect you
want.

**Corn with background —
Paint Behind**

**Sheath with gray
gradient — Paint Selection**

**Corn with bad kernels —
Paint Inside**

Brush Size

Click the Brush Size drop-down list and choose a size from the list of circles.
This list defines the width of the brush. If you use a brush mode that helps
you draw neatly, such as Paint Selection, you don't need to be too concerned
with the size of the brush. On the other hand, if you're creating an artistic
effect using the Paint Normal mode, the width of the brush is important.

Brush Shape

Flash offers several brush shapes that you can choose from. Click the Brush
Shape drop-down list and choose one of the shapes. Each shape produces a
different effect, especially when you paint at an angle — you just need to try
them out to see what works best. Figure 3-11 shows a scene drawn with various brush shapes.

Figure 3-11:
Each brush
shape
creates a
different
effect —
especially at
the ends of
the stroke.

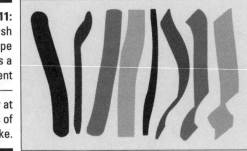

Pressure modifier

If you have a pressure-sensitive pen and tablet, Flash also displays a pressure modifier (refer to Figure 3-9) so that you can vary the width of your strokes according to the pressure you put on your pen as you draw.

Flash fully supports pressure-sensitive pens and adds some unusual features, such as the ability to use the opposite end of the pen to erase — just like a real pencil. Figure 3-12 shows such a pen and tablet.

Figure 3-12:
This Wacom
pen and
tablet is
easier to
draw with
than a
mouse and
enables you
to easily
vary brush
width as
you draw.

Photo courtesy of Scott Rawlings of Wacom.

A pressure-sensitive pen works together with a tablet to help you draw in Flash. The tablet tracks the movement and pressure of the pen as you draw. You can also use the pen as a mouse to choose menu and dialog box items. In other words, if you want, you can use the pen for all your Flash work. Alternatively, you can use the pen and tablet just for drawing and the mouse when you want to work with menus and dialog boxes.

See the section, "A Rainbow of Colors," later in this chapter, for an explanation of the Lock Fill modifier.

Pouring on the Paint

The Paint Bucket creates fills that fill shapes with color. You may create fills as you use other tools, such as the Rectangle and Oval tools, or you may want to fill an enclosed area that you created with the Line or Pencil tool. You can also fill enclosed shapes created with the Pen or Brush tools.

The Paint Bucket is also handy for changing existing fills. You can change the color as well as fiddle around with gradient and bitmap fills. (See Chapter 4 for more on editing fills.)

 To use the Paint Bucket, choose the tool from the Drawing toolbox. Set the color by clicking the Fill Color tool and choosing a color. Alternatively, you can use the Fill panel by choosing Window⇨Panels⇨Fill.

 Flash can fill areas that aren't completely closed. The Gap Size modifier determines how large a gap Flash will overlook to fill in an almost enclosed area. Choices range from Don't Close Gaps to Close Large Gaps. Because *small* and *large* are relative terms, you may have to experiment to get the result you want. After you choose the appropriate modifier, click any enclosed or almost enclosed area to fill it, as shown in Figure 3-13.

 After you use the Paint Bucket to fill a shape created with another tool, you can erase the outline of the shape and keep just the fill.

Strokes, Ink

You use the Ink Bottle tool to create an outline on an existing shape. You can also use the Ink Bottle tool to change an existing line (also called a stroke).

Figure 3-13:
You can fill
areas that
are not
completely
closed by
using the
Gap Size
modifier.

 To use the Ink Bottle tool, click it on the Drawing toolbox. Click the Stroke Color tool to choose a color. Use the Stroke panel, as explained earlier in the discussion of the Pencil tool, to choose a line thickness and line style. Then click anywhere on the shape. If the shape has no existing line, Flash adds the line. If the shape has a line, Flash changes its color, width, or style to the settings you created using the Stroke panel.

A Rainbow of Colors

Flash offers you lots of color options. You can work with the solid colors that come with Flash. By default, Flash uses a palette of 216 colors that are Web-safe, which means that they look good on all Web browsers. Or you can create your own colors.

Solid citizens

When you choose either the Stroke Color or Fill Color tool, Flash opens the *current color palette,* the active set of colors that Flash uses. If you want to stick with Web-safe colors, you should choose one of these colors.

Creating new or editing existing colors

Flash provides two ways for you to specify your own colors. First, you can choose the Stroke Color or Fill Color tool from the Drawing toolbox and click the Colors Window button at the top-right corner of the palette to open the Color dialog box. Alternatively, you can choose Window⇨Panels⇨Mixer to open the Mixer panel. These two methods duplicate each other; here we explain how to use the Mixer panel, shown in Figure 3-14.

If you select an object before you use the Mixer panel, the object's color changes immediately as you change the color in the Mixer panel.

Fill Color

Stroke Color

Figure 3-14:
Use the
Mixer panel
to create
your own
colors.

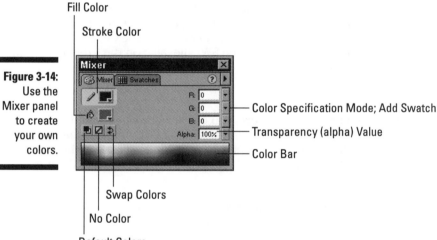

Color Specification Mode; Add Swatch

Transparency (alpha) Value

Color Bar

Swap Colors

No Color

Default Colors

To create a new color or edit an existing color, follow these steps:

1. **Click the right-pointing arrow at the top-right of the panel to open the pop-up menu; then choose the color mode.**

    RGB specifies a color according to red, green, and blue components; HSB specifies a color by hue, saturation, and brightness. Hex uses hexadecimal notation, which is the system used on the Web. The pop-up menu automatically closes when you choose a color mode, returning you to the Mixer dialog box.

2. **Click the Stroke Color or Fill Color box to specify which color you want to change.**

3. **Type in the color specs in the text boxes, use the sliders to drag to the desired color, or find a color in the Color Bar that's close to the one you want and click.**

4. **Set the level of transparency (also called *alpha*) by using the Alpha slider or by typing a number in the Alpha box.**

   A setting of 0% is completely transparent; 100% is completely opaque.

5. **If you want to create a new color swatch, click the right-pointing arrow at the top-right and choose Add Swatch from the list that appears.**

   Flash adds the new color to the color palette so that you can access it from the Stroke Color or Fill Color boxes in the Drawing toolbox, the Swatches tab of the Mixer panel, or anywhere else that Flash displays the color palette.

Look for `opening movie.fla` in the Ch03 folder of the CD-ROM for a great example of the use of transparency. The transparent rectangles pass by each other, creating constantly changing color effects. Choose Control⇨Text Movie to see the movie run or open the SWF file, also on the CD-ROM. (*Flash movie is courtesy of Jennie Sweo:* `http://sweo.tripod.com.`)

Managing colors

If you have added or changed colors, you can save this new palette. You can then save this palette for use in other Flash movies or import a color palette from another Flash movie (so you don't have to bother creating the color again). Color palettes are saved as CLR files and are called Flash Color Set files.

Macromedia Fireworks and Adobe Photoshop use Color Table files (ACT files), and Flash can import and save these as well.

To import a color palette, choose Window⇨Panels⇨Swatches or choose the Swatches tab of the Mixer panel. From the drop-down menu at the top-right of the panel, choose Add Colors if you want to append this imported palette to an existing palette. Choose Replace Colors if you want the imported palette to replace an existing palette. Choose Save Colors to save a palette to a file for use in another movie or program.

You can use the same Swatch panel drop-down menu to manage your color palettes. Choose from the following:

- ✔ **Duplicate Swatch:** Creates a duplicate of a swatch. Do this when you want to create your own color and use an existing color as a basis.

- ✔ **Delete Swatch:** Deletes a color.

- ✔ **Load Default Colors:** Replaces the active color palette with Flash's default palette of 216 Web-safe colors.

- ✔ **Save as Default:** Saves the active color palette as the default palette for any new Flash movies that you create.

✔ **Clear Colors:** Clears all colors except black and white. For when you really want to start from scratch.

✔ **Web 216:** Loads the Web-safe 216 color palette.

✔ **Sort by Color:** Sorts the display of colors by luminosity.

Gradient colors

So you're bored with solid colors and want something more interesting. *Gradients* are combinations of two or more colors that gradually blend from one to another. Flash can create gradients of up to 16 colors — quite a feat. Gradients are always used as fills. The gradient can be linear or *radial* (concentric), as shown in Figure 3-15. Because the figure isn't in color, it can't begin to show you the glory of gradients.

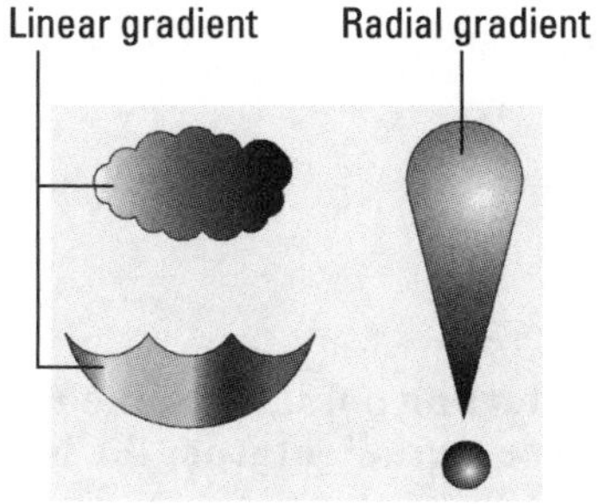

Figure 3-15:
Linear and
radial
gradients
make your
graphics
much more
interesting
than plain
solid colors.

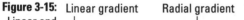

Linear gradient   Radial gradient

Flash offers a few standard gradients that you can find at the bottom of the color palette. But you often need a more customized look, and Flash has the tools to create just about any gradient you want.

First you need to understand a few terms:

✔ **Linear gradient:** A gradient whose transition is blended in straight bands of color.

✔ **Radial gradient:** A gradient whose transition is blended in concentric circles of color around a point.

✔ **Color pointer:** On the Gradient display of the Fill panel, the pointer defines the number and location of color changes in a gradient.

Radial gradients look best on curved objects. A circle suddenly looks like a sphere when you fill it with a radial gradient. Radial gradients give the impression of light highlights if you put white at the center of the gradient. Linear gradients look best on straight objects.

To create your own gradient, follow these steps:

1. **Choose Window➪Panels➪Fill to open the Fill panel. Then choose Linear Gradient or Radial Gradient from the drop-down list.**

   The Linear Gradient option is shown in Figure 3-16.

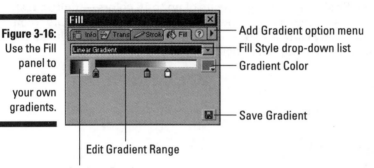

Figure 3-16:
Use the Fill panel to create your own gradients.

— Add Gradient option menu
— Fill Style drop-down list
— Gradient Color

— Save Gradient

Edit Gradient Range

Gradient Preview

2. **To use an existing gradient as a starting point, click the Fill Color box in the Drawing toolbox and choose a gradient from the bottom of the color palette.**

3. **To specify the color for each color pointer, click the pointer; then click the color box to the right of the gradient bar and choose a color from the color palette.**

   Note that when you click a pointer, its point turns black to indicate that it's the active pointer. The square beneath the point displays the color pointer's current color.

4. **To change the number of colors in the gradient, add or delete color pointers.**

   To add a color pointer, click where you want the pointer to appear, just below the gradient bar. To delete a color pointer, drag it off the gradient bar.

5. **To save the gradient, click the right-pointing arrow at the top-right corner of the Fill panel and choose Add Gradient.**

The new gradient now appears in the color palette of the Fill color box on the toolbox. Go ahead and fill something with it!

You can also move a gradient's center point, change its width and height, rotate it, scale it, skew it, and tile it. See Chapter 4 for more on editing gradients.

Bitmap fills

You can create the coolest, weirdest fills by importing a bitmap graphic and using the bitmap to fill any shape. For our hypothetical Web site protesting genetically engineered foods, for example, we could find a bitmap of a bug (representing the Bt bacteria genetically engineered into corn) and use it to fill a graphic of corn. Figure 3-17 shows the result.

Figure 3-17:
You can fill any shape with a bitmap, repeated over and over and over. . . .

To use a bitmap graphic to fill a shape, follow these steps:

1. **Create the object or shape that you want to fill.**

2. **Choose File⇨Import.**

   The Import dialog box opens.

3. **In the dialog box, choose the bitmap you want to use as the fill and click Open/Import.**

   The bitmap appears on the Stage.

   We explain more about importing graphics in the section, "The Import Business — Using Outside Graphics," at the end of this chapter.

4. **Choose Modify⇨Break Apart.**

   Flash breaks the bitmap into separate areas of color.

5. **Click the Eyedropper tool on the Drawing toolbox.**

6. **Click the bitmap on the Stage.**

   Notice that the Fill Color tool on the toolbox now shows a tiny picture of your bitmap. Flash also automatically switches you to the Paint Bucket tool so that you can immediately fill an object.

7. **Click the object you want to fill.**

Flash fills it with the bitmap. The bitmap is repeated over and over, in an effect called *tiling*.

Instead of using the Paint Bucket tool, you can switch to the Brush tool and then brush with the bitmap. Use a thick enough brush size so that the bitmap shows clearly.

Locking a fill

Flash has another trick up its sleeve for gradient or bitmap fills. A *locked fill* looks as if the fill is behind your objects and the objects are just uncovering the fill. As a result, if you use the same fill for several objects, Flash locks the position of the fill across the entire drawing surface, rather than fixing the fill individually for each object. Figure 3-18 shows an example of a locked fill. In this figure, you see some windows and portholes filled with a locked bitmap of the sky. Doesn't it look as if the sky is really outside the windows?

Figure 3-18:
When you lock a fill, the fill's pattern continues across the Stage but appears only where you use it.

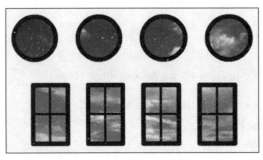

To lock a fill, choose the Brush or Paint Bucket tool with a gradient or bitmap fill, as explained in the two preceding sections. Then click the Lock Fill modifier. Start painting where you want to place the center of the fill and continue to other areas.

Drawing Precisely

If precision drawing in Flash seems too loosey-goosey to you, you need to know about a few features that can help you draw more precisely. Other programs do offer more precise tools, but Flash may have the tools you need.

The ruler rules

To help you get your bearings, you can choose View➪Rulers to display the Flash ruler along the top and the left side of the Stage, as shown in Figure 3-19.

To give yourself more room to work while you create drawing objects on the Stage, you can hide the Timeline by choosing View➪Timeline. Do the same to display the Timeline again when you need to work with layers or start animating your work.

By default, the ruler is measured in *pixels*. Computer screens are measured by how many pixels they display horizontally and vertically. Pixels are useful for Web site work because Web browsers work only with this unit. A pixel, however, is not a fixed physical size because it depends on the resolution capacity and settings of your screen. You may find it easier to think in inches or millimeters.

You can set the ruler to the unit of measurement that is most helpful to you. Choose Modify➪Movie to open the Movie Properties dialog box. From the Ruler Units drop-down list choose one of the units (pixels, inches, points, centimeters, or millimeters) and click OK.

Figure 3-19:
Display the ruler to help you draw more precisely; for further control, drag guides onto the Stage.

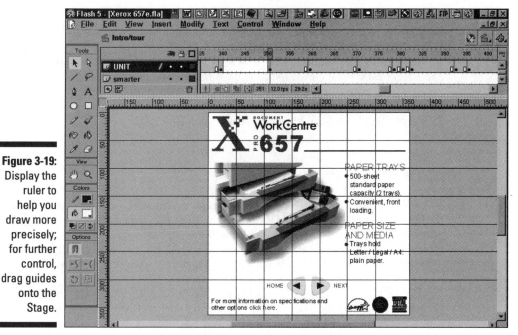

Figure courtesy of Phil Marinucci, Xerox.ca, and Julie Raymond, Xerox Canada.

When the ruler is displayed, lines appear on both the top and side rulers whenever you drag an object — either while creating it or editing it. For example, as you drag to create a square, you see a line on each ruler telling you where you started and where you end up. If you're moving the square, Flash displays two lines on each ruler indicating the outside dimensions of the square. You can easily move the square one inch to the left by looking at the lines on the top ruler.

Using guides

Guides are a new feature in Flash 5 to help you lay out the Stage more pre-cisely. Guides (refer to Figure 3-19) are horizontal and vertical lines that you can use as drawing aids while you work. Don't worry, guides never appear in the published Flash Player file. In order to use the guides, you must display the rulers, as described in the preceding section. To display guides, choose View⇨Guides⇨Show Guides. But that action simply turns on the guides feature; you still don't see anything!

To actually display the guides, you need to drag them from the rulers. Drag from the left ruler to create a vertical guide and drag from the top ruler to create a horizontal guide.

To customize the guides, choose View⇨Guides⇨Edit Guides to open the Guides dialog box where you can choose the guide color or clear all the guides. To force objects to *snap to* (attach themselves to) the guides, turn on guide snapping by choosing View⇨Guides⇨Snap to Guides. You can use the Snap Accuracy drop-down list in the Guides dialog box to choose how pre-cisely Flash snaps to the guides. To remove an individual guide, drag it back to its vertical or horizontal ruler. To lock the guides so that they don't move while you work, choose View⇨Guides⇨Lock Guides.

Working with the grid

You can display a grid on the Stage to help you draw more accurately and to gauge distances. The grid exists only to guide you and never appears when the movie is printed or published on a Web site. Simply displaying the grid doesn't constrain your objects to points on the grid. Use the grid by itself when you want a visual guide for sizing, moving, and laying out the Stage.

To display the grid, choose View⇨Grid⇨Show Grid. Use the same command to hide the grid again. You can set the size of the grid squares. Choose

View⇨Grid⇨Edit Grid to open the Grid dialog box. You can also change the color of the grid lines here.

You can change the units of measurement used for the grid by choosing Modify⇨Movie. In the Modify Movie dialog box, choose the unit you want from the Ruler Units drop-down list and click OK.

Snapping turtle

When you want even more precision, you can turn on snapping. Snapping tells Flash to snap objects to the intersections on the grid or to other objects. Usually you want the grid on when you use snapping so that you can see the snap points.

 To turn on snapping, choose the Arrow tool and click the Snap modifier in the Options section of the Drawing toolbox or Choose View⇨Snap to Objects. To snap to the grid, choose View⇨Grid⇨Snap to Grid. You can use either method to turn snapping off again.

Snapping pulls your cursor to the grid points and to existing objects as you work. You can take advantage of snapping both while drawing new objects and editing existing objects. When you have snapping on and select an object, Flash displays a small black circle and snaps that circle to the grid points.

Setting snap to grid preferences

You can get downright picky about how Flash snaps to grid points. Do you want the end of a line (for example) to always snap or only if it is close to a grid point or existing object? To set your preferences, choose View⇨Grid⇨ Edit Grid. From the Snap Accuracy drop-down list, choose one of the options between Must be Close and Always Snap.

Setting snapping to objects preferences

Because snapping applies to objects as well as grid points, you can separately set how Flash snaps to objects. Choose Edit⇨Preferences and click the Editing tab. Under Drawing Settings, click the Connect Lines drop-down list. Choose from Must be Close, Normal, and Can be Distant. Although Flash calls this the Connect Lines setting, it affects rectangles and ovals, as well as lines drawn with the Line and Pencil tools.

This setting also affects how Flash recognizes horizontal and vertical lines and makes them perfectly horizontal or vertical. For example, the Can be Distant setting adjusts a more angled line than the Must be Close setting.

Aligning objects

Flash gives you the tools to line up two or more objects vertically or horizontally and also lets you put equal space between three or more objects. Align and space objects to make your Flash movie look professional, as opposed to something you might create at 3 a.m. when your vision is too blurry for you to see straight.

To get those objects straightened out, select the objects and choose Window➪Panels➪Align to open the Align panel shown in Figure 3-20.

Distribute objects evenly

Align objects horizontally

Align objects vertically

Figure 3-20:
Use the
Align panel
to line up
and evenly
distribute
objects.

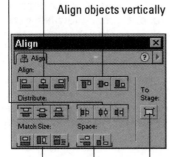

Align/distribute relative to Stage

Space objects evenly horizontally/vertically

Match size by width, height, both

To perfectly center one object on the Stage, select it and choose Window➪Panels➪Align. Click To Stage. In both the Align Vertical and the Align Horizontal sections, click the button that aligns objects through the middle. Flash centers the object on the Stage. A quicker way is to cut and paste the object because Flash automatically pastes objects at the center of the display (which is at the middle of the Stage if you don't pan the display vertically or horizontally).

The Import Business — Using Outside Graphics

So maybe you're the lazy type — or totally without artistic talent — and you really need help. Flash hasn't given up on you completely. Instead of creating your own graphics, you can use the work of others. Although Flash creates vector-based graphics, it can import both bitmap and vector graphic files.

When using others' artwork, be careful about copyright issues. For example, some graphics available on the Web can be used for personal, but not commercial, use. Most Web sites offering graphics for download have a written statement explaining how you can use their graphics.

Importing graphics

To import a graphic file, follow these steps:

1. **Choose File⇨Import.**

   The Import dialog box opens.

2. **In the dialog box, locate and choose the desired file.**

3. **Click Open/Import to open the file.**

A really cool feature of Flash is its capability to recognize and import sequences of images. If the image file you choose in the Import dialog box ends with a number, and there are other files in the same folder that have the same name but end with consecutive numbers (for example an1, an2, and so on), Flash asks whether you want to import the entire sequence of files. Click Yes to import the sequence. Flash imports the images as successive frames on the active layer so that you can use them as the basis for animation. (Chapter 9 explains more about frames and animation.) Table 3-1 provides a list of the types of files that you can import into Flash.

Table 3-1	Files That Flash Can Import	
File Type	*Windows*	*Mac*
Adobe Illustrator (.eps, .ai) (through Version 6.0)	X	X
AutoCAD DXF (.dxf) (2D only)	X	X
Bitmap (.bmp)	X	

(continued)

Table 3-1 *(continued)*

File Type	Windows	Mac
Enhanced Metafile (.emf)	X	
FutureSplash Player (.spl)	X	X
GIF/animated GIF (.gif)	X	X
JPEG (.jpg)	X	X
PICT (.pct, .pic)		X
PNG (.png)	X	X
Flash Player (.swf)	X	X
Windows Metafile (.wmf)	X	
QuickTime Movie (.mov)	X	X

You can also simply copy and paste graphics. From the other application, copy the graphic to the Clipboard; then return to Flash and choose Edit⇨Paste. (See Chapter 13 for details on exporting objects.)

For a nice example of imported bitmap graphics, see dc12_e_2.fla and Xerox 657e.fla in the Ch03 folder of the CD-ROM. In Xerox 657e.fla, Xerox is showing how the Docucolor 12 Copier/Printer can produce quality color printed output. To view these movies, choose Test⇨Movie or open the SWF file, also on the CD-ROM. (*Flash movies courtesy of Phil Marinucci and Julie Raymond, Xerox Canada.*)

Using imported graphics

Vector graphics from any drawing program become a grouped object that you can use like any other Flash object. The WMF format, a Windows vector graphics format, also imports in this way. These formats work especially well when imported into Flash. You can sometimes find WMF graphics in clipart collections and on the Web.

You can import text from a text editor and Flash turns it into a Flash text object so that you can edit and format it within Flash. See Chapter 5 for more on text and type objects.

When you import a bitmap graphic, you often need to take some steps before you can use the graphic in your Flash file. You can manipulate your graphics in several ways to make them more Flash-friendly:

- ✔ **Delete the background:** In many cases, Flash imports not only the shape you want, but also a rectangular background that you don't want. To get rid of that background, deselect the imported object, select just the rectangular background, and press Delete. If that doesn't work, read on.

- ✔ **Ungroup the graphic:** Ungrouping separates grouped elements into individual elements. Ungrouping retains most of the features of your graphic. Select the graphic and choose Modify➪Ungroup. If you find that you still can't work with your graphic properly, read the next item.

- ✔ **Break apart the graphic:** Break imported graphics to separate them into ungrouped editable elements. Breaking apart is useful for reducing the file size of graphics that you have imported. Breaking apart converts bitmaps to fills, converts text to outlines, and breaks the link between an OLE object and its source application. In other words, the Break Apart command is a powerful tool. Select the graphic and choose Modify➪ Break Apart.

- ✔ **Trace the bitmap:** Flash can work magic. If you want total control within Flash, convert a bitmap to a vector graphic.

To trace a bitmap, follow these steps:

1. **Import the bitmap — *don't deselect it or perform any other action on it.***

2. **Choose Modify➪Trace Bitmap.**

   The Trace Bitmap dialog box opens.

3. **In the Color Threshold text box, type a number to represent the threshold.**

   The higher the number, the fewer colors you get in the final vector graphic. For close results, try a value of 10.

4. **In the Minimum Area text box, type a number to represent the number of nearby pixels that Flash considers when assigning a color to a pixel.**

   For greatest fidelity, try a value of 1.

5. **From the Curve Fit drop-down list, choose an option to represent how smoothly Flash draws the outlines.**

   For the most exact results, choose Pixel.

6. **In the Corner Threshold drop-down list, choose an option to represent how Flash reproduces sharp edges.**

   For sharpest results, choose Many Corners.

7. Click OK to close the Trace Bitmap dialog box and then deselect the graphic to see the result.

When you import a bitmap graphic, Flash places the graphic in the current movie's Library. For best results, don't delete the original graphic from the Library, even if you have modified it. Flash continues to refer to the graphic after you have converted it to a symbol. (Chapter 2 explains all about the Library. See Chapter 7 for the total wisdom on symbols.)

If you're working in the Windows environment, you can also paste a graphic into Flash as an embedded object. To edit the object, double-click it to open the original application and use that application's tools.

To embed an object, follow these steps:

1. From within the object's native application, select the graphic and choose Edit⇨Copy.

2. Close the other application and return to Flash.

3. Choose Edit⇨Paste Special.

The Paste Special dialog box opens.

4. In the dialog box, select the type of object you want to embed, if you have a choice.

5. Click the Paste Link check box if you want to retain a link to the original file so that Flash updates the graphic if it changes.

6. Click OK to close the Paste Special dialog box.

Whether you created your graphics in Flash or imported them, you need to edit them in many ways. Chapter 4 explains the details of editing objects.

Chapter 4

You Are the Object Editor

*T*his chapter tells you all you need to know about editing objects. You can manipulate objects in a zillion ways to suit your artistic fancy. The Flash editing tools can give you precisely the results you want. Some of the more interesting features allow you to smooth curves, soften edges, and add interesting fills inside objects.

Sometimes you need to edit because you made a mistake (rarely, of course), but often editing is just part of the creation process. You may also find that you have to alter imported graphics so that they fit into the scheme of things.

Selecting Objects

Before you can edit any object on the Stage, you need to select it. Flash offers many ways to select objects. After you get the hang of using the Flash selection tools, you'll find them very efficient and easy to use.

Selecting with the Arrow tool

To select an object, choose the black Arrow tool. That sounds pretty basic. But just when you thought it was safe to skip the rest of this section, we've added some ifs and buts, so read on.

What is an object? If you draw a shape with an outline (also called a *line* or a *stroke*) and a fill, such as a filled-in circle, you have two objects — the outline and the fill. Here are some pointers for selecting objects:

✔ If the object doesn't have an outline and is just a fill, you're home free. Click the object with the Arrow tool, and it's selected.

✔ If the object has an outline and a fill, clicking the fill only selects the fill. The outline remains unselected. You can use this feature to move the fill away from its outline. To select both the fill and the outline, double-click the object.

✔ You can also use the Arrow tool to create a selection box. Click at one corner and drag to an opposite corner, making sure that the bounding box completely encloses the object or objects you want to select, as shown in Figure 4-1.

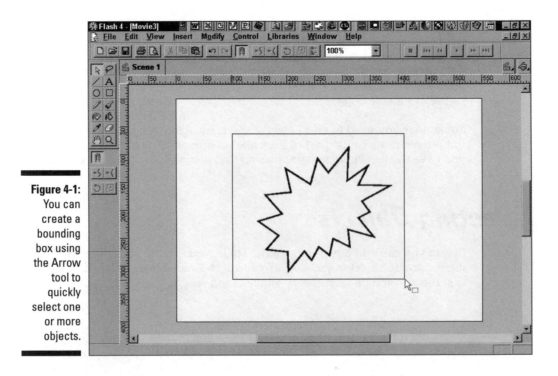

Figure 4-1:
You can create a bounding box using the Arrow tool to quickly select one or more objects.

- ✔ To select just a line, click the line with the Arrow tool. Still, you never know when an outline is really several objects, like the outline of the shape in Figure 4-1. To select the entire outline, double-click it. This technique applies to any connected lines.

- ✔ To select several unconnected objects, select one object, press and hold the Shift key, and select additional objects. When you press Shift, you can add to already selected objects and select as many objects as you want.

To deselect selected objects, click any blank area.

So you're happily drawing away, using the various drawing tools. Then you want to select one of the objects, but you forget to change to the Arrow tool. Oops! You draw another object by accident. Immediately, choose Edit➪Undo. Then use one of the Flash arrow shortcuts:

- ✔ Press the *V* key to switch to the Arrow tool.

- ✔ To temporarily switch to the Arrow tool while you're using another tool, hold the Ctrl (Windows) or ⌘ (Mac) key while you select an object or objects.

Lassoing your objects

For you rodeo types, you can lasso your objects so they can't escape. The Lasso tool creates a customized select area and selects everything inside. Use the Lasso tool when you want to select a number of objects that are near other objects that you want to remain free.

To lasso objects, click the Lasso tool on the Drawing toolbox.

To lasso freehand, make sure that the Polygon Modifier is not selected. Click anywhere on the Stage and drag around the objects you want to select. Flash creates a selection area as you drag. Release the mouse button close to where you started it to close the lasso's loop, as shown in Figure 4-2.

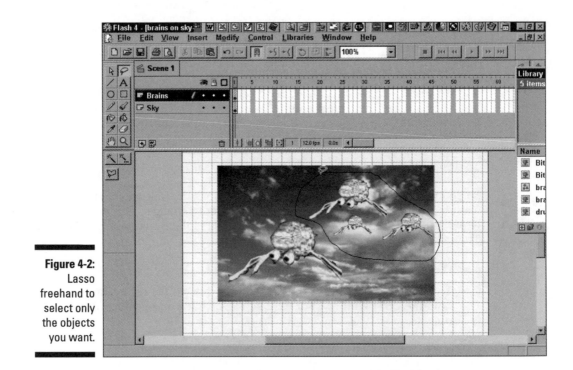

Figure 4-2:
Lasso
freehand to
select only
the objects
you want.

You may find that freehand lassoing is somewhat hard to control. If you find yourself inadvertently cutting across objects instead of around them, use the Polygon Modifier to draw straight-line polygons instead — like a lasso with a very stiff rope.

To lasso using straight lines, follow these steps:

1. **Click to choose the Lasso tool.**

2. **Click the Polygon Modifier.**
3. **Click where you want the first line of the polygon to start.**
4. **Click again where you want the line to end.**
5. **Continue to click, creating line segments as you go.**
6. **Double-click when you have finished lassoing the objects.**

Polygon lassoing may seem more complex than freehand lassoing, but it's easier to control because you aren't dragging with the mouse.

Selecting everything in one fell swoop

Suppose, for example, that you want to select or deselect all objects at once. Flash has some handy shortcuts to help you do that:

✔ To select everything, press Ctrl+A (Windows) or ⌘+A (Mac). Or choose Edit⇨Select All.

✔ Select All selects all objects on all layers except for objects on locked or hidden layers. (See Chapter 6 for an explanation of layers.)

✔ To select everything on one layer, click the layer name.

✔ To deselect everything, press Ctrl+Shift+A (Windows) or ⌘+Shift+A (Mac). Or choose Edit⇨Deselect All — who can remember those keyboard shortcuts anyway? Deselect All deselects all objects on all layers.

✔ To lock a group or symbol so that it can't be selected or edited, select the group or symbol and choose Modify⇨Arrange⇨Lock. To unlock a group or symbol, choose Modify⇨Arrange⇨Unlock All. (See the section, "Getting Grouped," later in this chapter, to find out about groups. Chapter 7 is all about symbols.)

Moving, Copying, and Deleting

The most common changes you make to objects are to move them, copy them, and delete them. Usually, moving, copying, and deleting are pretty straightforward tasks, but Flash has a few tricks up its sleeve, so keep on truckin'.

Movin' on down the road

Before you can move, you have to select. After you select your object or objects, place the mouse cursor over any selected object until your cursor displays the dreaded four-headed arrow. (Okay, most people don't dread it at all.) Then click and drag to wherever you're going. Press Shift as you drag to constrain the movement to a 45-degree angle.

For precision drawing, use the grid and turn on the snapping feature. (See Chapter 3 to find out about the grid and snapping.) You can also apply this technique to moving and copying objects. For example, you can attach one object to another by moving your first object until it snaps to the second, using the small black circle as a guide.

You can also use the four arrow keys on your keyboard to move a selected object or objects. Each press of an arrow key moves the selection one screen pixel in the direction of the arrow. Press Shift plus an arrow key to move the selection by eight screen pixels.

Moving with the Clipboard

You can move an object by cutting to the Clipboard and pasting if you want to move the object to another layer, scene, or to another file or application. After you select the object or objects, choose Edit⇨Cut. Alternatively, press Ctrl+X (Windows) or ⌘+X (Mac). Choose another layer or scene or open another file and do one of the following:

- To paste the selection in the center of the display, choose Edit⇨Paste or press Ctrl+V (Windows) or ⌘+V(Mac).

- To paste the selection in the same position relative to the Stage, choose Edit⇨Paste in Place.

Moving with the Info panel

If you want to place objects precisely, use the Info panel. After you select an object or objects, choose Window⇨Panels⇨Info to open this panel, as shown in Figure 4-3.

Figure 4-3:
Use the Info panel to place objects precisely — down to the pixel, if necessary.

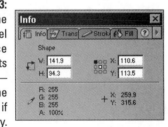

Use the X and Y text boxes to specify the location. The X setting specifies horizontal distance; the Y setting specifies vertical distance. Use the grid next to the X and Y text boxes to measure either from the top-left corner or the center of the selection — just click in the desired reference point on the grid. Flash uses the units that you specify in the Movie Properties dialog box. (See the section on drawing precisely in Chapter 3 for information on setting the units in the Movie Properties dialog box.)

Remember that when you move an object onto another existing object, it either joins it (if the objects are the same color) or cuts it out (if they are different colors). See the section on mixing and matching shapes in Chapter 3 for more information.

Copying objects

After you spend loads of time creating a cool graphic, you may want to copy it all over the place. The easiest way is to clone it directly, by dragging. Just select the object and press Ctrl (Windows) or Option (Mac) as you drag. Flash makes a copy and moves it wherever you drag.

You can also copy objects to the Clipboard. Select an object or objects and choose Edit⇨Copy or press Ctrl+C (Windows) or ⌘+C (Mac). You can paste the selection on the same layer or move it to another layer, scene, or file by using one of these techniques:

- ✔ To paste the selection in the center of the display, choose Edit⇨Paste or press Ctrl+V (Windows) or ⌘+V (Mac).

- ✔ To paste the selection in the same position relative to the Stage, choose Edit⇨Paste in Place. If you're on the same layer, scene, and file, you now have two copies, one on top of the other. The new object is selected, so you can immediately drag it to a new location.

Because Flash pastes objects from the Clipboard to the exact center of the display, cutting and pasting is a great technique to center objects on top of each other. For example, if you want to create two concentric circles, one on top of the other, create the circles in separate locations. Cut and paste the larger circle first, and then the smaller circle. You now have perfect concentric circles, and you can move them together to the desired location.

When you paste a new object, be sure to move the new object right away if it covers an existing object on the same layer. If you deselect the new object, it either joins the existing object (if the objects are the same color) or cuts it out (if they are different colors). Of course, that may be your intention. See the section on mixing and matching shapes in Chapter 3 for more information.

Makin' it go away

Making objects go away is easy. Just select them and press Delete or Backspace (Windows), or Delete or Clear (Mac).

Making Shapes More Shapely

You have created an object, but now you want to tweak it a bit. Flash has many techniques to help you perfect your artwork, and you can modify both lines and fills.

Reshaping shapes and outlines

To reshape an outline or a fill, choose the Arrow tool and place the mouse cursor on the object:

- ✔ If you see a corner next to the cursor, you can move, lengthen, or shorten an endpoint, as shown in Figure 4-4.

- ✔ If you see a curve next to the cursor, you can reshape a curve, as shown in Figure 4-5.

Figure 4-4: Use the Arrow tool on endpoints to move, lengthen, or shorten them.

Figure 4-5: Use the Arrow tool on curves to reshape them.

Now click and drag in the desired direction. Flash temporarily displays a black drag line to show you what the result will look like when you release the mouse button. If you don't like the result, choose Edit⇨Undo — or press Ctrl+Z (Windows) or ⌘+Z (Mac) — and try again.

When you reshape with the Arrow tool by dragging, you do *not* select the object. Dragging is the simplest and most direct way to reshape objects.

As with drawing, you may find it helpful to increase the zoom factor. Try editing at 200% or 400%.

Using the Subselect tool

You can use the Subselect tool to reshape strokes or fills created by using the Pen, Pencil, Brush, Line, Oval, or Rectangle tools. To use Subselect, follow these steps:

1. **Choose the Subselect tool (the white arrow on the Drawing toolbox).**
2. **Click the stroke (outline) or fill shape to display the anchor points on the line or shape outlines.**
3. **Drag the anchor points to modify the shape.**
4. **To change the direction of a curve, click any anchor point to display tangent lines and drag the tangent line handles (the little dots at the ends of the tangent lines).**

The tangent lines indicate the direction of the curve. See the section on drawing curves with the Pen tool in Chapter 3 for information on anchor points and tangent lines.

If you click a graphic with the Subselect tool and points aren't displayed on its edges, maybe you grouped it as we describe later in this chapter (or maybe you didn't create it with the Pen, Pencil, Brush, Line, Oval, or Rectangle tools). In any case, try choosing Modify➪Ungroup or Modify➪Break Apart, and then using the Subselect Tool.

You can also delete anchor points. Flash reshapes the shape without that anchor point. Select the object with the Subselect tool, select an anchor point, and press Delete.

Straightening lines and curving curves

Just as you can straighten and smooth strokes by using the Straighten and Smooth modifiers of the Pencil tool (see Chapter 3 for more about the Pencil tool), you can straighten and smooth strokes and fills of existing objects.

You can activate the Straighten and Smooth modifiers repeatedly and watch as Flash slightly reshapes your strokes or fills each time. Eventually, Flash reaches a point where it can't smooth or straighten any more.

Choose Edit➪Preferences➪Editing to adjust how Flash calculates straightening and smoothing. Change the Smooth Curves and Recognize Shapes settings.

To straighten a stroke, first select the object. With the Arrow tool active, click the Straighten Modifier button in the Options section of the toolbox. (You can also choose Modify➪Straighten if you're a menu nut.) Flash straightens out curves and recognizes shapes, if appropriate.

To smooth a curve, first select the object. With the Arrow tool active, click the Smooth Modifier button in the Options section of the toolbox. (You can also choose Modify➪Smooth.) Smooth softens curves and actually reduces the number of segments that create a curve.

You can use the smooth or straighten modifier to simplify a stroke or shape and then reshape it directly by using the Arrow or Subselect tool, as we describe in the previous sections.

Optimizing curves

Flash offers a technique called *optimizing* for curves. Optimizing reduces the number of individual elements in a curve. One advantage to optimizing is that it reduces the size of your file resulting in faster download times on your Web site. You can optimize repeatedly, just as you can with smoothing and straightening. Optimizing works best for complex art created with many lines and curves. The visual result is somewhat like smoothing but may be even subtler.

To optimize, select the object or objects and choose Modify➪Optimize. Flash opens the Optimize Curves dialog box, as shown in Figure 4-6.

Figure 4-6:
Optimize
curves to
reduce the
number of
curves and
smooth
them out.

Optimize Curves		
Smoothing: ———|———	OK	
None Maximum	Cancel	
Options: ☐ Use multiple passes (slower)		
☑ Show totals message	Help	

As you can see in the dialog box, you can choose how much you want Flash to optimize curves. If you mangle your work too much on the first try, undo it and try again using a different setting. You can generally leave the other settings as they are. Unless you have an extremely complex drawing, you won't have to wait very long so you can keep the Use Multiple Passes setting. And it's helpful to see the totals message that shows you how many curves Flash cut out and the percent of optimization that represents. (Why should you have to do the math?) Click OK to optimize.

Be careful to check the results after optimizing. Flash sometimes eliminates small objects that you may want to remain. Other changes may also be unwanted. If you don't like the results of optimizing, choose Edit⇨Undo.

Expanding and contracting filled shapes

You can expand and contract shapes. Expanding and contracting works best on shapes with no stroke (outline) because Flash deletes the outline while executing the command. If you want to expand or contract a shape with a stroke, scale it. We explain scaling later in this chapter.

Expanding and contracting is much like scaling but it's less flexible and intuitive. Therefore, you may want to consider scaling instead. The advantage of expanding and contracting is that you can specify a change in size in terms of pixels.

To expand or contract a shape, select it and choose Modify⇨Shape⇨Expand Fill. The Expand Fill dialog box appears. In the Expand Fill dialog box, shown in Figure 4-7, type a number in the Distance text box, using the units you have set for the entire movie. By default, movies are measured in pixels. (See the section on drawing precisely in Chapter 3 for the details on setting movie units.)

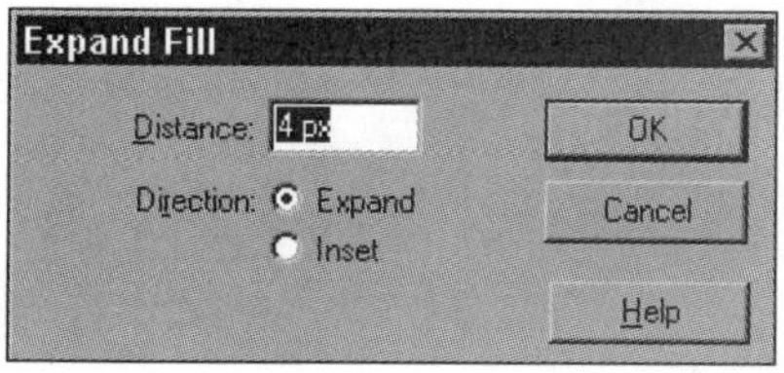

Figure 4-7:
Use the
Expand Fill
dialog box
to expand
or contract
fills.

Expand Fill	⊠
Distance: 4 px	OK
Direction: ⦿ Expand	Cancel
○ Inset	Help

To expand a shape, choose Expand. To contract a shape, choose Inset. Then click OK.

Softening edges

Softening edges is another shape modification tool. You can soften edges to get a graphic to look like you created it in some high-end program, such as Photoshop. Figure 4-8 shows some text before and after its edges are softened.

You can create this effect by breaking apart the text before softening the edges. Chapter 5 explains how to break apart text into editable shapes.

Figure 4-8:
You can soften the edges of objects to create cool effects.

To soften edges, select the object or objects and choose Modify⇨Shape⇨ Soften Fill Edges. Flash opens the Soften Edges dialog box, shown in Figure 4-9.

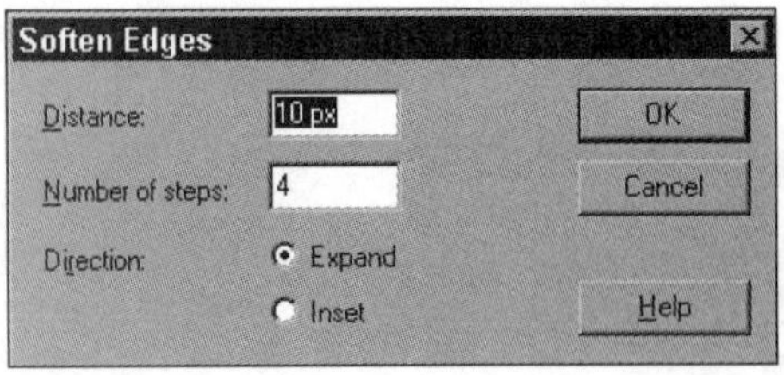

Figure 4-9:
Use the Soften Edges dialog box to soften up your boss — no, your graphics.

To soften edges, follow these steps:

1. **Set the distance, which is the width of the softened edge.**

   The distance is measured in pixels unless you have changed the movie units. (See the section on drawing precisely in Chapter 3 for information on setting the units in the Movie Properties dialog box.)

2. **Choose the number of steps, which means the number of curves that Flash uses to create the softened edge.**

   Try Flash's default first and change it if you don't like the result. You can increase the number to get a smoother effect, but the file size becomes larger.

3. **Choose either Expand to create the softened edge outside the shape or Inset to create the softened edge within the shape.**

   If you choose Expand, Flash expands the object. For example, if you used the Expand option in the example in Figure 4-8, the letters would run into each other. Therefore, inset is a better option.

4. **Click OK to return to your movie.**

   Your shape is still selected so click anywhere outside it to see the result. If you don't like it, choose Undo on the Standard toolbar (Windows) or press ⌘+Z (Mac) and try again using different options.

You can also create soft edges by using gradients that blend into the Stage color and with partially transparent colors. Chapter 3 explains more about using colors.

Converting lines to fills

Flash offers lots of great ways to fill a shape — for example, with gradients and bitmap images. But what about those poor strokes, or outlines? They're so *boring!* Flash doesn't want anything you do to be boring, so you can convert lines to fills and make them fun, fun, fun. (See Chapter 3 for an explanation of fills, including gradients and bitmap images.)

Mind you, there's not much point in converting a line to a fill if it's so thin that no one would ever see a fill in it. But by creating wide lines and converting them to fills, you can create interesting effects. Figure 4-10 shows some waves created with a line (using the Pencil tool) that's 10 points wide — the widest Flash allows. We converted the line to a fill and then used the Paint Bucket tool to fill the line with a gradient.

Figure 4-10:
Use the
Paint Bucket
tool to
change
the fill.

To convert a line to a fill, select the line and choose Modify⇨Shape⇨Convert Lines to Fills. That's all you have to do. You won't see any visible difference when you deselect the line, but now you can change the fill to anything you want.

Editing Fills

You can use the Paint Bucket tool to fill an outline. You can use the same tool to edit existing fills. For example, by changing the fill color of the Paint Bucket tool, you can change the fill color of a selected object. (For more information on the Paint Bucket tool, see Chapter 3.)

The Paint Bucket tool offers a unique way to edit gradient and bitmap fills. You can perform the following changes to a fill:

- Move its center point
- Change its width or height
- Rotate it
- Scale it
- Tile it
- Change the radius of a circular gradient
- Skew (slant) it

From the previous list, you can see that there's no point in fiddling with solid fills. They would look the same no matter what direction, size, or scale they were. (See the section on colors in Chapter 3 for colorful coverage of gradient and bitmap fills.)

To edit a fill, choose the Paint Bucket tool, and then click the Transform Fill modifier. Click any gradient or bitmap fill. Flash places an editing boundary and editing handles around the fill, as shown in Figure 4-11. The editing boundary is circular around a circular gradient fill but rectangular around a linear gradient or bitmap fill.

Figure 4-11:
The
Transform
Fill modifier
places an
editing
boundary
around
the fill.

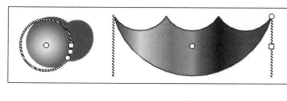

After you have a fill with an editing boundary, you're ready to go ahead and fiddle with the fills. Here's how to make changes:

- ✔ To move the center of the fill, drag the center point, marked by a small circle at the center of the fill. Try dragging to different center locations until you like the effect. You can move a center fill to change the apparent direction of light in a circular gradient or place a bitmap off-center.

- ✔ To change the width of a fill, drag the square handle on the side of the editing boundary. To change the height of a fill, drag the handle on the bottom of the editing boundary. If a fill doesn't have one of these handles, you can't edit the fill that way. Changing a linear fill perpendicular to its direction is the same as scaling the fill — the stripes get wider.

- ✔ To rotate a fill, drag the rotation handle, a small circle at the corner of the editing boundary. Figure 4-12 shows a linear gradient rotated 45 degrees.

Figure 4-12:
Rotate a
linear fill
to create
diagonal
fills.

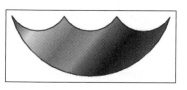

- ✔ To scale a bitmap gradient, drag the square handle at the corner of the editing boundary — inward to scale down and outward to scale up. To scale a circular gradient, drag the middle circular handle on the editing boundary. Scaling a circular gradient changes the radius of the gradient. Figure 4-13 shows a bitmap gradient at original size and scaled down. Flash tiles the bitmap if you scale down significantly.

Figure 4-13:
You can scale a bitmap fill to make it larger or smaller.

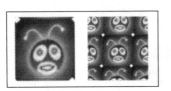

✔ To skew (slant) a fill, drag one of the circular handles on the top or right side of the editing boundary. You can only skew a bitmap. Skewing is different from rotating because the bitmap is distorted. Figure 4-14 shows an example of a skewed bitmap.

Figure 4-14:
You can skew a bitmap fill for really weird results.

When rotating a fill, you can press and hold the Shift key as you drag to constrain the rotation of the fill to multiples of 45 degrees.

If you scale down a bitmap so that you see many tiles, the next time you want to edit the bitmap, Flash places an editing boundary around each tile so that you have to edit each one individually. That could take a long time! If you want to edit a bitmap in several ways, save scaling down for last.

Later in this chapter, we explain how to rotate, scale, and skew entire objects.

Transferring Properties

You can use the Eyedropper tool to copy outline and fill properties from one object to another. Used that way, the eyedropper is like the Format Painter you may see in other applications. (See the section on bitmap fills in Chapter 3 for instructions on using the Eyedropper tool to create bitmap fills.)

To transfer properties, follow these steps:

1. **Choose the Eyedropper tool.**

2. **Select an outline or a fill.**

   If you select an outline, Flash activates the Ink Bottle tool. If you select a fill, Flash activates the Paint Bucket tool and turns on the Lock Fill modifier. (For more information, see the section that discusses locking a fill in Chapter 3.)

3. **Click another outline or fill.**

   Flash transfers the properties of the original outline or fill to the new object.

Transforming Objects

To scale, rotate, and flip objects, choose Modify⇨Transform. When you scale, rotate, or skew an object, Flash kindly remembers the object's qualities so that you can return the object to its original state before you fiddled around with it.

You can also rotate and scale by using the shortcut buttons at the bottom of the Drawing toolbox.

Scaling, scaling . . .

If you want to scale by eyeballing the result and don't care a whit about exact scaling percentages, use the Scale modifier of the Arrow tool. Select the object and then select the Arrow tool's Scale modifier. (If you used the Lasso tool to select the object, you must first activate the Arrow tool to display the Scale modifier.)

You can select as many objects as you want, and Flash scales them all. When you select more than one object, Flash places the handles around an imaginary bounding box that encompasses all the objects. Sometimes you may not get exactly the result you want using this method, so check carefully.

Flash places side and corner handles on the object, as shown in Figure 4-15.

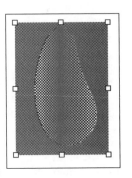

Figure 4-15:
Flash places handles on the object so that you can drag inward or outward to scale the object.

To scale the object proportionally, maintaining the relationship between the horizontal and vertical dimensions, drag any corner handle. Drag outward to enlarge the object and drag inward to shrink it.

You can also scale only the horizontal or vertical dimensions by dragging a handle on the side of the bounding box. Drag on the left or right handle to scale horizontally. Drag on the top or bottom handle to scale vertically.

Most of the time, scaling by using the Scale Modifier button is the easiest, fastest way to go. But sometimes you may want more precision. To rotate and scale at the same time, choose Modify⇨Transform⇨Scale and Rotate. In the Scale and Rotate dialog box, type a new scale as a percentage of the current scale. Type a rotation angle. (Flash rotates the object clockwise.)

For more options, select an object and choose Window⇨Panel⇨Transform to open the Transform panel, shown in Figure 4-16.

The controls in the Transform window work only if an object is selected. If you forgot to select an object, you don't need to close the window; just select an object.

To scale the selected object or objects, type a scale value between 1 and 1000. Any value under 100 reduces the size of the object, so a value of 10 creates a new object 10 percent of the original object and a value of 1000 multiplies the object's size by a factor of 10. Then press Enter (Return).

Figure 4-16:
The
Transform
panel lets
you scale,
rotate,
and skew
objects
with great
precision.

To make a copy of an object at a scaled size, click the Copy button (the left button at the bottom-right corner of the panel). The copy appears on top of the original object but is selected so that you can immediately move it if you want. Figure 4-17 shows an example of how you can use scaling and copying together to create the impression of objects at varying distances. When you make the copy, just move it to a new location.

Figure 4-17:
The brain
creatures
are
attacking!

Would you like to set the exact size of the object in pixels (or the current units for the movie)? Perhaps you need the object to fit into a certain space whose size you know. In that case, choose Window➪Panels➪Info to open the Info panel (refer to Figure 4-3).

Use the *w* (width) and *h* (height) settings to change the width and height of your object and press Enter (Return).

'Round and 'round and 'round we rotate

 The easiest way to rotate objects is by using the Rotate modifier of the Arrow tool. Select the object and then select the Arrow tool's Rotate modifier. (If you used the Lasso tool to select the object, you must first activate the Arrow tool to display the Rotate modifier.)

 You can select as many objects as you want, and Flash rotates them all. Sometimes you may not get exactly the result you want by using this method, so look carefully.

Flash places side and corner circular handles on the object, as shown in Figure 4-18.

Figure 4-18:
Use the circular handles on the object to drag it 'round and 'round.

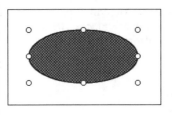

To rotate an object, drag any corner handle. The object moves as you drag so that you can see the result in real-time. Release the mouse button when you like what you see.

If you want to rotate and scale at the same time, choose Modify⇨Transform⇨ Scale and Rotate as we explain in the previous section on scaling.

If you want to rotate something exactly 20 degrees or rotate and skew at the same time, use the Transform panel. Select the object and choose Window⇨ Panels⇨Transform to open the Transform panel (refer to Figure 4-16).

To rotate the selected object or objects clockwise, type a value between 1 and 359. To rotate counterclockwise, type a value between –1 and –359. Then press Enter (Return).

 If you don't like the results, click the Undo button at the bottom-right corner of the panel and try again.

To make a copy of an object at a different rotation, click Copy (the left button at the bottom-right corner of the panel). The copy appears on top of the original object but is selected so that you can immediately move it.

If you want to rotate a section by 90 degrees quickly by using the menu, follow these steps:

✔ To rotate right (clockwise), choose Modify➪Transform➪Rotate 90° CW.

✔ To rotate left (counterclockwise), choose Modify➪Transform➪ Rotate 90° CCW.

When you rotate, Flash rotates the object around its center. To rotate around a different point on the object, you can convert the object to a group or symbol and change its *registration point,* the point on an object that Flash references when rotating. See the section on changing the registration point later in this chapter.

You can create groovy circular patterns by using the rotate and copy functions, as shown in Figure 4-19. Unless the object you're working with is completely symmetrical, you need to change the registration point.

Figure 4-19: By rotating an object and copying it at the same time, you can add flower power to your Web site.

Getting skewy

Skewing is a variation of rotating. Instead of rotating an entire object, you slant it horizontally, vertically, or both. Skewing a square creates a rhombus (diamond). In Figure 4-20, you see a simple arrow before and after skewing.

Figure 4-20:
After
skewing,
a boring
arrow looks
like it's in
a hurry.

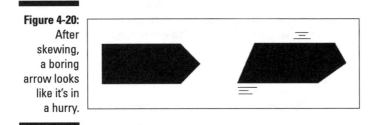

The easiest way to skew objects is by using the Rotate modifier of the Arrow tool. Select the object and then select the Arrow tool's Rotate modifier. Flash places side and corner circular handles on the object (refer to Figure 4-18).

To skew, drag any side handle. Drag either the top or bottom handle to skew horizontally (refer to Figure 4-20). Drag either the left or right handle to skew vertically.

Usually, you can eyeball the skewing process. If you want precision or to combine skewing with scaling, use the Transform panel. Select the object and choose Window➪Panels➪Transform to open the Transform panel. To skew the selected object or objects, click Skew.

Use the left box to skew horizontally. To skew clockwise, type a value between 1 and 89. To skew counterclockwise, type a value between –1 and –89. Then press Enter (Return).

To skew vertically, type a value in the right text box. Positive values skew clockwise, and negative values skew counterclockwise. If that sounds confusing, just try something out and see if you like it. If you don't, click Undo (the right button at the bottom-right corner of the panel) and try again.

To make a copy of an object at a skewed angle, click the Copy button (the left button at the bottom-right corner of the panel). The copy appears on top of the original object but is selected so you can immediately move it.

Flippety, floppety

Flipping reverses an object so that you have a mirror image of your original object. You can flip both horizontally (left to right or vice versa) and vertically (up to down or vice versa). Flash flips objects about their center so that they stay in their original position on the Stage.

Figure 4-21 shows a curlicue design in its original form, flipped horizontally, and flipped vertically. If you flip an object horizontally and then vertically, you end up with an object that has been mirrored in both directions.

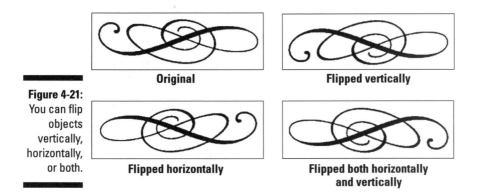

Original	**Flipped vertically**
Flipped horizontally	**Flipped both horizontally and vertically**

Figure 4-21:
You can flip objects vertically, horizontally, or both.

To flip an object, select it and choose Modify⇨Transform⇨Flip Vertical or Flip Horizontal. To flip an object in both directions, flip it in one direction, and then in the other.

You can use flipping to create symmetrical objects. To create symmetrical objects, you need to change the object's registration point from the center to one side or corner, as explained in the next section. Later in this chapter, in "Changing the registration point," we explain how to use flipping to create symmetrical objects.

Getting Grouped

After you know how to create objects, you can get carried away and create so many objects on the Stage that they're hard to manage. You may want to move a number of objects at once. Although you can select them all and move them, that technique may not be enough. For example, you may inadvertently leave behind one piece and discover it's hard to move that piece in the same way you moved the rest. That's why Flash provides grouping.

Grouping is a common concept in graphics programs. You select a group of objects and group them one time. From then on, you can select them with one click. If you move one, the rest come along for the ride.

In Flash, grouping has an additional advantage. If you put objects on top of each other, they merge if they're the same color or create cutouts if they're different colors. One way you can keep the integrity of objects is by grouping them. (Another way is by putting them on different layers, as explained in Chapter 6.)

It's easy to group objects. Select them and choose Modify⇨Group. For you shortcut types, press Ctrl+G (Windows) or ⌘+G (Mac).

After you group objects, you can ungroup them at any time. Select the group and choose Modify➪Ungroup.

You can also break apart groups as well as symbols, bitmaps, and text. (See the section on using imported graphics in Chapter 3 for more information.)

If you want to edit a component of the group without ungrouping first, Flash lets you do so. To edit without ungrouping, follow these steps:

1. **Using the Arrow tool, double-click the group.**

   Alternatively, you can select the group and choose Edit➪Edit Selected.

   Flash dims other objects on the Stage and displays the Group symbol above the layer list.

2. **Edit any of the group components.**

3. **To return to regular editing mode, double-click any blank area on the Stage with the Arrow tool or click the current scene symbol to the left of the group symbol.**

   You can also choose Edit➪Edit All.

Changing the registration point

When Flash rotates or scales an object, it uses a point as a reference. This is generally the center of the object. For positioning and certain transformations of lines and shapes, Flash uses the top-left corner. You may find that the point Flash uses isn't suitable for your needs. For example, you may want to rotate an object around its bottom-left corner.

Flash stores a registration point for the following types of objects:

✔ Groups

✔ Instances of symbols

✔ Type blocks (text)

✔ Bitmaps

(Symbols are explained in Chapter 7, text is just one chapter away in Chapter 5, and bitmaps are covered in Chapter 3.)

Flash needs this registration point to animate and transform these objects. The registration point is at the center by default. But if your object is any of the types just listed, you can change the registration point.

To change a registration point for a different type of object, such as a shape, group it.

To change an object's registration point, follow these steps:

1. **Select the object.**

   Remember, it must be a group, symbol instance, text, or bitmap.

2. **Choose Modify⟹Transform⟹Edit Center.**

   Flash places a crosshair on the current registration point, as shown in Figure 4-22.

3. **Drag the crosshair to the desired location.**

   As you drag, Flash displays a small circle at the mouse cursor, representing the new registration point location.

4. **Click anywhere else on the Stage to hide the registration point.**

Sometimes, turning on Snap or the Grid helps to place the registration point accurately. For more information, see the section on drawing precisely in Chapter 3.

Figure 4-22:
Use the
Edit Center
command
to drag an
object's
registration
point.

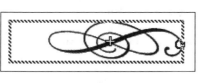

Changing the registration point is useful when you want to create symmetrical objects by flipping. To use flipping to create symmetrical objects, follow these steps:

1. **Select the object.**

2. **Choose Edit⟹Copy to copy the object to the Clipboard.**

3. **Choose Edit⟹Paste in Place to paste the copy on top of the original.**

4. **Choose Modify⟹Transform⟹Flip Vertical or Flip Horizontal.**

   You see your original and the copy. The copy has been flipped so that it's a mirror image of its original.

5. **To create a four-way symmetrical object, group both objects and change the registration point to one side of the combined group; then repeat Step 4 in the other direction.**

Figure 4-23 shows a weird creature created this way.

Figure 4-23:
Create scary, symmetrical creatures by copying and then flipping.

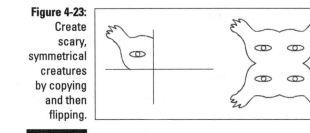

Locking objects

You can lock groups and symbols so you (or some other interfering person) cannot accidentally change it. When a group or symbol is locked, it cannot even be selected.

Here's how to lock or unlock a group or symbol:

✔ To lock a group or symbol, select it and choose Modify➪Arrange➪Lock.

✔ To unlock a group or symbol, choose Modify➪Arrange➪Unlock All. Flash unlocks all locked groups and symbols.

Establishing Order on the Stage

Flash stacks objects in the order that you create them. If you draw a circle and then an overlapping square, the square looks like it is on top of the circle because you created it more recently.

If you place an object on top of another object, the objects become one if they're the same color. If they're different colors, the top object cuts out the underlying object.

One way to keep the integrity of objects is by grouping them. Symbols also maintain their integrity. (Symbols are covered in Chapter 7.) Groups and symbols are always stacked on top of regular objects. Therefore, ungrouped objects must be grouped or converted to a symbol to move them above existing groups or symbols. Some imported graphics may also need to be turned into a symbol or group before you can move them in the stack.

If you draw an object and it immediately disappears beneath another object, it's often because you tried to draw the object on top of a group or symbol. It doesn't work. Group the object or change it to a symbol if it must be on top. (You can also convert the group or symbol back to individual objects.)

Another way to reorder objects is by putting them on different layers. You can then reorder the objects by reordering their layers. (See Chapter 6 for the details.)

As long as you have objects that can maintain their integrity, you can change their stacking order. You can move them up or down in the stack or move them to the top or bottom of the stack.

To change the stacking order of an object, select the object and choose Modify⇨Arrange. Then choose one of the four options:

- ✔ Bring to Front brings the selected object to the tippy top of the stack.

- ✔ Bring Forward brings the selected object one level up.

- ✔ Send Backward moves the selected object one level down.

- ✔ Send to Back sends the selected object down, down, down to the very bottom of the stack.

Figure 4-24 shows an example of two objects stacked in two different ways.

Figure 4-24:
The big, old-fashioned bitmap star and the small, up-and-coming vector star vying to be in front.

Chapter 5

What's Your Type?

*W*e assume that occasionally you want to say something on your Web site. So this chapter covers text in all its forms and formats. You can use Flash to create the text for your Web pages if you want to (you don't have to). But if you want flashy text effects, Flash is the way to go.

Typography is the art or process of arranging text on a page, and basically that's what this chapter is all about. Many graphics programs call text *type*. We use the words interchangeably here — we don't care what you call it.

Presenting Your Text

The majority of text on most Web sites is formatted using HTML coding that sets the text's font, size, and color. Using HTML code is ideal for larger amounts of text because it's simple to code and loads fast.

For smaller amounts of text that you want to have special formatting or effects, Flash offers more options than HTML. (Almost anything offers more options than HTML.) Of course, if you want to animate your text, you can use Flash. You can animate text just as you do other objects. For example, an animated logo usually includes not only the graphic art but also the name of the organization, which is, of course, text.

Here are some innovative things you can do with text:

✔ You can rotate, scale, skew, or flip text without losing the ability to edit the text.

✔ You can turn text into shapes and modify them any way you want. But after you turn text into shapes, you can't edit the text's characters simply by typing. Figure 5-1 shows some text that was modified in this way.

✔ You can create transparent type.

✔ You can create hyperlinked text that links users to other Web pages when they click the text.

Figure 5-1:
You can turn text into a shape and edit it to your heart's content.

Creating text

Creating text in Flash is simple. Follow these steps:

1. **Click the Text tool.**

2. **Specify the text starting point on the Stage.**

   • To specify the width of the text, click the Stage at the top-left corner where you want your text to start and drag to the right until you have the width you want. Flash places a square block handle at the top right corner of the text block.

   • To create a text block that expands as you type, just click the Stage at the desired starting point. Flash places a round block handle at the top-right corner of the text block.

3. **Start typing; to force a return to the left margin, press Enter (Return).**

4. **After you finish typing, click anywhere off the Stage to deselect the text.**

Congratulations, you've just said something. We hope it was worthwhile!

Editing text

After you type text, it never fails that you want to change it. Editing text is easy in Flash, but first you have to select it. Here are the selection techniques:

✔ To edit an entire text block the same way you would edit an object, choose the Arrow tool and click the text. Flash places a selection border around the text. You can move, rotate, and scale all the text in a text block this way.

✔ If you want to edit the content of the text itself, double-click the text using the Arrow tool. Flash switches you to the Text tool automatically. (Or, choose the Text tool and click the text.) Flash places the text cursor where you clicked or double-clicked the text, more or less.

✔ Choose the Text tool and drag across one or more characters to select them individually. Do this when you want to edit only those characters.

✔ Choose the Text tool and double-click any word to select that word.

✔ Choose the Text tool and click at the beginning of text you want to select, and then Shift+click at the end of the desired selection.

✔ Choose the Text tool and click in a text block, and then press Ctrl+A (Windows) or ⌘+A (Mac) to select all the text in the text block.

To change the content of the text, select a text block and then select the characters or words that you want to change, as explained in the preceding list. Type to replace the selected text. Other text editing techniques are the same as in your word processor. For example, you can press the Delete key to delete characters to the right of the text cursor (Windows only) or press the Backspace key (Windows) or Delete key (Mac) to delete characters to the left of the cursor.

Setting character attributes

Of course, you won't always want to use the Flash default font and size for your Web site. Boring! You can set the attributes before you start typing or edit the attributes of existing text. To edit existing text, double-click the text block and then select the characters or words you want to format. Then choose Window➪Panels➪Character or press Ctrl+T (Windows) or ⌘+T (Mac) to open the Character panel, as shown in Figure 5-2.

Setting the font, font size, and font style

Usually, the first step in formatting text is selecting a font. To select a font for your text, simply choose one from the Font drop-down list of the Character panel. Flash changes the font of the selected text.

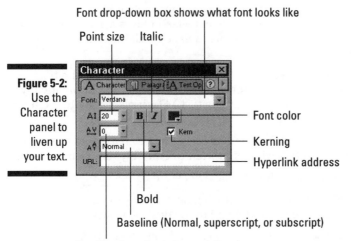

Font drop-down box shows what font looks like

Point size   Italic

Font color

Kerning

Hyperlink address

Bold

Baseline (Normal, superscript, or subscript)

Tracking (spacing between letters)

Figure 5-2:
Use the
Character
panel to
liven up
your text.

You can change the font characteristics that control specific properties of the font, such as size and style:

✔ To choose a font size, type a font size in the text box or drag the slider to the desired value.

✔ To choose a font style, click Bold, Italic, or both. Flash applies the style to selected text.

You can also choose fonts, font sizes, and font styles directly from the Text menu. This menu, new for Flash 5, is devoted entirely to help you format your text.

Specifying text color

Black is the Flash default color, but you have lots of additional options. The first concern is that the text is legible against its background. Yellow text looks great in front of black, but it's almost invisible against white. Also consider that text is often unreadable in front of complex graphic images, no matter what the color.

To set text color, select the text that you want to change. Open the Character panel as described in the previous section. Click the Text Color button to open the Color palette. Click a color. (For more information on colors, see Chapter 3.)

You cannot fill text with gradients without breaking it apart. At the end of this chapter, we explain how to break apart text.

To create transparent (or semi-transparent) text, choose Window⇨Panels⇨ Mixer to open the Mixer panel. Type a new Alpha percentage and press Enter. A 100% alpha setting results in opaque text. Text with a 0% alpha setting is completely transparent. A setting of 50% results in text that looks somewhat transparent but is still visible. To see the results, deselect the text by choosing the Arrow tool and clicking outside the text.

For a great example of text animation, open `time.fla` from the Ch05 folder of the CD-ROM. Then choose Control⇨Test Movie from within Flash. You can contact the animation's creator, Stefano Gramantieri, directly at `gramants@cine.ra.it`. To see the complete site online with the rest of the animation, the music, and all the links intact, go to `www.timeonline.it` and click the Flash site button. (The site is in Italian.)

Adjusting kerning and tracking

To get the look you want, you can adjust the spacing between letters of your text. *Kerning* reduces the spacing between certain letters, such as V and A. Because of the diagonal line on the left side of the A, without kerning, the V and the A may look too far apart. Figure 5-3 shows an example of text with and without kerning.

By default, Flash uses a font's kerning information, which is embedded in the font definition. Using the default setting is usually sufficient. Sometimes, with smaller font sizes, kerning can make text hard to read, so you can turn it off. Without kerning, text takes up slightly more space.

Figure 5-3:
First line uses kerning, second line doesn't.

VACATION

VACATION

To turn off kerning, select the characters you want to adjust and open the Character panel as previously described. Uncheck the Kern check box.

You can adjust the spacing between all the letters, also called *tracking*. Perhaps you need the text to fit into a tight space or you want to s t r e t c h it out without changing the font size. Figure 5-4 shows some text with a variety of letter spacing.

To change tracking, open the Character panel as explained earlier and type a value in the Tracking text box or drag the slider bar to the desired value.

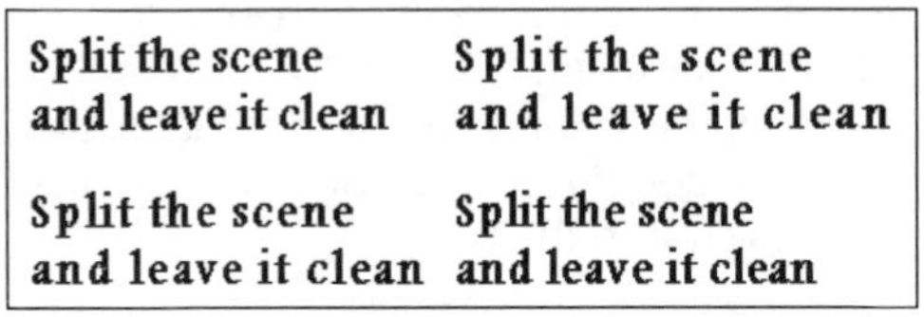

Figure 5-4:
Four
variations of
stretched or
condensed
text.

Split the scene and leave it clean	Split the scene and leave it clean
Split the scene and leave it clean	Split the scene and leave it clean

Hyperlinking text

You can create text that links users to other Web pages when they click the text. Flash underlines linked text, following the universal convention on Web sites.

To create text with a hyperlink, follow these steps:

1. **Select the text.**

2. **If necessary, choose Window⇨Panels⇨Character to display the Character panel.**

3. **In the URL text box, type the URL (Web address) of the Web page you want to use.**

   Flash creates a hyperlink to the URL. When your Flash movie appears on a Web site, clicking the text links users to the Web site with the URL you specified.

Checking text appearance in a browser

Although Flash offers lots of fonts, you don't know whether viewers will be able to see the fonts as you have created them. Viewers must have the fonts installed to see them properly. Moreover, fonts you create on one platform (that is, Windows or Mac) may not display identically on the other platform. As a result, you need to consider how your text will appear when published and viewed in a browser.

As a workaround to avoid possible problems with viewing fonts, Flash includes three *device fonts* that the Flash player always converts to the closest available font on the local computer:

✔ _sans: A sans-serif font similar to Arial (Windows) and Helvetica (Mac).

✔ _serif: A serif font similar to Times New Roman (Windows) and Times (Mac).

✔ _typewriter: A font that looks like it's been typed on a typewriter. (Are you old enough to remember what that is?) It's similar to Courier New (Windows) and Courier (Mac).

Another advantage of using device fonts is that the resulting published movies are smaller, so download time is shorter.

One way to avoid font incompatibility is to break apart the type into shapes, as described at the end of this chapter. But breaking apart text increases the size of your movie file.

To test whether a font can be exported with a movie, choose View⇨Antialias Text. You should see the text become smoother, less jagged. If the text remains jagged, Flash cannot export the text with the movie.

 Rather than give up all those wonderful fonts, try testing them instead. Publish the movie (see Chapter 13 for the full story on publishing your movie) and send the movie as an e-mail attachment to friends who use a different platform or who use different fonts. They can open the movie in their browsers and report on the results.

When you publish your movie, you can turn on the Device Font setting (Windows only). The Flash player substitutes system fonts for fonts that aren't installed on the user's system. (Chapter 13 tells more about publish settings.)

Setting up paragraph formats

You can set paragraph attributes such as alignment, margins, indents, and line spacing. Use these settings when you type more than one line of text.

Setting text alignment

You can align text along the left margin (*left justification*) or right margin (*right justification*) of the text block. You can also center text. You can create an even edge along both margins, called *full justification* or *justified text*. By default, text is left-justified.

To align text, select it and choose Window⇨Panel⇨Paragraph to open the Paragraph panel, as shown in Figure 5-5. (If you have the Character panel open, you can simply click the Paragraph tab. Then click one of the alignment buttons: left, center, right, or full.)

Left margin

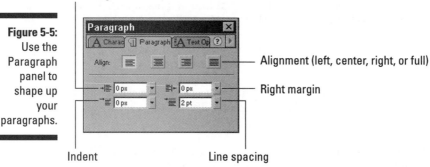

Figure 5-5:
Use the
Paragraph
panel to
shape up
your
paragraphs.

Alignment (left, center, right, or full)

Right margin

Indent   Line spacing

Setting margins and indents

The margin is the space between the text block border and your text. By default, the margin is 0 pixels. (The margin is measured in the unit used for the movie. See the discussion on drawing precisely in Chapter 3.) You can increase the margin to guarantee some space around the text. You can set only the left and right margins (not the top or bottom ones).

To set the left margin, select the paragraph and type a value in the Left Margin text box or click the arrow and use the slider to specify a value. Then press Tab or Enter (Windows)/Return (Mac). To set the right margin, use the Right Margin text box.

Indentation creates an indented first line. It's equivalent to placing a tab at the beginning of a paragraph. (Remember your sixth grade teacher who told you to always start each paragraph with an indent?) Indentation is measured in the movie units. For example, you can indent the first line 15 pixels. To indent the first line, select the paragraph and type a value in the Indent box or click the arrow and drag the slider bar. Press Tab or Enter (Return).

Specifying line spacing

Line spacing determines the space between lines. Flash measures line spacing in points (1/72 of an inch) because font size is measured in points. For example, if your text is 18 points high and you want to double-space the lines, use a line spacing of 18 points so that a space exactly one line high exists between each line of text.

To set line spacing, select the paragraph and type a value in the Line Spacing box or click the arrow and drag the slider bar. Press Tab or Enter (Return).

Flash remembers paragraph properties from movie to movie. When you change paragraph properties for one movie, you'll see them rear their ugly heads in your next movie. If your text looks strange, for example, automatically indents at the beginning of paragraphs or comes out double-spaced, check out the Paragraph panel.

Creating Cool Text Effects

Flash wouldn't be worth its salt if you couldn't create some flashy effects with text. You can manipulate text in two ways:

- ✔ Transform text just like other objects. In other words, you can scale, rotate, skew, and flip type. Figure 5-6 shows an example of skewed text.

- ✔ Convert type to shapes by breaking it apart. Select the text and choose Modify⇨Break Apart. You can then edit the text in the same ways that you edit shapes (as explained throughout Chapter 4). However, you can no longer edit the text as text— for example, correct a spelling mistake — so check your words before converting them! Refer to Figure 5-1 for an example of text turned into a shape.

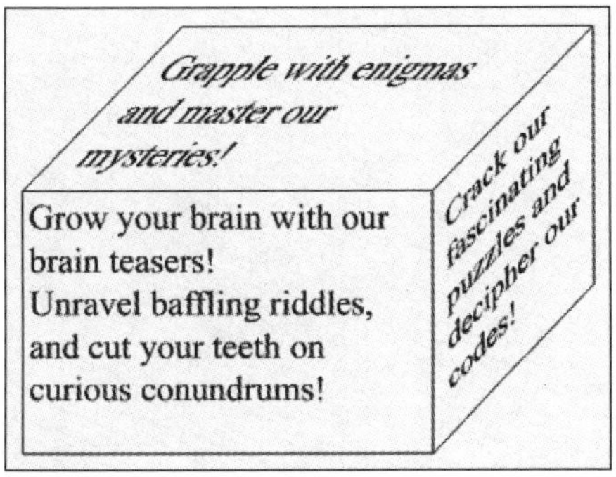

Figure 5-6:
Text skewed to match the angles of the skewed rectangles, creating a 3-D effect.

Grapple with enigmas and master our mysteries!

Grow your brain with our brain teasers! Unravel baffling riddles, and cut your teeth on curious conundrums!

Crack our fascinating puzzles and decipher our codes!

To animate text, you usually break it apart so that you can move letters individually. You can create animation where the letters of a word fly in toward the sentence to create the whole word, or, vice versa, where a word explodes, sending the letters flying outward. (See Chapter 9 for the details on animation.)

Chapter 6

Layer It On

· ·

In This Chapter

▶ Working with layers

▶ Modifying layers

▶ Using guide layers

▶ Creating holes with mask layers

· ·

*F*lash lets you organize objects on the Stage in *layers.* Layers keep objects separated from each other. Remember that Flash either combines or creates cutouts when two objects overlap. By placing the two objects on different layers, you can avoid this behavior, yet retain the appearance of overlapping objects.

Layers are also important for error-free animation. To move one object across the stage in front of other objects, such as a background, you need to put the object on its own layer. If you want to animate several objects across the Stage, you usually put each object on a separate layer.

You can also hide layers. Flash doesn't display objects on hidden layers. Hidden layers are valuable when you create motion guides that tell Flash where your objects go during animation. You want to see the object moving, but not the line (or curve) it's following. Hidden layers are also great for hiding some objects temporarily while you figure out what to do with all the rest of the stuff on the Stage. In other words, hiding layers helps unclutter the Stage so you can work more easily.

Finally, layers are great places to put sounds and actions. For example, you can name a layer Music and put your music there. Then you can easily find the music if you want to change it. Layers provide a great way to keep the various components of your movie organized. (See Chapter 10 to find out more about actions.)

In this chapter, you get all the information you need to use layers effectively.

Creating Layers

Flash lists layers at the top left of the Stage. New movies start out with one layer, creatively named Layer 1. You can, and should, change the name of this layer and new layers to something more descriptive, as shown in Figure 6-1.

Figure 6-1:
Flash keeps you organized by listing all layers.

If you're the organized type, it's a good idea to think about your animation in advance and decide which layers you need. For some reason, it doesn't often work that way and you may find yourself creating layers after you've created objects. In that case, you then need to move the existing objects onto those new layers. Either way, you create the layer in the same way.

To create a layer, click the Insert Layer button at the bottom of the layer list (or choose Insert➪Layer). Flash displays the new layer above the currently active layer and makes the new layer active.

If the Drawing toolbar isn't docked, it may cover up your layer listing. Try to drag it up and to the left to dock it on the left margin of your screen. You can also drag the entire Timeline, including the layer listing, to the right so it's not covered by the toolbox. To close any open panels, press Tab or choose Window➪Close All Panels.

To name the layer, double-click its name, type something meaningful, and press Enter (Return).

Using layers

Any object you create goes on the active layer. You can tell which layer is active because it's highlighted black and has a pencil icon next to its name (refer to the Rainbow layer in Figure 6-1). To change the active layer, just click any inactive layer on its name. You can also click anywhere in the layer's row on the Timeline.

To help make your work easier, Flash automatically changes the active layer to match any object that you select. So, if you're working on a layer that you named Text and select a shape on a layer that you named Shapes, Flash automatically switches you to the Shapes layer. Any new objects you create are now on the Shapes layer. Of course, if that's not the layer you want, you can switch to any other layer at any time by clicking its name.

If you click a layer to make it active, Flash selects all the objects on that layer. (Even if a layer is already active, you can click its name to select all its objects.) This feature is helpful for working with all the objects on a layer and discovering which objects a layer contains.

Changing layer states

Besides being active or inactive, layers have three *states* that determine how objects on that layer function or look. Use these states to help you organize how you work. The more objects and more layers you have, the more you need to use these layer states.

To the right of the layer name you see an eye, a lock, and a box. These aren't mystical symbols. The following sections explain how to use them.

Show/hide

You can hide all objects on a layer (also called hiding a layer). Hide a layer to reduce the clutter while you work. To hide a layer, click beneath the eye icon on that layer's row. Flash places a red X under the eye icon. All the objects on that layer disappear. Click the X to get them back again. To hide (or show) *all* the objects on the Stage, click the eye icon itself; but keep in mind that you can't work on a hidden layer.

To show or hide all layers *except* one, Alt+click (Windows) or Option+click (Mac) beneath the eye icon of that layer's row. You can also right-click (Windows) or Control+click (Mac) on a layer and choose Hide Others from the shortcut menu.

Lock/unlock

You can prevent objects from being edited by locking their layers. Lock a layer when you want to avoid changing objects by mistake. To lock a layer, click beneath the lock icon on that layer's row. Flash places a lock in the layer's row. Click the lock to unlock the layer again. The lock disappears and you can now edit objects on that layer. You can lock *all* the layers by clicking the lock icon directly. Click the lock icon again to unlock all the layers, but remember that you can't work on a locked layer.

To lock or unlock all layers *except* one layer Alt+click (Windows) or
Option+click (Mac) beneath the lock icon on that layer's row. You can also
right-click (Windows) or Control+click (Mac) a layer and choose Lock Others
from the shortcut menu.

Outlines

You can display objects as outlines of different colors. Outlines help you see
which layers objects are on because each layer uses a different color, as shown
in Figure 6-2. (Okay, you can't *really* see the colors in a black-and-white book,
but you can probably tell by the variations in gray that *Youth, Evolution,* and
2000 aren't the same color.) To display outlines, click beneath the outline (box)
icon on that layer's row. Flash puts a colored box in the layer's row, and all
objects on that layer are now shown as outlines in that color. (Text is still
filled in, however.) Click the box to display objects on that layer normally. To
display *all* layers as outlines, click the outline icon directly. Click it again to
see your objects as normal. You can work on outlined layers except that all
new objects appear as outlines, so it's hard to tell how they appear when displayed normally.

In Figure 6-2, the word *Evolution* has been broken apart for animation and is
therefore outlined like other objects.

To display all layers except one layer as outlines, Alt+click (Windows) or
Option+click (Mac) beneath the outline icon on that layer's row.

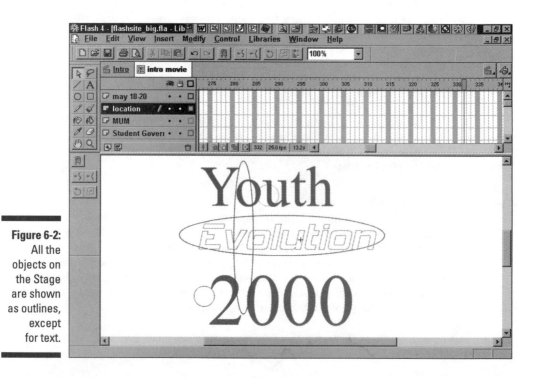

Figure 6-2:
All the
objects on
the Stage
are shown
as outlines,
except
for text.

Getting Those Layers Right

Good layer housekeeping can help keep you sane. Delete layers you no longer need. You can rename layers as their content changes; you can copy layers with their entire contents (rather than re-create them from scratch). Here we explain how to keep control over layers.

 You can select more than one layer at a time. To select a contiguous group, click the first layer, hold down the Shift key and click the last layer in the group. To select more than one layer when they're not all together in a group, click the first layer, press and hold the Ctrl key (Windows) or ⌘ key (Mac), and click any additional layers that you want to select.

Deleting layers

 As you work, you may find that a layer no longer has any objects. It's a layer without a purpose in life, so delete it. Select the layer and click the Trash button at the bottom of the layer list. You can also drag the layer to the Trash button; those of you who use Macs are accustomed to dragging items to the Trashcan.

 When you delete a layer, you delete everything on the layer. Not everything on a layer may be visible. You see only what exists on the Stage in the current frame. For example, if you introduce a circle in frame 15 of a layer named Circle, but you're currently in frame 1, you won't see that circle. Deleting the Circle layer, however, deletes the circle, although you can't see it.

 To check for objects on a layer, right-click the layer and choose Hide Others. Click the first frame in the Timeline and press Enter to run any existing animation. Objects on that layer will appear during the animation if they exist. To properly see the animation, you may need to choose Control⇨Test Movie to run the movie in the Flash Player — especially if you used ActionScript to control the animation. (Chapter 10 explains how to use ActionScript to control animation.)

Copying layers

You can copy a layer along with its entire contents, throughout all frames. If you have created a great bouncing ball, and now want two balls, copy the layer. You can then modify the position of the second ball throughout the timeline without having to re-create the ball itself. Now you have two bouncing balls.

To copy a layer, follow these steps:

1. **Click the layer name to select the layer.**
2. **Choose Edit⇨Copy Frames.**
3. **Click the Insert Layer button to create a new layer.**
4. **Choose the new layer to make it active.**
5. **Choose Edit⇨Paste Frames.**

Renaming layers

Rename a layer whenever you want. By default, Flash names layers Layer 1, Layer 2, and so on. As you use a layer, rename it to reflect its contents. To rename a layer, double-click the layer name and type a new name. Then press Enter (Return).

You can rename a layer as many times as you want.

Reordering layers

In Chapter 4, we explain how to change the order of objects on the Stage when they're on the same layer. When objects are on different layers, a new rule applies.

The order of the layers indicates the display order of objects on the Stage. Therefore, objects on the first layer on the list are always on top, objects on the second layer appear one level down, and so on. Objects on the last layer on the list appear on the bottom level of the Stage.

In fact, a simple and effective way to control object stacking is to put objects on different layers and then move the layers higher or lower in the layer list.

To move a layer, just click and drag it to the desired location. Figure 6-3 shows an example before and after moving a layer. The rabbit and the heart are on different layers. When you reorder the layers, their objects are reordered as well.

Changing layer order can help you select and edit objects covered up by other objects more easily. Simply drag the layer to the top of the list and the objects on that list now appear on top. When you finish editing the objects, drag the layer back to its original location.

Figure 6-3:
By changing
the order of
the layers,
you change
the order of
the objects
on those
layers.

Modifying layer properties

You can use the Layer Properties dialog box, shown in Figure 6-4, to change certain layer properties, such as the color used for the layer's outlines and the layer height. Most of the settings, however, are easily accessible from the layer list. Choose Modify⇨Layer to open the Layer Properties dialog box.

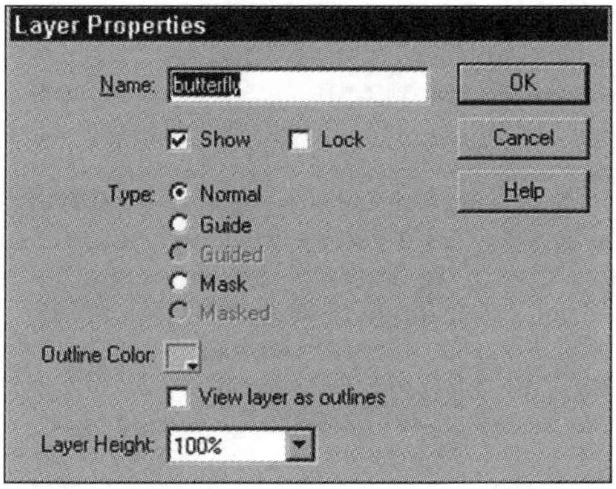

Figure 6-4:
The Layer
Properties
dialog box
lets you
fine-tune
layer
settings.

Here's how to use this dialog box to get the most out of your layers:

✔ **The Name text box displays the current name of the layer.** You can rename the layer here if you want.

✔ **Change the Show/Hide and Lock/Unlock layers states by checking (or unchecking) the appropriate check boxes.** Usually, you change these states directly on the layer list, as explained earlier in this chapter.

✔ **You can change the type of layer by choosing from the list of layer types.** Guide and mask layers are covered later in this chapter.

✔ **You can change the color Flash uses when the layer is displayed as outlines.** Click the Outline Color swatch and choose another color from the color palette.

✔ **Check the View Layer as Outlines check box to turn on outlines.** As explained earlier in this section, you can accomplish this task easily from the layer listing.

✔ **You can change the layer height to two or three times normal.** The main purpose of changing the height of a layer is to view sound waves on a layer containing a sound.

After you finish using the Layer Properties dialog box, click OK.

Creating Guide Layers

A guide layer is a layer that's invisible in the final, published animation. Although Flash 5 lets you display guides on the screen (as described in Chapter 3), you can also use guide layers to place gridlines on to help you lay out the Stage. Graphic designers use such gridlines to create a balanced, pleasing effect in their art. You can also import a bitmap graphic onto a guide layer and draw over the graphic on a regular layer, using the Flash drawing tools. This technique of drawing over a graphic can be a big help when creating your artwork.

Of course, you could use a regular layer and then erase whatever you don't want to appear in the final movie. But if you need to go back and make changes, you would have to create the guide layer over again. Using a guide layer gives you the flexibility of keeping the layer in the movie file, knowing that it will never appear in the published animation.

Layers that are hidden appear in the published SWF file.

You can place a path on a guide layer to control the motion of an object during animation. Figure 6-5 shows such a guide layer that contains a motion guide for the skateboarder. When animated, the skateboard does a flip, following the motion guide. (Chapter 9 explains how to create motion guides.)

To create a guide layer, create a new layer. Then right-click (Windows) or Control+click (Mac) and choose Guide from the menu. The layer is now a guide layer.

Use the same steps to convert a guide layer back to a regular layer. The Guide item on the menu is a toggle, so when you click it again, Flash removes the guide status of the layer.

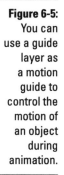

Figure 6-5:
You can use a guide layer as a motion guide to control the motion of an object during animation.

When you use a guide layer as a motion guide, Flash links the guide layer to a layer that contains the objects you want to guide. The layer with the guided objects is called a *guided* layer. In Figure 6-5, the loops are on a guide layer and the skateboarder is on a guided layer. All objects on a guided layer automatically snap to the motion path of the motion guide on the guide layer. To link a layer to a guide layer, creating a guided layer, you can do any of the following:

✔ Create a new layer under the guide layer.

✔ Drag an existing layer under the guide layer.

✔ Alt+click (Windows) or Option+click (Mac) the layer.

✔ Choose Modify➪Layer and choose Guided in the Layer Properties dialog box.

Flash indents the guided layer beneath the guide layer to help you see that they are linked.

If you want to unlink a guided layer, drag the layer above the guide layer or choose Modify➪Layer and choose Normal in the Layer Properties dialog box. You can also Alt+click (Windows) or Option+click (Mac) on the layer — this keyboard shortcut acts as a toggle to change the layer's status.

Opening Windows with Mask Layers

A *mask layer* hides every object on its related layers except inside a filled shape or text object. You can use mask layers to create peepholes or spotlight effects. Figure 6-6 shows a keyhole shape on a mask layer that hides the entire garden scene except for the part within the keyhole. The garden scene is actually a rectangle much larger than the section displayed through the keyhole.

Figure 6-6:
You can use a mask layer to create a hole through which you can see the layer or layers beneath.

Creating a mask layer

To create a mask layer, including the object on the mask layer and the objects behind the mask layer, follow these steps:

1. **Create the objects you want to show through the "hole" in the mask layer.**

   These objects can be on one or more layers. Place all the layers that you want to be masked next to each other and at the top of the layer list.

2. **Select the topmost layer on the layer list and click the Add Layer button to create a new layer at the top of the list.**

   This layer will become the mask layer.

3. **Create, insert, or import one filled shape, text, or an instance of a symbol on the new layer (see Chapter 7 for more about symbols).**

   The filled part of the shape, text, or instance becomes the hole — in other words, transparent. Unfilled portions of the objects become opaque. So everything becomes the opposite of its current state.

4. **Right-click (Windows) or Control+click (Mac) the layer's name and click Mask from the menu.**

   Flash turns the layer into a mask layer and locks the mask layer as well as the layer just beneath it on the layer list. The masked layer is indented. You see the mask effect displayed. (To link more than one layer to the mask layer, see the next section on editing mask layers.)

Editing mask layers

Because Flash locks both the mask layer as well as the layer or layers that are masked, you cannot edit them. To edit them, click the lock symbol above the layer list. Flash unlocks the layers and removes the mask effect.

After you finish editing the layers, lock them again to redisplay the mask effect.

When you create a mask layer, Flash only links the layer directly beneath it to the mask layer. A layer linked to a mask layer is *masked.* If you place objects on several layers that you want to be masked, you need to change the property of all those layers from normal to masked.

All the layers that you want to be masked must be directly under the mask layer.

You can link a layer to a mask layer in several ways:

✔ If you drag a normal layer directly beneath a mask layer, Flash links it to the mask layer, in addition to existing masked layers.

✔ Alt+click (Windows) or Option+click (Mac) the layer that you want to be masked.

✔ Right-click (Windows) or Control+click (Mac) the layer and choose Properties. Choose Masked in the Layer Properties dialog box.

Similarly, you can unlink a layer from its mask layer by using one of these methods:

✔ Drag the linked layer above the mask layer.

✔ Right-click (Windows) Control+click (Mac) the layer and choose Properties. Choose Normal in the Layer Properties dialog box.

✔ Alt-click (Windows) or Option+click (Mac) the layer. If it's masked, Flash changes its status to normal.

Animating mask layers

Mask layers are more fun when you animate them. You can move them, change their size, and change their shape. If you create a keyhole like the one shown in Figure 6-6, you can move the keyhole past the masked layers, revealing what lies beneath as the keyhole moves. You can use the same technique to create an effect of a spotlight moving around a stage, revealing whatever it lights up. The only thing you can't do is to animate the mask layer objects along motion paths. (Chapter 9 explains how to animate masks along with other objects.)

Look for di.swf in the Ch06 folder of the CD-ROM. This movie from Dennis Interactive, at www.dennisinteractive.com, starts with a good example of a mask. This is a Flash Player file, so you can view it by double-clicking the file. *(Thanks to Leslie Allen-Kickham for this file.)*

Part III
Getting Symbolic

The 5th Wave   By Rich Tennant

"Look into my Web site, Ms. Carruthers. Look deep into its rotating, nicely animated spiral, spinning, spinning, pulling you in, deeper... deeper..."

In this part . . .

Symbols teach us about the deeper levels of life, and Flash symbols let you get down deep into the mechanics of animation. In this part, you learn about the three kinds of symbols — graphic, button, and movie clip symbols and how to use them.

Manipulating symbols is a critical feature of Flash. Symbols let you easily place duplicate graphics in your movie without significantly increasing the movie's size, and you use symbols when you start to animate. This part also gives you the lowdown on buttons, which are so central to the Web lifestyle in the 21st century. Flash lets you create buttons that change as you pass the mouse cursor over them and again as you click them. You can even make animated buttons. Part III provides you with the basis for creating great animations.

Chapter 7

Heavy Symbolism

● ●

● ●

*F*lash offers a way to simplify your work, called *symbols*. A symbol can be any object or combination of objects, animation, or a Web button. When you create a symbol, the objects (or animation) become one symbol. Sounds like grouping, yes? The difference is that Flash stores the definition of the symbol in the Library. From the library, you can now effortlessly insert multiple copies of the symbol into your movie. Each copy is called an *instance*.

Besides making your life easier when you want to use a set of objects more than once, symbols have another advantage — they significantly reduce the size of your files. Instead of storing each instance you use, Flash stores one definition for the symbol and only references to the symbol for each instance. Turning objects into symbols helps reduce file size even when you use the symbol only once, because Flash remembers only one object instead of many. Backgrounds that aren't animated can therefore be combined into one symbol. In our test, we created a simple animation and turned the background into a symbol. The file size went from 77K to 60K.

You can place symbols inside other symbols. Used this way, symbols are the building blocks for complex graphics and animation. Motion-tweened animation requires symbols, groups, or text, so you often create symbols when preparing to animate. (Chapter 9 explains tweened animation.)

So, symbols are all-around good guys and you should use them as much as possible.

Understanding Symbol Types

Flash offers three types of symbols. Each type is made up of a group of objects or animation, but each type has a different purpose. Understanding these types is very important to understanding symbols and Flash animation in general.

Using graphic symbols

Graphic symbols are the simplest and most obvious type of symbol. When you create a Flash movie, you create objects on the Stage. Some objects may remain still, such as backgrounds. You animate other objects — after all, what is Flash for? When you create a symbol from either objects or animation, you're creating a graphic symbol. Figure 7-1 shows a graphic symbol created from several curves and circles.

Figure 7-1:
A graphic symbol, created from several objects, has a single selection border.

You create graphic symbols to reduce the size of your file and to make it easier to add multiple copies of a graphic to your movie. Symbols are stored in the Library and are not only available to the movie in which you created them but also to any other movie. Therefore, using symbols is a good way to store graphic images for use in Flash movies. You don't have to re-create the wheel.

Flash ignores sounds or actions inside graphic symbols. Actions (which we explain in detail in Chapter 10) are the key to creating interactive movies. For that reason, turn animation into graphic symbols only when the animation is simple.

Using movie clip symbols

Movie clips were introduced with Flash 4. A *movie clip* is like a movie within a movie that you can manipulate by using interactive controls (also called *actions,* and created with *ActionScript,* which you can read about in Chapter 10). Movie clips are crucial for complex animation and especially interactive animation. A movie clip doesn't take place on the main Timeline. Instead, you can go to the movie clip at any time, play it, and then return to where you left off in the Timeline. You can also attach movie clips to buttons. We explain how to create movie clips in this chapter. Chapter 8 discusses using movie clips with buttons. Chapter 9 covers using movie clips in animation. Chapter 10 explains how to use and control movie clips using interactive controls.

With Flash 5, you can give a movie clip custom properties. Right-click (Windows) or Control+Click (Mac) the movie clip in the Library and choose Define Clip Parameters. You can then assign specific values to individual instances of movie clips. Select the instance and choose Window⇨Panels⇨ Clip Parameters. You can add actions to instances of a movie clip; in Flash 4 you were able to place actions only on frames or in buttons. (See Chapter 10 for more information.)

Using button symbols

Button symbols create *buttons* — those little graphics that you click in Web sites to take you to other places on the site or the Internet. In Flash you can use buttons in the same way, but you can also use buttons to let viewers decide if they want to see a movie — when they click the button, the movie starts. You can also use advanced scripting to create buttons that control interactive games and other viewer activities. However you want to use buttons, button symbols are the way to start. You can add movie clips and interactive controls to buttons. Find out all about buttons in Chapter 8.

Creating Symbols

In most cases, you create the objects that you need and then turn them into a symbol. However, creating a movie clip symbol is different because it's a type of animation. Either create animation on the Stage and then convert it to a movie clip symbol, or create the movie clip symbol, create the initial objects, and then create the animation.

To create a symbol from objects that you've already created, follow these steps:

1. **Select the objects on the Stage that you want to convert to a symbol.**

2. **Choose Insert⇨Convert to Symbol or press F8.**

   The Symbol Properties dialog box opens, as shown in Figure 7-2.

Figure 7-2:
Use the
Symbol
Properties
dialog box
to specify
the name
and type of
the symbol.

Symbol Properties

Name: [Symbol 2]

Behavior: ⦿ Graphic
○ Button
○ Movie Clip

3. **In the Name text box, type a name for the symbol.**

4. **In the Behavior list, choose the type of symbol that you want to create: graphic, button, or movie clip.**

5. **Click OK to create the symbol and close the Symbol Properties dialog box.**

   The objects you selected become one object, indicated by a single selection border around all the objects. Flash also stores the symbol in the Library. (Chapter 2 explains how to use the Library.)

Each type of symbol has its own icon that's used in the Library. While the second column of the Library tells you the type of symbol, often you want to keep the Library window as narrow as possible so that it doesn't cover up the Stage. So, if you can't see the second column, you can just look at the symbol icon to know its type. The following list shows what type of symbol each icon represents:

Graphic

Button

Movie clip

Smart clip

Instead of creating a symbol from existing objects, you can create an empty symbol and then create the objects for the symbol. If you know in advance that you want to create a symbol, you can use this method.

To create an empty symbol, follow these steps:

1. **With no objects selected, choose Insert⇨New Symbol.**

   The Symbol Properties dialog box opens.

2. **In the Name text box, type a name for the symbol.**

3. **In the Behavior list, choose the type of symbol that you want to create: graphic, button, or movie clip; then click OK.**

   Flash switches to symbol-editing mode, which we describe in the section, "Editing symbols," later in this chapter.

4. **Create the objects or animation for the symbol in the same way that you do in regular movie-editing mode.**

5. **Choose Edit⇨Edit Movie to leave symbol-editing mode and return to your movie.**

   Your new symbol disappears! Don't worry, Flash saved the symbol in the Library. To insert the symbol on the Stage, see the section, "Inserting instances," later in this chapter.

You can create a movie clip symbol by converting regular animation to a movie clip. Use this method when you already have the animation created on your Timeline.

To convert an animation on your Stage to a movie clip symbol, follow these steps:

1. **On the layer listing, select all frames in all layers containing the animation by clicking the first layer and pressing Shift while you click the last layer in the group.**

   Alternatively, you can press Ctrl (Windows) or ⌘ (Mac) and click additional layers.

2. **On the Timeline, right-click (Windows) or Control+Click (Mac) and choose Copy frames to copy all the frames of the animation to the Clipboard.**

   Alternatively, you can choose Edit⇨Copy Frames.

3. **With no objects selected, choose Insert⇨New Symbol.**

   The Symbol Properties dialog box opens.

4. **In the Name text box, type a name for the movie clip.**

5. **From the Behavior list, choose Movie Clip as the type of symbol.**

6. **Click OK to close the Symbol Properties dialog box.**

   Flash switches to symbol-editing mode so that you can edit the symbol.

7. **Click the first frame of the Timeline to set the start of the movie clip symbol.**

8. **Choose Edit⇨Paste Frames to paste the animation into the Timeline and create the symbol.**

9. **To return to the main movie and Timeline, choose Edit⇨Edit Movie.**

10. **To delete the animation from the main movie (now that you've saved it in a movie clip), select all layers as you did in Step 1 and choose Insert⇨Remove Frames.**

    Flash deletes the animation from the main movie because you now have a movie clip in your Library containing that animation.

The final way to create a symbol is to duplicate an existing symbol. To duplicate a symbol, follow these steps:

1. **Open the Library (Window⇨Library).**

2. **Select the symbol that you want to duplicate.**

3. **Click the Options menu in the upper-right corner of the Library window and choose Duplicate.**

   Flash opens the Symbol Properties dialog box.

4. **In the Name text box, type a name for the duplicate and choose the type of symbol that you want to create if you want a different kind than the original.**

5. **Click OK to close the dialog box and create the duplicate symbol.**

Changing the type of symbol

You may need to change a symbol's type. For example, you may create a graphic symbol and then realize that you need it to be a movie clip. No problem!

To change the symbol type, follow these steps:

1. **Choose Window⇨Library to open the Library.**

2. **Right-click (Windows) or Control+click (Mac) the symbol's icon (not its name) and choose Properties from the menu.**

   The Symbol Properties dialog box opens.

3. **From the Behavior list, choose the type of symbol you want and click OK.**

Look in the Ch07 folder on the CD-ROM for `invent.fla` and `invent.swf` for a good example of a short movie with lots of different types of symbols. This movie is taken from the beginning of the `www.omm.ch` Web site, with a humorous twist (press the Enter button). *(Flash movie is courtesy of Stephan Oppliger of OMM Oppliger Multimedia.)*

Editing symbols

Part of the power of symbols lies in their control over instances. If you edit a symbol, Flash updates all instances of that symbol in the movie. You can change a symbol once and save yourself the time of creating the same change for every instance of that symbol. For that reason, it's worthwhile to make a symbol every time you want to use a certain shape or group of shapes more than once.

You can edit a symbol in three different modes:

- ✔ **Edit in Place:** Lets you edit a symbol while still viewing other objects on the Stage. Other objects are dimmed while you edit the symbol.

- ✔ **Edit in Symbol-Editing Mode:** Switches you to symbol-editing mode. You see only the symbol.

- ✔ **Edit in a New Window:** Opens a new window where you can edit your symbol. You see only the symbol.

The value of editing in place is that you can see how your change works with the rest of the objects you have on the Stage. For example, if you want to make your symbol bigger, you need to make sure that it doesn't obscure some nearby text. If you have lots of stuff on the Stage, however, editing in symbol-editing mode or in a new window can help you focus more easily on the symbol itself.

To edit a symbol, follow these steps:

1. **Select any instance of the symbol on the Stage and right-click (Windows) or Control+click (Mac).**

2. **Choose Edit in Place, Edit in New Window, or Edit. (Choosing Edit puts you into symbol-editing mode.)**

   Flash displays the symbol name (Capsule) above the layer list, as shown in Figure 7-3.

3. **Edit the symbol in any way you want.**

4. **After you finish editing (from Edit or Edit in Place), click the scene name to the left of the symbol name or choose Edit⇨Edit Movie; from a new window, click the Close button.**

   You are now back in your main Movie.

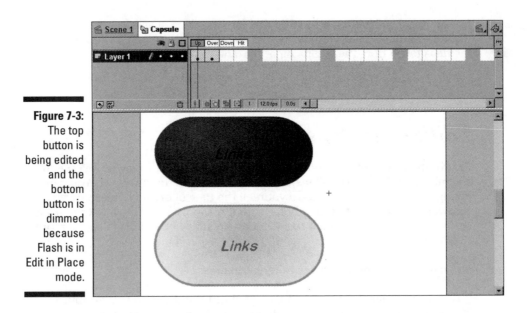

Using symbols from other movies

After you create a symbol and store it in the Library, you can use the Library
in any other movie. You can also open the Library from any other movie and
use its symbols in your current movie.

To use a symbol from the Library of another movie, follow these steps:

1. **Choose File⇨Open as Library.**

   The Open as Library dialog box opens.

2. **Select the movie file.**

3. **Click Open.**

   Flash displays the Library of the other movie in a new Library window.

The new Library may completely hide your current movie's Library. Just drag
it to a new location. In the new Library, many of the Option menu items and
icons are disabled to prevent you from making changes in the other movie's
file.

To use a symbol, drag it onto the Stage. When you do this, Flash places a
copy of the symbol in the current movie's Library.

Using the Flash Library

Flash comes with several libraries that you can use in your movie. To access these libraries, choose Window➪Common Libraries and then select one of the libraries. Flash includes buttons, graphics, movie clips, smart clips, and sounds. These libraries are also a good place to pick up ideas and see what you can create in Flash.

Using the Flash For Dummies Library

The Flash libraries contain lots of good examples, but they miss many basic shapes and simple objects that you could use for your own movies. We decided to fill in the gaps! So we created a library of geometric and fun shapes that you can use in your movies. The Flash For Dummies Library is called Flash For Dummies Library.fla. You can find it in the Library folder of the CD-ROM.

To use this library, copy Flash For Dummies Library.fla from the Library folder of the CD-ROM to the Macromedia\Flash 5\Libraries folder on your hard drive. After that, you can always open this library the same way that you open other common libraries — choose Window➪Common Libraries➪Flash For Dummies Library.fla. We hope you enjoy it!

Working with Instances

After you create a symbol, you can use it in many ways. You can insert it in your movie or inside other symbols or even in other movies. Each copy of the symbol is called an *instance*. You can change the properties of an instance so that the symbol differs from its parent symbol. For example, you can change the color of an instance color — the original symbol remains unchanged.

Inserting instances

To insert an instance of a symbol, follow these steps:

1. **Choose Window➪Library (Ctrl+L for Windows or Û+L for Mac) to open the Library, as shown in Figure 7-4.**
2. **Choose the layer where you want the instance to be placed.**

3. **Click a keyframe on the Timeline where you want the instance to be placed.**

   Flash places instances only in keyframes. If you don't select a keyframe, Flash puts the instance in the first keyframe to the left of the current frame. (See Chapter 9 for more about keyframes.)

4. **Drag the symbol from the Library to the Stage.**

Figure 7-4:
Insert an instance of a symbol by dragging it from the Library.

When you insert a graphic instance, you need to consider how it fits within your entire animation. For example, the instance may be the starting point for some animation, or it may be part of the background that remains static throughout the animation. Perhaps you want the instance to suddenly appear at some point in the animation. If it contains animation, you need to insert it at its proper starting point. (Chapter 9 explains how to copy graphics across any number of frames to create a static background and covers the entire topic of animation in detail.)

A movie clip instance, on the other hand, takes up only one frame on the Timeline. It plays and loops automatically unless you create actions to control it. (Chapter 10 talks about actions.)

Editing instances

A symbol's *children* don't have to be carbon copies of their parents, thank goodness. Instances of a symbol can differ from their parent symbol by color, type, and play mode. You can also rotate, scale, or skew an instance, leaving the parent symbol unchanged.

When you edit an instance, Flash remembers the changes. If you go back and edit the symbol, Flash doesn't forget. Suppose, for example, that you create a red circle graphic symbol and change an instance to pink. Then you edit the circle symbol to change it to an oval. The instance is now a pink oval. Its shape has been updated, but the color remained.

No matter what change you want to make to an instance, you do it in the Instance panel or the Effect panel. Use the Effect panel to change the color, brightness, or transparency of an instance. To change the instance type, you would use the Instance panel. These two panels appear as tabs on the same window, so you can move from one to the other easily. For more on using the Instance panel, see the section "Changing an instance's type," later in this chapter.

You can change an instance's color (or tint), brightness, or transparency. Flash controls aren't necessarily easy to use, but they offer a great deal of control.

To change an instance's color, brightness, or transparency, follow these steps:

1. **Select the instance.**
2. **Choose Window⇔Panels⇔Effect to open the Effect panel.**
3. **From the drop-down menu, choose one of these options:**
   - **None:** Adds no color effect
   - **Brightness:** Changes the lightness or darkness of the instance
   - **Tint:** Enables you to change the color of the instance
   - **Alpha:** Changes the transparency of the instance
   - **Advanced:** Enables you to change both the color and the alpha at once
4. **Make the desired changes.**

   You see the changes that you make in the Effect panel immediately in your selected instance.

When you choose Brightness on the drop-down list, a slider and a text box appear. Type in a brightness percentage or drag the slider and see the result immediately in the symbol instance. High brightness makes the image light. Low brightness makes the image dark.

When you choose Tint on the drop-down list, you can pick the color and then the amount of the color (the tint), by percentage, that you want to apply. Figure 7-5 shows the controls for this option. You can pick a color in the color picker, type red, green, and blue values (if you know them), or choose from the color swatches.

Figure 7-5:
The Tint
option
changes
both the
color and
amount of
the color
(tint) used
on an
instance of
a symbol.

Tint Color

Color Picker

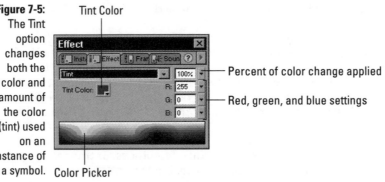

Percent of color change applied

Red, green, and blue settings

The Tint Color button, undocumented in Flash Help, has two functions: It shows you the color you have created (using the Color Picker or text boxes) and opens color swatches so that you can easily pick the color you want.

Specify the percentage of the color that you want to apply by typing a value in the box to the right of the Color Effect drop-down list (the box above the R box) or by clicking the drop-down arrow and dragging the slider to choose a percentage. When the percentage is set to 100%, the instance completely changes to the color you specified. If the percentage is set to 0%, Flash leaves the instance unchanged.

The Flash method of specifying a color gives you great flexibility and precision. You can choose a color and use the tint control to create a meld of the current color and your chosen color.

If you want to stick to Web-safe colors, just choose a color swatch from the ones displayed when you click the Tint Color button, and then slide the tint control all the way up to 100%.

Changing transparency

Choose Alpha on the Color Effect drop-down menu to change the transparency of an instance. Use the slider or type a value in the text box. A value of zero means your instance becomes completely transparent. When you return to the Stage, all you see is the selection border and the small plus that marks the symbol's registration point. When you deselect the instance, you see absolutely nothing! (Chapter 4 explains more about a symbol's registration point, including how to move it. See the section on Groups.)

Partial transparency lets your background show through. A partially transparent instance blends in with your background, creating a softer effect.

Changing color and transparency at the same time

Choose Advanced on the Color Effect drop-down menu to change both the
color and the transparency at the same time, using red, green, and blue
values. Figure 7-6 shows the controls, which are complex.

Figure 7-6:
The
Advanced
option lets
you change
the color
and
transpar-
ency at the
same time.

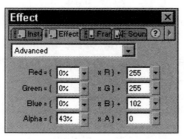

 Use the controls on the left to reduce the color or transparency by a specific
percent compared to the current values. Use the controls on the right to
change the color or transparency to a specific, absolute amount. Flash then
calculates the new color value by multiplying the current value by the percentage you specified and then adding the value from the right side. As you
can see, this method provides lots of control — but it may make you crazy
first.

To simply change both the color and the transparency of an instance, use the
Tint controls to change the color and then just change the left Alpha setting
in the Advanced controls.

Changing an instance's type

The instance type — that is, graphic, movie clip, or button — comes from the
symbol type, but you may want to change it. For example, if you created some
animation and saved it as a graphic symbol, you may want to use it as a movie
clip. Instead of changing the symbol type, you can change only the type of
the instance that you have inserted.

To change the instance type, follow these steps:

1. **Select the instance.**

2. **Choose Window⇨Panels⇨Instance to open the Instance Panel, as
   shown in Figure 7-7.**

3. From the Behavior drop-down list, choose one of the following types:

- **Graphic:** If the graphic contains animation, choose Graphic in the Behavior box and then determine how the animation will run in the drop-down list located in the bottom section of the Instance panel. Here are your choices:

  Loop — Plays the animation contained in the instance over and over during the frames occupied by the instance.

  Play Once — Plays the animation one time from the frame you specify.

  Single Frame — Displays any one frame of the animation. In other words, the animation doesn't play; you specify which frame the movie displays.

- **Button:** Choose the Button option to determine how the button is tracked in the Tracking Options section. From the Options drop-down list, choose Track as Button when you're creating single buttons. Choose Track as Menu if you're creating pop-up menus.

- **Movie Clip:** Choose the Movie Clip option and specify an Instance name in the Name text box. You use this name with certain actions (interactive controls) so that you can refer to and control the instance. (For more information about actions, see Chapter 10.)

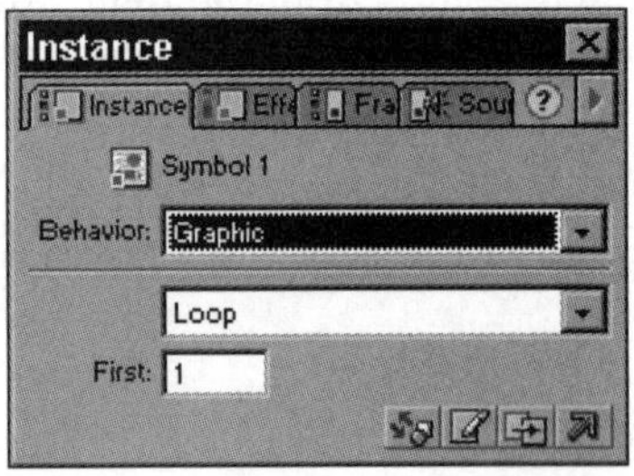

Figure 7-7:
Use the
Instance
panel's
Behavior
menu to
change the
instance
type.

Replacing or duplicating an instance

Suppose that you create a complex animation with bouncing bunnies all over the Stage. Suddenly, your boss decides the animation should have bouncing squirrels instead. Meanwhile, you had already edited all the bunnies to make them different sizes and colors.

To replace an instance, follow these steps:

1. Create the squirrel symbol (or whichever new symbol you need).

Flash stores the new symbol in the Library.

2. **Select an instance of the bunny, that is, your original instance, on the Stage.**

3. **Choose Window⇨Panels⇨Instance to open the Instance panel.**

4. **Click the Swap Symbol button to open the Swap Symbol dialog box.**

5. **In the dialog box, select the squirrel or any other symbol.**

6. **Click OK to swap the symbols and close the Swap Symbol dialog box.**

   Flash retains your color effects and size changes, but changes the symbol.

Unfortunately, you must repeat this process for all your bunnies on the Stage, but it's better than reinserting all your instances and re-creating the instance changes.

You can use the same procedure to duplicate a symbol. Select any instance and click the Duplicate Symbol button in the Instance panel. Note that you're duplicating the symbol, not the instance. Flash asks you to name the new symbol. Do so and click OK.

Duplicate a symbol when you want to use one symbol as a springboard for creating a new symbol. Make any changes that you want to the new symbol and place instances on the Stage.

Breaking apart an instance

You can break apart an instance into its component objects. The original symbol remains in the movie's Library. You may want to use the instance as a starting point for creating a completely new symbol or you may want to animate the components of the symbol so that they move separately. Other instances remain unchanged.

To break apart an instance, select it and choose Modify⇨Break Apart. If an instance contained symbols or grouped objects within it, you can use the Break Apart command again to break apart those internal objects as well.

Chapter 8

Pushing Buttons

· ·

· ·

*W*hen you view a Web page, you see buttons that you can click to move to other pages or sites. These buttons are graphic images, but they're hyperlinks as well. If you start to pay attention to these buttons, you'll see that some of them change when you pass your mouse cursor over them. They change again when you click them. Sometimes they make a sound when you click them.

Flash can create these types of buttons and more. You can animate Flash buttons, for example, so that they move or rotate when viewers pass over or click them. You can add interaction controls (actions) to buttons so that passing over or clicking them starts other movies.

In this chapter, you find out how to create buttons that look the way you want. You also learn how to make more complex buttons that include sounds, movie clips, and simple actions. To discover more about actions and interactivity, see Chapter 10.

Creating Simple Buttons

Before you create a button, stop and think about what you want the button to accomplish on a Web page and how you want it to look. Web page designers often create a series of buttons which look similar and which lead to various Web pages. Buttons often include some text to identify the button's purpose.

But you can use buttons for lots of other, more advanced purposes than navigating to Web pages. A button can start a Flash movie, indicate a choice in a survey or game, or be dragged around on a puzzle or game Web page.

A *button* is a symbol. (See Chapter 7 for the lowdown on how to create and edit symbols.) Here we cover the entire process of creating buttons.

Understanding button states

A button has four *states* that define characteristics of the button:

- ✔ **Up:** Defines what the button looks like when the mouse pointer is not over the button. The viewer initially sees the Up state of a button.
- ✔ **Over:** Defines what the button looks like when the pointer is over the button (but it hasn't been clicked).
- ✔ **Down:** Defines what the button looks like when the button is clicked.
- ✔ **Hit:** Defines the area of the button that responds to the mouse. The user doesn't see this area — it's invisible.

Figure 8-1 shows a button in its four states. A typical, simple button may show a lit up effect for the Over state and an indented look (as if the button is pressed in) for the Down state. In this example, the Down state moves the highlight to the right, giving the impression of movement as the button is clicked.

Radial gradients are useful for creating a lit-up or pushed-in look. Use a light color or white to create the appearance of a highlight. Use a dark color or black to create an indented look. Just changing the color of the fill (often to a lighter color) is often enough to make it seem lit up.

Up   **Over**

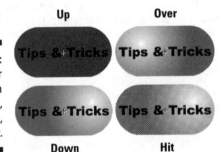

Figure 8-1:
The four states of a button: Up, Over, Down, and Hit.

Down   **Hit**

The button shown in Figure 8-1 is on the CD-ROM. Look for `capsule.fla` in the Ch08 folder. To try it out, choose Control⇨Test movie.

Making a basic button

To create a simple button, follow these steps:

1. **Choose Insert➪New Symbol to open the Symbol Properties dialog box.**

2. **In the Name text box, type a name for the button.**

3. **In the Behavior section, choose Button and click OK.**

   You're now in symbol-editing mode. Flash displays the special Timeline for buttons, with four frames: Up, Over, Down, and Hit, as shown in Figure 8-2. Note the dot in the Up frame, indicating that the frame is a keyframe. A keyframe appears as soon as you create any object on the Stage. The word *Up* is highlighted, indicating that the Up frame is active.

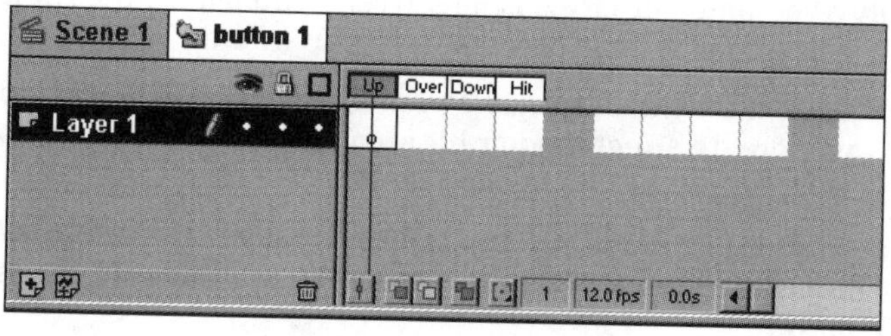

Figure 8-2:
The Flash symbol-editing mode for buttons displays a Timeline with four frames.

4. **Create the graphic for the Up state.**

   You can use the Flash drawing tools, an imported graphic, or an instance of a symbol. You can create as many layers as you want for the button. For an animated button, use a movie clip symbol. We explain how to create an animated button in the "Adding a movie clip to a button" section, later in this chapter.

   If you want the button image for the four states to be in the same place, place the graphic in the center of the display and build the other states in the center as well. To do this, cut and paste the graphic. (See Chapter 4 for more about centering objects on the display.) If the button images aren't in the same place, the button appears to shift as the viewer passes the cursor over or clicks the button.

5. **Right-click (Windows) or Control+click (Mac) the Over frame and choose Insert Keyframe.**

   Flash inserts a keyframe in the Over frame of the button. You can also choose Insert➪Keyframe or press F6. The graphic for the Up state remains on the Stage.

6. **Create the graphic for the Over state.**

   You can use the graphic for the Up state as a starting point and change it (or leave it the same if you don't want the button to change when the mouse pointer passes over the button). You can also delete the graphic and put a new one in its place. If you have more than one layer, place a keyframe on each layer before creating the artwork for that layer.

7. **Right-click (Windows) or Control+click (Mac) the Down frame and choose Insert Keyframe.**

8. **Create the graphic for the Down frame.**

   Repeat as in Step 6.

9. **Right-click (Windows) or Control+click (Mac) the Hit frame and choose Insert Keyframe.**

10. **Create the shape that defines the active area of the button.**

    This shape should completely cover all the graphics of the other state. Usually a rectangle or circle is effective. If you ignore the Hit frame, Flash uses the boundary of the objects in the Up frame.

    If you use text for the button, viewers have to hit the letters precisely unless you create a rectangular hit area around the text. To cover an area of text, create a filled-in shape on a new layer.

11. **Click the scene name at the top left of the layer list or choose Edit⇨Edit Movie to return to the regular Timeline and leave symbol-editing mode.**

12. **If the Library isn't open, choose Window⇨Library and drag the button symbol that you just created to wherever you want it on the Stage.**

    You just created a button!

A button is a symbol, but when you want to place a button on the Stage, you must drag it from the Library to create an instance of the symbol. See Chapter 7 for a full explanation of symbols and instances.

Putting Buttons to the Test

After you create a button, you need to test it. You can choose from a couple of methods.

The fastest way to test a button is to *enable* it. An enabled button responds to your mouse as you would expect — it changes as you specified when you pass the mouse over it and click it. To enable the buttons on your Stage, choose Control⇨Enable Simple Buttons. All the buttons on the Stage are now enabled.

Have fun with your button! Pass the mouse over it, click it, and watch it change.

After you test your button, suppose that you want to select the button to move it. You try to click it to select it and it only glows at you, according to the Down frame's definition. Choose Control➪Enable Buttons again to disable the buttons. Now you can select a button like any other object. In general, enable buttons only to test them.

However, if you really want to select an enabled button, you can do so with the Arrow tool by dragging a selection box around it. You can use the arrow keys to move the button. If you want to edit the button further, choose Modify➪Instance to edit the button's properties in the Instance Properties dialog box.

If you have other animation on the Stage, you can play the animation with the buttons enabled. Choose Control➪Play or press Enter. By playing the animation, you can see how the buttons fit in with the rest of your movie.

Another way to test a button is to test the entire movie. Choose Control➪Test Movie. Flash creates an SWF file just as it would if you were publishing the movie — except that this SWF file is temporary. Any animation plays and you can test your buttons as well. When you're done, click the Close box of the window.

Note for Windows users: this is not the topmost Close box that closes Flash.

If your button contains movie clips, you must use this method of testing the button because the animation doesn't play on the Stage.

Creating Complex Buttons

Buttons can do more than just change color or shape. You can enhance a button in three ways:

- ✔ **Add a sound:** For example, you can add a clicking sound to the Down frame of a button so that users hear that sound when they click the button.

- ✔ **Add a movie clip:** To animate a button, you add a movie clip to it. You can animate the Up, Over, and Down frames if you want.

- ✔ **Add an action (interactive control):** To make a button do something, you need to add an action to it. Actions are covered in Chapter 10, but we discuss some of the basic concepts here.

Adding a sound to a button

For fun, you can add a sound to a button. Usually, sounds are added to the Over or Down frame — or both, if you want. Chapter 11 explains lots more about sound, but here we explain how to add a simple sound to a button.

Look in the Ch08 folder for click.wav. You can add this sound to the Down frame of a button.

To add a sound to a button, follow these steps:

1. **Create the button symbol.**

2. **Choose File⇨Import to open the Import dialog box.**

3. **Select the sound file (in WAV, AIFF, or MP3 format) and click Open.**

   Flash stores the file in the Library.

4. **Choose Window⇨Library to open the Library.**

5. **If you aren't in symbol-editing mode, use the Arrow tool to double-click the button's icon in the Library to enter symbol-editing mode.**

6. **Click the plus sign at the bottom of the layer list to add a new layer.**

7. **Name the new layer Sound or something similar.**

   See Chapter 6 for a full explanation of layers.

8. **In the new layer, right-click (Windows) or Control+click (Mac) the frame where you want to place the sound — for example, the Down frame — and choose Insert Keyframe from the menu.**

9. **Choose Window⇨Panels⇨Sound to open the Sound panel, as shown in Figure 8-3.**

   The sound is inserted into the frame you selected in Step 8.

10. **From the Sound drop-down list, choose the sound file you want.**

    Flash lists all sounds that you have imported into the Library. When you choose the sound file, you see the sound wave indicator on the Sound layer in the frame where you inserted the sound, as shown in Figure 8-4.

Figure 8-3:
Use the Sound panel to insert a sound into your button.

Sound	☒
Inst Effe Fran Sound ?
Sound: Click.wav ▼
22 kHz Mono 8 Bit 0.1 s 1.3 kB
Effect: None ▼ Edit...
Sync: Event ▼
Loops: 0

11. **From the Sync drop-down list, choose Event.**

    The Event setting synchronizes the sound to the occurrence of an event, in this case, the clicking of the button. Event is the default setting.

12. **Click the scene name at the top left of the layer list or choose Edit⇨Edit Movie.**

    Flash returns you to the regular timeline and leaves symbol-editing mode.

13. **Drag the button symbol you just created from the Library to wherever you want the button on the Stage.**

    You're done! Now test the button as explained in the previous section, "Putting Buttons to the Test."

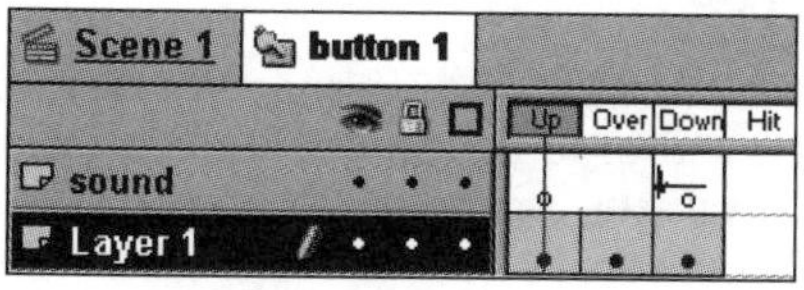

Figure 8-4:
When you add a sound to a button, the sound wave appears in the Timeline.

Be sure to look in Chapter 11 for more information on adding sounds to buttons and movies.

If you've already added the sound to another movie, choose File⇨Open as Library and open the other movie. Click the desired keyframe and drag the sound from the Library to anywhere on the Stage. Flash places the sound in the selected keyframe.

Adding a movie clip to a button

If you think simple buttons are b-o-r-i-n-g, you can animate them. To animate a button, you must create a movie clip symbol and then insert the movie clip into one of the frames. Generally, button animation is localized in the area of the button. If you want to make an elaborate button, you can animate all three frames — Up, Over, and Down.

In order to add a movie clip to a button, you must first create the movie clip. Chapter 7 explains how to create a movie clip symbol, and Chapter 9 explains how to create the animation to put in the movie clip.

For the following steps, you can use the movie clip that we provide in the Ch08 folder of the CD-ROM. Open `flower power.fla`. This is a blank movie whose Library contains the symbols necessary to create a button with a movie clip.

If you've never created a button before, review the steps in the section, "Making a basic button," earlier in this chapter. Then, to create a button with a movie clip, follow these steps:

1. **If you're using the movie file included on the CD-ROM, open** `flower power.fla` **from the Ch08 folder; otherwise, open any new movie file.**

2. **Choose Insert⇨New Symbol to open the Symbol Properties dialog box.**

3. **In the Name text box, type a name for the button.**

   In this example, we used Flower Button.

4. **In the Behavior section, choose Button and click OK.**

5. **Create the graphic for Up state.**

   If you're using the movie from the CD-ROM, choose Window⇨Library and drag the flower graphic symbol to the Stage. Click anywhere on the Stage to make it active and press the arrow buttons on the keyboard (left, right, up, and down, as necessary) to center the flower symbol's registration point (shown by a little plus sign) exactly over the registration point (also a plus sign) on the Stage (see Figure 8-5). The flower graphic symbol is static, not animated.

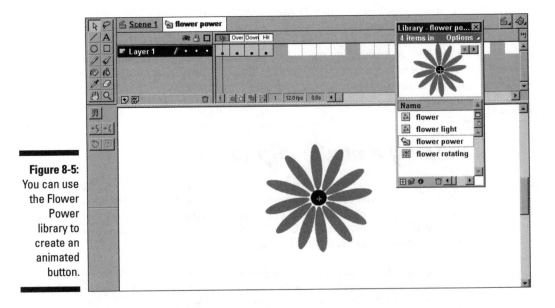

Figure 8-5:
You can use the Flower Power library to create an animated button.

6. **Right-click (Windows) or Control+click (Mac) the Over frame and choose Insert Keyframe.**

   Flash inserts a keyframe.

7. **Create the graphic for the Over state.**

   For this example, delete the graphic on the Stage (still there from the Up frame) and drag the movie clip called Flower Rotating to the center of the Stage. Click the Stage and use the arrow keys to perfectly center the flower. Flower Rotating is a movie clip that animates the flower by rotating it.

8. **Right-click (Windows) or Control+click (Mac) the Down frame and choose Insert Keyframe.**

9. **Create the graphic for the Down state.**

   In this example, delete the graphic on the Stage and drag the Flower Light graphic symbol to the exact center of the Stage.

10. **Right-click (Windows) or Control+click (Mac) the Hit frame and choose Insert Keyframe.**

11. **Use the Rectangle tool and drag a square to cover the entire area of the symbol, leaving the symbol on top; use the Arrow tool to select and delete the symbol, leaving only the square.**

    If you don't perform this step, viewers must place the mouse cursor exactly over one of the petals to see the animation. By defining the Hit frame as a square, placing the cursor anyplace within that square activates the button.

12. **Click the scene name (Scene 1) at the top left of the layer list to return to the regular timeline.**

13. **Drag the button symbol that you just created from the Library to wherever you want the button placed on the Stage.**

    Congratulations! You have just created a button with a movie clip.

To test the button that you just created, choose Control⇨Test Movie. Place the cursor over the button and click it and watch the animation. If you used the Flower Power library from the CD-ROM, the flower rotates when you pass the cursor over it and also lightens. When you click the flower, it just lightens. Click the window Close box to close the testing window. If you want, you can save the file on your computer by choosing File⇨Save As and choosing a location on your hard drive.

If you want to see the final result of the preceding steps, check out flower power final.fla in the Ch08 folder on the CD-ROM.

Testing your button's Get URL action

To properly test a button with a Get URL action, you need to publish your movie, upload it to your Web page, go online, and try it out. You can test the button on your hard drive first, however, so that you can be fairly sure it will work when you put it on your Web page.

Suppose, for example, that you want your button to link to another Web page on your Web site. Perhaps that page's local URL is `tips.html`. Assume that `tips.html` is in the same folder as the Web page containing your Flash button, so that you can use this simple local URL.

To test your button's Get URL action, follow these steps:

1. **After creating the button and its Get URL action with a URL of tips.html (or whatever's appropriate in your situation), choose File⇨Save to save the movie file.**

2. **Choose File⇨Publish.**

   Flash publishes the file, creating an HTML and an SWF file in the same folder as your FLA file. (These are default settings. See Chapter 13 for more information on publishing movies.)

3. **To test the button, you need a file on your hard drive with the same URL you used in your button. Create a file named tips.html (or whatever URL you used) on your hard drive in the same folder as your movie. You can use either of two methods:**

   ✔ Make a copy of the existing `tips.html` (if you have it on your hard drive) and move it to the folder containing your movie.

   ✔ Create a new HTML document and save it as `tips.html` in the same folder as your movie. This document can be a *dummy* document — you can put any text you want in it. For example, you can type, **This is a test HTML document.** If you create this document in a word processor, be sure to save it as an HTML document. Otherwise, use the software that you normally use to create HTML documents.

4. **Working offline, open your browser, choose File⇨Open, and open the HTML file for your Flash movie (it has the same name as your movie).**

5. **Click your button.**

   You should see `tips.html` displayed. If you don't, go back and check your action settings.

In Flash 5, you can also test your button without publishing it by choosing Control⇨Test Movie and clicking a button with a Get URL action.

Adding an action to a button

A button doesn't do anything except look pretty until you give it the proper instructions. Most buttons either link you to another Web page or start a movie. Actions are covered in Chapter 10, but here we explain the basic principle of adding an action to a button — in this case, an action that links the user to another Web page.

To add an action to a button, follow these steps:

1. **If you haven't already done so, drag an instance of the button onto the Stage. If not already selected, select the button.**

2. **Choose Window⇨Actions to open the Object Actions window.**

3. **Click Basic Actions.**

4. **Double-click the action you want; to use the button to link to another page, double-click Get URL from the list.**

   Figure 8-6 shows the Object Actions window with the Get URL action selected.

5. **In the URL text box at the bottom of the dialog box, type the URL that you want to create a hyperlink to.**

   If the bottom parameters pane is not displayed, click the arrow at the bottom-right corner of the dialog box. When typing the URL, follow the same rules you would to create any hyperlink on your Web site. For example, usually you can use local URLs (referring just to the page, for example) for other pages on the same Web site, but you need absolute URLs (complete, starting with http://) for hyperlinks to other sites.

6. **From the Window drop-down list, choose Self to use the same window for the new URL.**

7. **For this example, leave the Variables setting at the default Don't Send.**

8. **Close the Object Actions window using the Close box.**

You can add your button to an existing Web page. In such a case the button may be the only Flash element on the page. You can also include buttons as part of an environment completely created in Flash. Either way, buttons are a valuable piece of the Flash arsenal.

You can also create pop-up menus using buttons. In a pop-up menu, viewers click on a button to reveal several other buttons each of which executes some type of action. The buttons function like a menu, to offer your viewers a set of choices. You should have a good understanding of symbols, buttons, movie clips, and actions before you try to create a pop-up menu. (See Chapter 15 for a step-by-step example.)

For a gorgeous example of a button, shown in Figure 8-7, look for nav_button.fla in the Ch08 folder of the CD-ROM. Open the FLA file and choose Control⇨Test Movie to see how the button works. (Clicking the button results in your computer trying to go to the URL of the button's action.) Then close the window. Choose Control⇨Enable Buttons to turn off the button. Right-click the button (not the entire symbol) and choose Actions. Now you can see the Get URL action attached to this button. *(The nav_button.fla file is courtesy of Jeremy Wachtel, Vice President of Project Management at Macquarium Intelligent Communications.)*

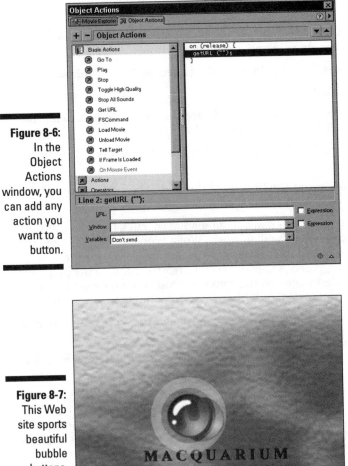

Figure 8-6:
In the Object Actions window, you can add any action you want to a button.

Figure 8-7:
This Web site sports beautiful bubble buttons.

Part IV
Total Flash-O-Rama

The 5th Wave   By Rich Tennant

"Evidently he died of natural causes following a marathon session animating everything on his personal Web site. And no, Morganstern—the irony isn't lost on me."

In this part . . .

Animation is the heart and soul of Flash, and in this part you let it rock 'n' roll. You find out about moving objects, changing their shape (or *morphing* them), and letting Flash create animation for you.

After you create animation, you can make it interactive so that the Web experience is more meaningful and engaging. Flash 5's new ActionScript offers infinite potential, so let your imagination soar. We show you how to combine your animation with your symbols and then add actions to script your entire movie.

The world is not silent, and your Flash movies don't have to be either. Find out how to add sounds and music from the simplest click of a button to a full-fledged symphony.

Chapter 9

Getting Animated

● ●

In This Chapter

▶ Understanding animation in Flash

▶ Getting ready to animate

▶ Animating with keyframes

▶ Using motion tweening

▶ Editing your animation

▶ Managing scenes

● ●

*W*hy do you create graphics in Flash? To animate them, of course. In this chapter, we explain animation — the heart and soul of Flash — and make your graphics move. Hold on to your hats!

We start by explaining the basics of animation, including how to prepare for animation and how to work with the Timeline. Then we go into the specific techniques — mainly frame-by-frame and tweening — that you can use to create great, animated effects in Flash. We cover both motion and shape tweening and then give you the details of editing your animation. So let's get moving!

Who Framed the Animation?

The secret of animation in Flash, as in the movies, is that ultimately nothing ever really moves. A Flash movie creates the illusion of movement by quickly displaying the sequence of still images. Each still image is slightly different. Your brain fills in the gaps to give you the impression of movement.

One of the great things about Flash is that you can easily create complicated, spectacular extravaganzas of animation. Flash stores lots of information in super-compact vector format. Because the files are so small, they download quickly. So Flash = spectacular animation + fast download. That's good for your Web site viewers.

Just as in a movie, each still image is contained in a frame. Each frame represents a unit of time. You create the animation by placing images in the frames. A frame may contain one object or none or many, depending on how crowded a scene you want to create.

Time is your ally in Flash because you have complete control over it. You can look at each individual image in time and tweak it to your heart's content. Then you can step on the gas, play everything back at high speed, and watch everything appear to move.

In Flash, you create animation in two ways:

- **Frame by frame:** You move or modify objects one frame at a time. This frame-by-frame animation is time consuming, but often the only way to create complex animated effects. It can certainly satisfy your appetite for total control.

- **Tweening:** You create starting frames and ending frames and let Flash figure out where everything goes in the in-between frames, which is why it's called *tweening.* Tweening is a lot more fun and easier than frame-by-frame animation. If you can create the animation you want by tweening, it's definitely the way to go. Flash offers two types of tweening: *motion tweening* and *shape tweening,* both described later in this chapter.

In tweening, your starting and ending frames are called *keyframes,* because they are the key moments in time that the software uses to calculate the in-between frames. Tweening not only means less work for you, it also creates smaller files (which download faster), because you're describing your animations more concisely. In frame-by-frame animation, every frame is a keyframe, because every frame defines a change in the action.

Preparing to Animate

You probably want to get started animating already, but you need to set the stage first so that your animation works properly. Here are the steps you need to take before you can begin creating your animation:

1. **Choose Insert⇨Layer to create a new layer for your animation and put your starting graphic or graphics on that layer.**

   You get best results if you animate on a layer that has no other objects on it. Otherwise, your animated objects may erase, connect to, or segment other objects, with messy results. See Chapter 6 for more information on layers.

2. **If you plan to use motion tweening, turn your graphic into a symbol or group; if you plan to use shape tweening, make sure that your graphic is a shape; and if you plan to do frame-by-frame animation, your graphic can be anything you want.**

   See the section, "The Animation Tween," a little later in this chapter to find out more about motion tweening and shape tweening. Your graphic absolutely must be a symbol or a group for your motion tweening to work properly. (See Chapter 7 for more about symbols and Chapter 4 for the lowdown on grouping objects.) For shape tweening, the rule is the opposite of motion tweening. If your graphic is a symbol and/or a group, you aren't able to shape tween it. So just draw a shape by using the drawing tools.

3. **Set a frame rate (see the section, "Turtle or hare?" for more information).**

When you animate, you often need to play back your animation during the process. The simplest way is to press Enter, which plays the movie. Sometimes, however, you may want more control, perhaps to play part of your movie. In this case the Controller is invaluable. The Controller, shown in Figure 9-1, is a very simple toolbar that looks like the controls on a tape recorder. Use it to play, rewind, fast-forward, and stop your animation.

Figure 9-1:
The
Controller
gives
control
over
animation
playback.

Master of the Timeline

The Timeline is the map of your animation sequence. If the Timeline isn't visible, choose View⇨Timeline. Each layer has its own Timeline row. The Timeline has its own coding to help you understand the structure of your animation, as shown in Figure 9-2.

Incomplete tweened animation (no ending keyframe)

Unchanged content (light gray, ending with rectangle)

Playhead (current frame marker)

Scene name   Frame label   Frame action (a)

Layers   Keyframe   Empty keyframe

Figure 9-2:
Use the
Flash
Timeline to
control your
animations.

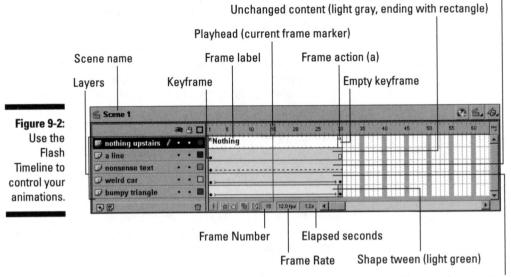

Frame Number   Elapsed seconds

Frame Rate   Shape tween (light green)

Motion tween (light blue)

Half the power of the Timeline is that it divides motion into frames — bits of time that you can isolate and work with — one at a time. The other half of the Timeline's power is that you can organize different components of your animation into different layers.

Always animate one layer at a time.

Click any frame to make it active. Remember to click in the row of the layer containing the graphics that you want to animate. By clicking any frame, you can view your animation frozen in a moment of time.

As you read through the examples and steps in this chapter, you'll quickly get the hang of working with the Timeline.

Hide the layers you're not interested in (click beneath the Eye icon) to help you visualize the animation. But don't forget to check the animation with all the layers displayed to see how everything looks together. You should also lock layers when you're finished with them to avoid unwanted changes. See Chapter 6 for further instructions on hiding and locking layers.

Turtle or hare?

All that you need to do to make animation work is to view your sequence of still images over time at high speed. Unless you have a remarkable attention span, one image per second is way too slow. Silent movies were typically 16 or 18 frames per second. With the arrival of talkies, the speed got bumped up to 24 frames per second for better quality sound. On your television, the speed is roughly 30 images per second.

On the Web, to cut down on the amount of data your viewers need to download, you should set your speed lower than that. In fact, 12 frames per second (fps) is usually a good choice. Luckily, that's the default rate in Flash.

To change the frame rate for your animation, follow these steps:

1. **Double-click the Frame Rate box (which displays a number and fps) at the bottom of the Timeline to open the Movie Properties dialog box.**

   Alternatively, you can choose Modify⇨Movie.

2. **In the Frame Rate text box, type a new number (in frames per second).**

   You can set only one frame rate for the entire movie, and it's best to set the frame rate before you start animating.

3. **Click OK to set the new speed and close the dialog box.**

A Flash movie's frame rate represents the maximum speed at which the movie runs. Flash animation has no guaranteed minimum speed. If your animation is lagging or bogging down, increasing the frame rate doesn't help at all; in fact, it may make things worse. *(Thanks to Mark Clarkson, author of* Flash 5 Cartooning, *published by IDG Books Worldwide, Inc., for this tip. To find out more about Flash cartooning, pick up a copy of this book.)*

Animating with Keyframes

Keyframes are the frames that are key to your animation. In frame-by-frame animation, every frame is a keyframe. In tweened animation, only the first and last frames of a tween are keyframes. By creating keyframes, you specify the duration and therefore the speed of an animated sequence.

To create a keyframe, select a frame on the Timeline and choose Insert⇨ Keyframe. For faster service, right-click (Windows) or Control+click (Mac) a frame in the Timeline and choose Insert Keyframe from the shortcut menu. You can also press F6.

Frame after frame after frame

If your animation isn't a simple motion in an easily definable direction or a change of shape (or color), you probably need to use frame-by-frame animation.

If you must, you must. Some complex animations just have to be created frame by frame. The basic procedure is simple.

To create an animation by using the frame-by-frame technique, follow these steps:

1. **Select a frame in the row of the layer you want to use.**

    The animation will start in that frame.

2. **Right-click the frame and choose Insert Keyframe from the menu.**

    The first frame in a movie's Timeline is automatically a keyframe, so you don't have to create it.

3. **Create the graphic for the first frame.**

    You can import a graphic, paste a graphic from the clipboard, or use the Flash drawing tools. (See Chapter 3 for help with creating or importing a graphic.)

4. **Right-click (Windows) or Control+click (Mac) the next frame and choose Insert Keyframe again.**

    The next frame on the Timeline now has the same graphic as the previous one.

5. **Modify the graphic to create the second frame of the animation.**

6. **Repeat Steps 4 and 5 until you've created all the frames that you need for your animation.**

7. **As you work, you can continually check your cool animation by pressing Enter to play it back.**

Figure 9-3 shows frames of an animation as the Word *New!* is created from a few specs on the page.

Stillness in the night

Regular frames cannot contain changes. Therefore, if you insert a graphic in the first keyframe, it remains throughout the Timeline until it reaches another keyframe with a new graphic.

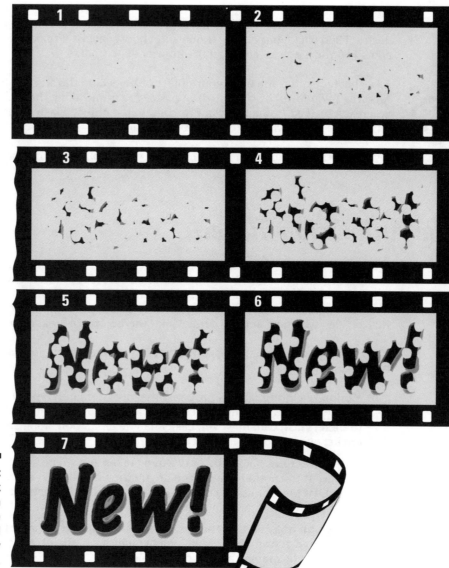

Figure 9-3:
A complex
animation
must be
created
frame by
frame.

There are several reasons why you may need to copy objects over a number of frames. Sometimes you want a still image to sit unmoving for a while on a layer of your animation — as a background image for example — while your animation moves in front. A background gives context to your animated objects. Even animated objects often need to remain on the Stage after they've finished moving about.

To make this happen, add a new layer for your background or other object. With that layer active, create or paste your object(s) at the starting frame you desire. Then click your ending frame and choose Insert➪Frame. Flash duplicates your image throughout all the intermediate frames.

As a shortcut, after you have your object or objects in the starting frame, Alt+drag (Windows) or Option+drag (Mac) the frame along the Timeline until you reach the last frame you want to contain the object. Flash copies the contents of the first keyframe through all the frames.

If you copy the objects to a keyframe, they remain on the Stage until the next keyframe.

The Animation Tween

If your animation follows some simple guidelines, you can save lots of work (and control file size, too) by asking Flash (say please) to interpolate the in-between frames for you automatically. You just create the first and last keyframes and Flash figures out what should go in-between. In animation techno-babble, that's called tweening and it's a quick, fun way to create great animations.

The Flash tweening capabilities are impressive. Here's what you can do with tweening:

- **Motion tweening:** This is probably the most common type of tweening. Simple motion tweening moves your objects in a straight line from here to there. Flash can, however, easily handle animation along any path you create, even one with lots of curves.

- **Shape tweening:** This type of tweening takes any shape and gradually changes it to another shape. You create the first and last shapes. Your kids call it morphing. You can add *shape hints* to tell Flash exactly how you want your shape to morph.

- **Change an object's size (both motion and shape tweening):** For example, if you make an object smaller as you move it, the object often appears to be moving away from the viewer.

- **Rotate an object (both motion and shape tweening):** You specify the amount of the rotation. Flash combines the motion or shape tweening with the rotation so that you get both effects at once.

- **Change color and/or transparency (both motion and shape tweening):** Flash creates a gradual change in color based on your starting and ending colors.

Animating your graphic's transparency is a particularly cool effect because it lets you fade objects in and out, making them magically appear and disappear at just the right moment.

Of course, you can create several animations, one after another to mix and match the effects. You can also combine frame-by-frame animation with tweened animation. Let your imagination soar!

From here to there — motion tweening

In motion tweening, you move an object from one place to another. The movement can be a straight line or any path that you can draw with the pencil tool. Figure 9-4 shows a few frames from a motion tween that uses a looped path. The skateboarder is also scaled down to 50 percent of its original size so that it appears to be moving away from you. Here the path is made visible so that you can see how the animation works. You usually hide the layer containing the path.

Moving symbols, groups, and type

You can motion tween instances of symbols, objects that you have made into a group, or type (text). Not only can you move them, but you also can change their size, rotation, skew, and color.

To *skew* an object means to slant it along one or both axes.

To create a simple motion tween animation, follow these steps:

1. **Right-click (Windows) or Control+click (Mac) an empty frame where you want the animation to start and choose Insert⇨Keyframe.**

   The Timeline's first frame is always a keyframe, so if you're starting from the first frame, just click the frame.

2. **Create a group or text block or drag a symbol instance from the Library.**

   See Chapter 7 for the details on creating symbols and instances. See Chapter 2 for the lowdown on using the Library.

3. **Create another keyframe where you want to end the animation.**

4. **Move the object to a new position.**

5. **If you want to change the object's size, rotation, or color (as explained in the sections that follow) make the adjustments at this point.**

   See the next two sections of this chapter for details.

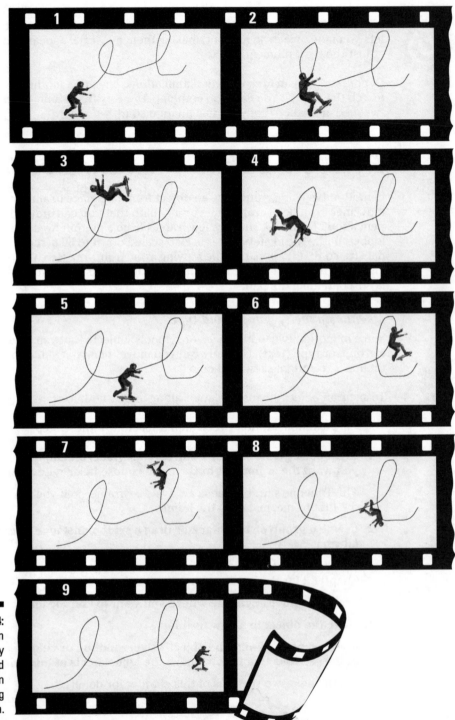

Figure 9-4:
You can draw any path and animate an object along the path.

6. **Click anywhere between the keyframes (you'll see a hand cursor) to select the entire range of frames. If necessary to select the very last keyframe, press Shift and click that keyframe.**

   All the frames in the animation tween should be selected.

7. **Choose Window⇨Panels⇨Frame to open the Frame panel.**

8. **From the Tweening drop-down list, choose Motion.**

   Flash creates the motion tween. If you change the object's size or rotation, specify the settings in the Frame panel, as explained in the next section.

You're done! Click the first frame and press Enter to play the animation.

Here's a silly phrase to help you remember the procedure for creating a motion tween:

Funny	First keyframe
Objects	Object — place it
Love	Last keyframe
Moving	Move object
So	Select range of frames
Tween	Tween — choose Motion from the Tweening drop-down list

Scaling and rotating an animated object

Okay, so you're creative and ambitious and want to do more. Changing other properties of your graphic while you're moving it is easy. In Step 5 of the procedure just listed, you can scale and rotate (including skewing) your object.

Use the Scale or Rotation (or both) modifiers on the Toolbox or any other method of change size or rotation. (See Chapter 4 for instructions on scaling and rotating objects.)

Then in Step 7 of the motion tweening procedure just listed, complete the rest of the settings in the Frame panel, as shown in Figure 9-5 (and described in the following text).

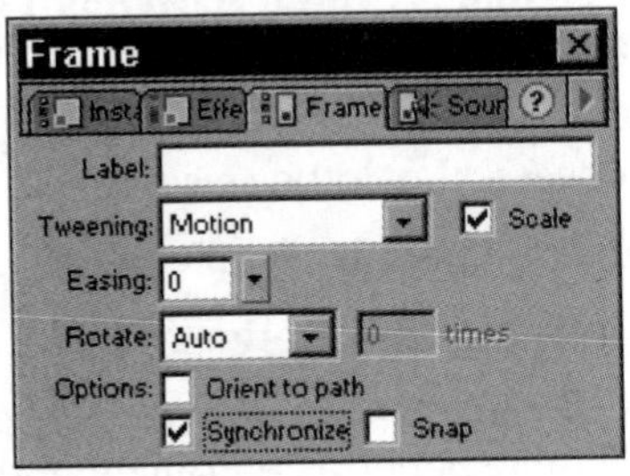

Figure 9-5:
Use the
Frame panel
to create
motion
tweening
and specify
scaling and
rotation.

After you specify motion tweening, settings in the Frame panel appear that let you specify how your motion tweening will work:

- ✔ **To put any scaling changes you made into effect, click Tween Scaling.** Checking Tween Scaling has no effect if you don't change the object's size when you created the motion tween. But unchecking Tween Scaling disables the scaling.

- ✔ **To rotate your graphic, choose one of the Rotate options from the drop-down list.** This automatically rotates the graphic once in the direction that uses the least movement. You can also choose to rotate clockwise or counterclockwise. Then type the number of times you want to rotate your graphic. This option rotates your object even if you didn't rotate it in Step 5 of the motion tweening procedure. If you did rotate the object, however, Flash adds the two rotations to end up with the rotation angle you specified.

- ✔ **To control acceleration or deceleration of the movement, use the Easing slider.** By default, the slider is in the middle, which creates a constant rate of movement throughout all the frames. Move the slider towards In to start slowly and get faster at the end. Move the slider towards Out to slow down at the end. You can create a sense of anticipation or excitement by using this technique.

- ✔ **To ensure that your graphic symbol animation loops properly, check the Synchronization box.** If your animation is in a graphic symbol, and the number of frames it takes up isn't an even multiple of the frames that the symbol occupies in the main Timeline, Flash synchronizes the two timelines so that the graphic symbol loops properly in the main Timeline.

The Snap setting is covered later in this chapter, in the section "Tweening along a path."

If you're doing a motion tween and the object refuses to move smoothly between keyframes — instead popping suddenly from one position to another — your problem is usually that more than one object is on the layer. *(Thanks to Mark Clarkson, author of* Flash 5 Cartooning, *published by IDG Books Worldwide, Inc., for this tip.)*

Look for `weldersmall.fla` in the Ch09 folder of the CD-ROM for a nice example of a motion tween that includes rotation. This animation is part of the `www.weldersmall.com` Web site *(Thanks to George Andres of Acro Media Inc. at `www.acromediainc.com` for this Flash file.)*

Another cool example of motion tweens is `thevoid.fla`, part of the `www.thevoid.co.uk` Web site. Look in the Ch09 folder of the CD-ROM. *(Thanks to Luke Turner, Creative Director of thevoid new media, for this Flash movie.)*

Tweening colors and transparency

To change an object's color, choose Window⇨Panels⇨Effect to open the Effect panel. Choose one of the effects (such as Tint or Alpha) and make the desired adjustments. (Chapter 7 explains how to modify instances of symbols and provides much more detail about using the options in the Effect panel.)

You can mix and match motion animation with scaling, rotation, and color/transparency changes to create exciting effects. If an object spins and gets smaller as it moves, it can seem to be rolling away from the viewer. Animating semi-transparent objects in front of each other creates interesting mixtures of color and gives a semblance of texture and depth in the 2-D world of the Web. Increasing alpha (that is, transparency) during a tween makes the object appear to fade. Try out some possibilities and come up with ideas of your own.

Color fades are faster than alpha fades. If you need an object to fade in or out, your movie loads faster if you tween to or from the background color rather than tweening to or from transparency. *(Thanks to Mark Clarkson, author of* Flash 5 Cartooning, *for this tip.)*

Tweening along a path

You can create animation that doesn't move in a straight line by motion tweening along a path that you draw. For example, suppose that you want to get the skateboarder shown in Figure 9-4 to do some tricks. The following steps show you how to do that.

If you want to follow along with these steps, you can import the skateboarder from the CD-ROM. Choose File⇨Import and look in the Ch09 folder for `skateboarder.bmp`. (We made him in Poser — a cool program for generating 3-D people, in case you're interested.)

To tween along a path, follow these steps (the first steps are the same as the ones provided earlier for motion tweens):

1. **Create the first keyframe (if necessary).**

2. **Place your instance, text block, or group on the Stage.**

   If you're using the skateboarder, drag it from the Library onto the left side of the Stage.

3. **Create the ending keyframe.**

   Don't move the object as you usually would when creating a motion tween.

4. **Select the entire range of frames.**

5. **Choose Window⇨Panels⇨Frame to open the Frame panel.**

6. **From the Tweening drop-down list, choose Motion.**

   You now have a motion tween with no motion.

7. **On the Frame panel, click to place a check mark in the Snap box to snap the registration point of the object to the motion path.**

8. **Click to place a check mark in the Orient to Path box if you want to rotate the object with the angle of the motion path.**

9. **Right-click (Windows) or Control+click (Mac) the object's layer and choose Add Motion Guide.**

   A new layer appears in the Timeline. It's labeled Guide and has a motion guide icon. (If you want, you can create this layer before you start the process of creating the animation.)

10. **Draw your path, making a few curves or loop-the-loops, if you want.**

    You can use any of the drawing tools: Pencil, Line, Circle, Rectangle, or Brush. You can also use the Straighten or Smooth modifiers if you're using the Pencil tool. (The path in Figure 9-4 was created by using the Pencil tool with the Smooth modifier.)

    Lock the object's layer while you're drawing the guide path so that you don't move the object by accident.

11. **Click the first frame of the animation and drag the object by its registration point (shown by a small plus) to the beginning of your path; let go when the registration point snaps to the beginning of the path.**

12. **Click the last keyframe and drag the object by its registration point to the end of the path; let go when the registration point snaps to the end of the path.**

13. **Press Enter to play the animation — you should see three seconds of death-defying skateboarding (or whatever animation you've created).**

You can find the completed animation, skateboarder.fla, in the Ch09 folder of the CD-ROM.

Not quite ready for prime time — yet

The steps just listed in the previous section for tweening along a path provide only the basic process. You often need to make several refinements to motion animation along a path.

Not satisfied with your motion path? No problem. Here's a really great feature that lets you easily modify your path. Select the motion guide layer. Choose the Arrow tool and reshape the line by dragging from any point on the line. (Just be sure not to break the line apart!) Press Enter again, and the skateboarder follows the revised path.

Want to get rid of that unsightly motion guide? That's easy, too. Click the eye column of the motion guide layer to hide it. Press Enter to play back the animation.

Symbols, groups, text, and bitmap images have a registration point that's usually at the center of the graphic. When you tween along a path, you may want another point to follow the path. In the section on groups in Chapter 4, you find out how to change the registration point to get the results you want.

What if you've already got a motion guide and you want to link it to an object on a different layer? Perhaps you drew an oval and then decide that you want an electron revolving along the oval, so you make its layer a motion guide layer. You have several choices:

- ✔ Create a new layer under the motion guide layer. The new layer appears indented under the motion guide layer, showing that it's linked to the motion guide, as shown in Figure 9-6. Then any objects you put on the new layer automatically snap to the motion guide. After putting your objects on the new layer, all you need to do is click the starting keyframe, drag your object to snap to the beginning of the path, click the ending keyframe and snap to the end of the path.

- ✔ If you already have a layer that you want to attach to your path, drag the layer with your graphics so that it's under the motion guide layer. When the new layer appears indented under the motion guide layer, you know it's linked.

- ✔ A third option to link a graphics layer to a path is to choose your graphics layer and then choose Modify➪Layer. The layer must be listed somewhere under the guide layer. In the Layer Properties dialog box, select Guided. Then Alt+click (Windows) or Option+click (Mac) the Motion Guide layer.

For a nice example of a motion tween along a path, open `flashsite_big.fla` from the Ch09 folder of the CD-ROM. The motion tween is hidden in a movie clip, so you have to find it. Choose Window⇨Library and select the Intro movie clip. (It has the movie clip symbol.) On the Stage, use the Arrow tool to create a selection box around the little plus and circle. Choose Edit⇨Edit Selected. You should now be in the Intro movie clip. Choose Control⇨Test Movie to watch the "electrons" revolve around their orbits. *(Flash movie is courtesy of Daniel Zajic.)*

Tweening shapes

In shape tweening, you change an object's shape at one or more points in time in the animation, and the computer creates the in-between shapes for you. You can get some great animation effects by using shape tweening. This is often called *morphing*. You can see an example in Figure 9-7.

You can combine shape tweening with motion tweening as well as changes in size and color/transparency. Like motion tweening, working with one shape per layer avoids problems.

You can only shape tween objects that you have created by using the Flash drawing tools. You can't shape tween a symbol, text (type), bitmap image, or group.

To create a simple shape tween, follow these steps:

1. **Right-click (Windows) or Control+click (Mac) an empty frame where you want the animation to start and choose Insert⇨Keyframe.**

2. **Use the drawing tools to create the beginning shape.**

   You can create complex objects by merging objects of the same color or creating cutouts with objects of differing colors. (See Chapter 3 for details.)

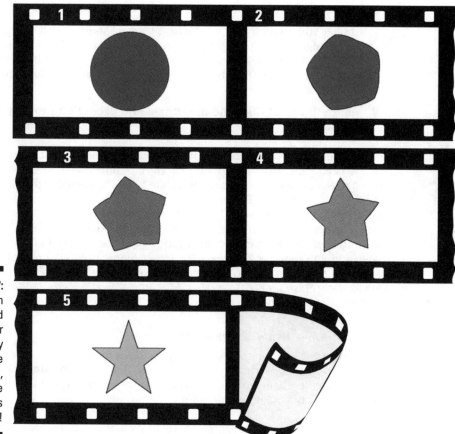

Figure 9-7:
You can
twist and
deform your
objects by
using shape
tweening,
and a circle
becomes
a star!

3. **Create a new keyframe after the first keyframe wherever you want it on the Timeline by using the same technique you used in Step 1.**

4. **Create the ending shape.**

   You can erase the old shape and draw a new one, or use the first shape, still on the Stage, and modify it. You can also move the shape and change its color/transparency. You can quickly change the color by using the Color modifiers on the Toolbox. Use the Mixer panel to change transparency (alpha). See Chapter 3 for more information on colors and transparency.

5. **To select the range of frames for the animation, click somewhere between them. If necessary, add the last keyframe by pressing Shift and clicking the last keyframe.**

6. **Choose Window➪Panels➪Frame to open the Frame panel.**

7. **Choose Shape from the Tweening drop-down list.**

8. **Choose whether you want an Angular or Distributive Blend type.**

   Choose the Angular Blend type for blending shapes with sharp corners and straight lines. It preserves corners and straight lines in the in-between shapes of your animation. If your shapes don't have sharp corners, then use the Distributive Blend type (the default) for smoother in-between shapes.

9. **You're finished! Click the first frame and press Enter to play the animation.**

Look in the Ch09 folder of the CD-ROM for a great example of shape tweening. The file is called `opening movie.fla`. Here, Jennie Sweo takes two circles and changes them into words using shape tweening. Amazingly, Flash handles this automatically. To shape tween one circle into a word, start with a circle. When you get to Step 4 of the shape tweening process, delete the circle and create the text wherever you want. Choose any size, color, and font, and then break apart the text (Modify⇨Break Apart). Finish the shape tween and you're done! To create the effect Jennie created, create a second similar shape tween on another layer. To view the effect, choose Control⇨ Test Movie. *(Flash movie is courtesy of Jennie Sweo. You can see this movie on the Web at http://sweo.tripod.com)*

Get the hint — using shape hints

Now you've got your shape animation, but does its transformation from one shape to another look strange? Flash tries to figure out the simplest and most probable way to change one of your shapes into another, but this may not turn out the way you expect or want.

Never fear. You can use the Flash shape hints feature to fix this up. A *shape hint* is a marker you attach to a point on a shape at the start and end of a shape change. This signals to Flash exactly how you want this point and the area around it to move from start to end of the shape tweening process.

You can use up to 26 shape hints per layer. Shape hints are displayed on the Stage as small colored circles with a letter (a–z) inside. On the starting keyframe, the shape hint is yellow, and on the ending keyframe, it's green. When you first insert a shape hint, before you move it onto your shape, it's red. Figure 9-8 shows an example of beginning and ending shapes with shape hints.

Figure 9-8:
Shape hints
guide Flash
as it tweens
your shape.

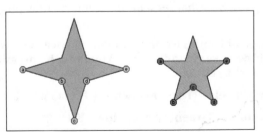

You can find the beginning and ending shapes on this book's CD-ROM in the Library folder, in `Flash 5 for Dummies Library.fla`. (Appendix D explains how to use this Flash movie as a permanent library.) Also look for the Flash movie file `4 to 5 point star with shape hints.fla` in the Ch09 folder.

To use shape hints, follow these steps:

1. **Create a shape animation by using shape tweening (refer to the preceding set of steps if you need help with this task).**

2. **Click the keyframe where you want to add your first shape hint.**

3. **With the object selected, choose Modify⇨Transform⇨Add Shape Hint or press Ctrl+Shift+H (Windows) or ⌘+Shift+H (Mac).**

   Your beginning shape hint appears as the letter *a* in a small red circle somewhere on the Stage.

4. **Click the small red circle and drag it to the part of your graphic that you want to mark.**

5. **Click the keyframe at the end of the shape animation.**

   The ending shape hint appears somewhere on the Stage, again as the letter *a* in a small red circle.

6. **Click the small red circle and drag it to the point on your shape to which you want your beginning point to move.**

   When you do this, the ending shape hint turns green. If you go back to the first frame of the animation, the beginning shape hint turns yellow.

7. **Press Enter to play your movie.**

You can drag shape hints off the Stage to remove them. Or choose Modify⇨Transform⇨Remove All Shape Hints to nuke them all — but the layer and keyframe with shape hints must be selected. Choose View⇨Show Shape Hints to see all the shape hints in your current layer and keyframe. Choose it again to hide them. (Again, the layer and keyframe with shape hints must be selected.)

Adjusting shape hints

To tweak your animation, click the keyframe at the start or end of your shape animation and move your shape hint. Then play your animation again to see the new result. The more complicated your shape animation, the more shape hints you need to use. For more complicated shape animations, you can also use more keyframes. Do this by creating intermediate shapes and tweening them (using plenty of shape hints, of course). In other words, you can create two shape tweens, one immediately following the other.

If you aren't getting the results you want, make sure that you have placed your shape hints logically. If you have a curve with shape hints a, b, and c in that order, don't have them tween to a curve with the shape hints in c, b, a order unless you want some unusual effects. Flash does a better job with shape hints when you arrange them in counter-clockwise order, starting from the top-left corner of your object.

Editing Animation

Of course, nothing is perfect the first time, and Flash is quite forgiving. You can edit keyframes in assorted ways.

You can't edit tweened frames directly — you can view them, but you can only edit the keyframes, not the tweened frames. You can overcome this restriction and edit your tweened frames by inserting a new keyframe between your beginning and ending keyframe, and then editing the new keyframe. You do this by choosing Insert⇨Keyframe. Don't choose Insert⇨Blank Keyframe unless you want to nuke your existing tween animation. Of course, you can always edit tweened frames simply by changing the starting or ending keyframe that defines them. When you edit a keyframe of a tweened animation, Flash automatically recalculates the entire tween.

The following sections explain some useful techniques for editing and managing your animations.

Adding labels and comments

Animation can get confusing after a while. You may find it helpful to add comments to your Timeline to explain what each part of the Timeline is doing. Also, when you start adding interactivity to your movies, you can add labels to frames and then refer to them in your ActionScripts. (You can find out more about ActionScripts in Chapter 10.)

To add a label or a comment to a frame, follow these steps:

1. **Select a frame.**

   See the next section for information on selecting a frame.

2. **Choose Window⇨Panels⇨Frame to open the Frame panel.**

3. **In the Label text box, type the text for the label or comment.**

   To make the text function as a comment, type two slashes (//) at the beginning of the comment. (If you get long-winded and go to a new line, type the two slashes at the beginning of the new line as well.)

Selecting frames

In Flash 5, the way you work with the Timeline has been changed somewhat. To select a frame or an individual keyframe, you click it, as you did in Flash 4. But in Flash 5, if you place the mouse cursor over a selected layer, between two keyframes, you see a hand cursor instead of the pointer, as shown in Figure 9-9. Clicking and dragging moves the entire sequence (between the keyframes) along the Timeline in either direction. To change the cursor back to an arrow to select an individual frame, you need to press Ctrl (Windows) or ⌘ (Mac).

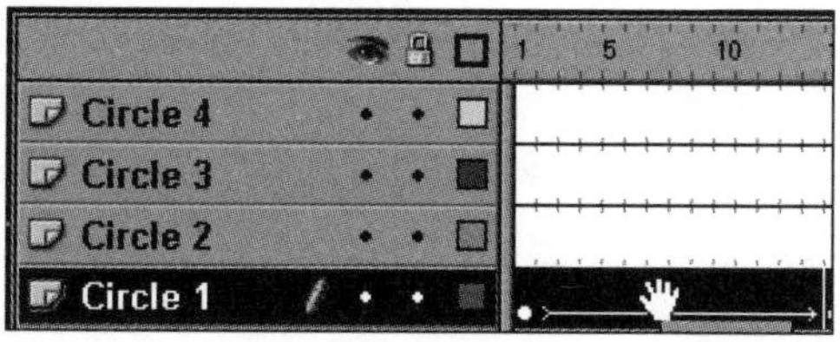

Figure 9-9:
Use the
Flash 5
hand cursor
to move a
sequence
between
keyframes
on a
selected
layer.

To select a range of frames, you can Ctrl+click (Windows) or ⌘+click (Mac) and drag. You can also click the first frame, press Shift, and then click the last frame in the range.

When you click the first or last keyframe of a tween and drag, you change the length of the tween instead of just selecting frames.

Copying and pasting

You can copy frames that contain contents that you want elsewhere. Then you can paste the frame in another location.

To copy and paste frames, follow these steps:

1. **Select one or more frames.**

2. **Choose Edit⇨Copy Frames to copy the frames to the Clipboard.**

3. **Select the first frame of your destination, or select a sequence of frames you want to replace.**

4. **Choose Edit⇨Paste Frames to paste the frames into their new location.**

You can also copy frames by pressing and holding Alt (Windows) or Option (Mac) while you drag the keyframe or range of frames to a new location. You see a small plus sign (+) as you drag.

Moving frames

You can move frames and their contents. Select the layer and place the cursor over a frame or range of frames. You see the hand cursor described previously in the section on selecting frames. Then drag them to their new home.

Adding frames

You can stretch out your animation by right-clicking (Windows) or Control+clicking (Mac) and choosing Insert Frame. Because you now have more frames between your first and last keyframes, the animation takes longer to complete, and therefore appears to be slower. Use this technique to slow down the rate of animation.

Deleting frames

Delete frames by selecting one or more frames. Then right-click (Windows) or Control+click (Mac) on one of the frames, and choose Remove Frames from the shortcut menu. If you delete frames within a tweened animation, the animation completes more quickly, and appears to be faster.

Turning keyframes back into regular frames

If you don't like a keyframe, you can change it back to a regular frame by right-clicking (Windows) or Control+clicking (Mac) the offending keyframe and choosing Clear Keyframe. Changing a keyframe into a regular frame removes the change that occurred at that keyframe. You can use this technique to merge two consecutive tweens into one tween — change the keyframe in the middle to a frame.

Reversing your animation

You can make your animation play backwards by selecting the relevant frames in one or more layers and choosing Modify⇨Frames⇨Reverse. Your selection must start and end with keyframes.

Faster or slower?

After you set up your animation, it's good to play your movie to check the speed. If one part of your tweened animation is too fast or too slow, you can slide keyframes around on the Timeline to shorten or lengthen the time between keyframes. You can do this simply by clicking a keyframe and dragging it to another point on the Timeline. This gives you a lot of control of the timing of your animation.

If you have difficulty dragging an ending keyframe, create a new keyframe somewhere to the keyframe's right and then drag the obstinate keyframe.

Figure 9-10 shows two possible versions of the Timeline for the shape tween shown in Figure 9-8. To create the version on the bottom, we dragged the last keyframe to the right, thereby lengthening the tween. Because the same change in shape now occurs over a longer period of time, the tween appears slower.

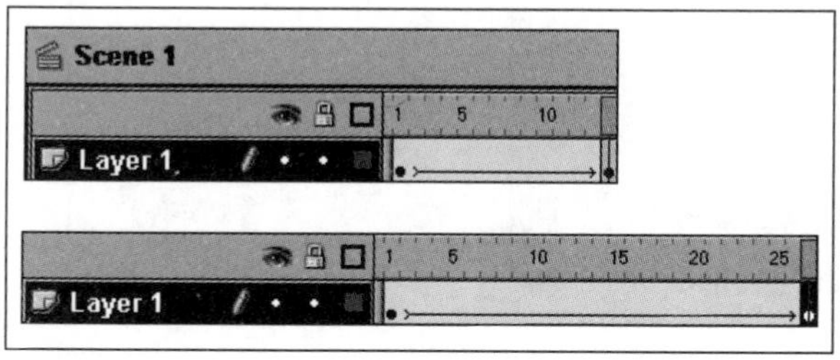

Figure 9-10:
You can change the length of a tween.

The effect is even more noticeable with a motion tween. For example, if a symbol moves from the left of the Stage to the right and you shorten the tween, the symbol now appears to move across the Stage more quickly because it must get from the left to the right in fewer frames.

Changing the animation settings

You can always go back and change some of the settings in the Frame panel. For example, you can add easing or change the Blend type of a shape tween in the Frame panel. These settings were explained earlier in this chapter.

Onion skinning

To help you visualize the flow of your animation, you can turn on the onion-skinning feature. Onion skinning lets you see a "ghost-image" of some or all of the frames in your animation. (Normally you only see the current frame on the Stage.) Figure 9-11 shows an example of both regular and outlined onion skinning. As you can see, it displays frames as transparent layers, like the transparent layers of an onion skin.

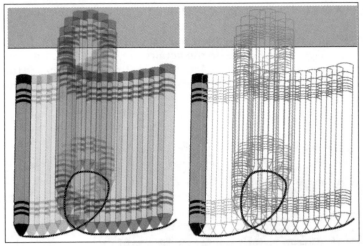

Figure 9-11: Onion skinning helps you to see where your animation is going.

 To display onion skinning, click the Onion Skin button at the bottom of the Timeline.

 To display onion skinning with outlines, click the Onion Skin Outlines button.

When you display onion skinning, Flash places markers at the top of the timeline around the frames that are displayed as onion skins (see Figure 9-12). Usually these markers advance automatically as the current frame pointer advances. You can manually adjust the beginning and ending of the onion skinning effect by clicking and dragging either the left or right marker to a new location on the Timeline.

Figure 9-12:
When you
display
onion
skinning,
markers are
placed on
the Timeline.

 To edit any of the frames on the Timeline no matter where your current frame pointer is, click the Edit Multiple Frames button. If you also have onion skinning turned on, you can then edit any frame while viewing all the other onion-skinned frames.

Click Modify Onion Markers to display a menu to help you adjust the way your onion markers work:

- ✔ **Always Show Onion Markers:** Shows onion markers even when you have turned off onion skinning.

- ✔ **Anchor Onions:** Lock the onion markers in their current position and prevents them from moving along with the current frame pointer as they normally do.

- ✔ **Onion 2:** Applies onion skinning to the two frames before and the two frames after the playhead (the current frame pointer).

- ✔ **Onion 5:** Applies onion skinning to the five frames before and the five frames after the playhead.

- ✔ **Onion All:** Applies onion skinning to all the frames in your Timeline.

 Hidden or locked layers never show as onion skinned. Hide or lock layers to isolate them from the layers you really want to change and to keep your onion skinning from getting out of control. Chapter 6 explains how to hide and lock layers.

Moving everything around the Stage at once

If you move a complete animation on the Stage without moving the graphics in all frames and all layers at once, you may quickly go nuts as you discover that every little thing must be realigned. Instead, retain your sanity and move everything at once.

To move a complete animation, follow these steps:

1. **Unlock all layers that contain the animation you want to move, and lock or hide any layers you don't want to move.**

2. **Click the Edit Multiple Frames button at the bottom of the Timeline.**

3. **Drag the onion skin markers to the beginning and ending frames of your animation.**

   Alternatively, if you want to select all frames, click the Modify Onion Markers button at the bottom of the Timeline and choose Onion All.

4. **Choose Edit⇨Select All.**

5. **Drag your animation to its new place on the Stage.**

Making the Scene

Animations can get complicated fast, and one way to manage that complexity is by organizing them in layers. (See Chapter 6 for the low-down on layers.) Another great way to manage the complexity of your animations is to break them into chunks of time, into scenes. You can then use scenes as the modular building blocks of your movies, which you can then rearrange in any way you want.

When's a good time to break up your movie into scenes? If your movie's simple, then one scene may be all you need. But if it gets more complex, you may want to break it up into a loading message, an introduction, the main act, the ending, and the credits.

Or, if your Timeline is starting to get longer than one screen will hold at once, you may want to find logical places to separate it into scenes. If your cast of graphics characters changes at a particular time, that may be a good place to break into a new scene. And if a section of your movie can conceivably be reused elsewhere in other movies, you may have an excellent reason to break it out into its own scene.

Breaking your movie into scenes

When you create a new Flash file (by running Flash for the first time or by choosing File⇨New), by default the file contains one empty scene, cleverly titled Scene 1. Any animations you create then become part of Scene 1.

If you want to add a scene, choose Insert⇨Scene, the Stage clears and the timeline is labeled Scene 2.

Manipulating that scene

To keep track of your scenes, open the Scene panel by choosing Window⇨ Panels⇨Scene, as shown in Figure 9-13. The Scene panel lists all the scenes in your movie. When you choose Control⇨Test Movie, the scenes play in order from the top of the list down.

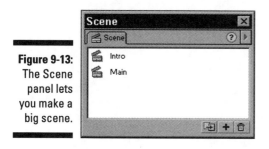

Figure 9-13:
The Scene panel lets you make a big scene.

Here's how to use the Scene panel to control your scenes:

- ✔ To change the order in which scenes play, drag a scene's name in the Scene panel to a new place in the list.

- ✔ To rename a scene, double-click the scene's name in the Scene panel, type the new name, and press Enter or Return.

 To delete a scene, select that scene and click the Delete Scene button at the bottom of the Scene panel. Or, open the scene and choose Insert⇨Remove Scene. Flash warns you that deleting a scene cannot be undone.

To duplicate a scene, click the Duplicate Scene button at the bottom of the Scene panel.

To view a particular scene, click its name in the Scene panel. Or, choose View⇨Goto and the name of the scene you want on the submenu.

 Look in the Ch09 folder of the CD-ROM for picturetour.fla, a nice example of a Flash movie divided into scenes. This movie is part of The Raj's Web site at www.theraj.com. *(Thanks to Lindsay Oliver of The Raj and Jesse Spaulding, the movie's creator, for this Flash movie.)*

Chapter 10

Getting Interactive

● ●

In This Chapter

▶ Getting familiar with actions

▶ Adding frames

▶ Using actions with buttons

▶ Adding actions to movie clips

▶ Working with actions

▶ Investigating advanced actions

● ●

*T*he real fun with Flash begins when you start to make your art and animations interactive. *Interactivity* means that your viewers interact with your
Web site. Examples include clicking a button to go to another Web page and
choosing to stop the music.

Flash uses *actions* to specify how the interactivity works. Actions are simply
short instructions that tell Flash what to do next. By combining actions, you
can create very complex sets of instructions that are like programming. You
can use actions to control your animation without interactivity, if you want.
Flash actions offer a great deal of flexibility, and only your imagination limits
what you can do.

In Flash 5, you can write actions from scratch in Expert mode. The language
is called *ActionScript* and its structure is similar to JavaScript, which is used
to program Web pages. You can, however, still build Action scripts by using
the dialog box as in Flash 4. (Whew!)

Understanding Actions

Flash lets you put actions in only three places:

- ✔ A frame on the timeline
- ✔ A button
- ✔ A movie clip

You cannot assign actions to graphics.

When you create an action, you first specify what has to occur for the action to be executed. This is the *when* part of the process. For example, if you add an action to a button instance, you can specify that the action will happen *when* the user releases the mouse button after clicking it.

Next you specify the action itself — *what* will happen. The action must come from the list of actions in Flash. Many of the actions have parameters that you must add. For example, to get a button to bring your viewer to another Web page, you use the Get URL action and add the exact URL (Web page address) as a parameter.

Adding Actions to Frames

You add an action to a frame to control what happens when the movie reaches that frame. Frame actions are often used to play a movie clip or to loop a movie so that a certain section of the animation is repeated. Another use for frame actions is to stop a movie or to automatically link to another URL (such as a Web page address). You can also use frame actions for more complex programming of Flash.

To add a basic action to a frame, follow these steps:

1. **Create a new layer for your actions (if you haven't already done so).**

   Chapter 6 explains how to add a new layer.

2. **Double-click a keyframe, which opens the Frame Actions window (see Figure 10-1).**

   If the frame you want to use is not a keyframe, right-click it (Windows) or Control+click it (Mac) and choose Insert Keyframe. Then choose Window⇨Actions to open the Frame Actions window.

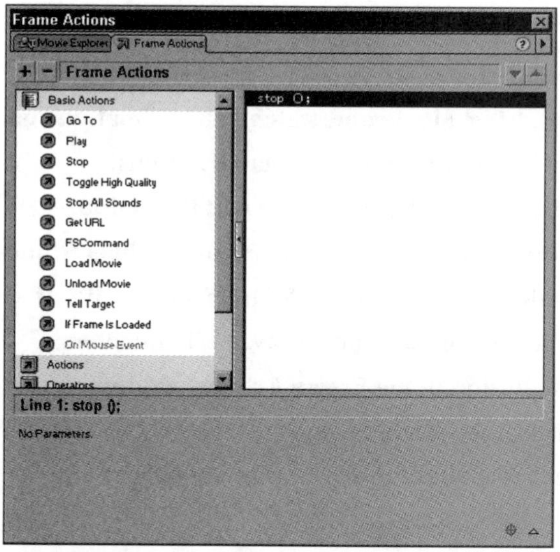

Figure 10-1:
The Frame
Actions
window is
your key to
adding
actions to
frames.

3. **Click Basic Actions on the left side and either double-click an action or drag the action to the right side.**

   You can also click the plus (+) button, choose Basic Actions, and then choose an action from the submenu.

4. **If the action requires parameters, type the required information at the bottom of the window.**

   If the Parameters area is not displayed at the bottom of the window, click the triangular arrow in the bottom-right corner of the window. We list the details of the specific actions and their parameters later in this chapter. You can continue to add additional actions by repeating Steps 4 and 5.

5. **If you want to get the Frame panel out of the way, click the Close box at the top of the window.**

A simple example of using a frame action is to place a Stop action at the beginning of the movie, as is illustrated in Figure 10-1. You may provide a button that starts the movie so that viewers can choose whether or not they want to see it. (They may want to get down to business right away and purchase something. Who are you to make them wait?) In this example, the movie loads, but the first thing it encounters is a command to stop. Nothing happens until someone clicks a button to start the movie. Of course, the Web page should contain other buttons and information that viewers can use to navigate through your Web site.

To add the Stop action to your movie, follow these steps:

1. **Create your animation.**

2. **Choose Control⊏>Test Movie and watch your animation run.**

3. **Create a layer for your action and name it** Actions.

4. **Click the keyframe where you want to add the action.**

5. **Choose Window⊏>Actions to open the Frame Actions window.**

6. **Click Basic Actions and double-click Stop from the list of actions.**

   Note that the bottom of the window says No Parameters.

7. **Click the Close button of the Frame Actions window.**

8. **Choose Control⊏>Test Movie again.**

   This time, the movie doesn't run because of the Stop action.

You can add many actions to frames. Later in this chapter, we list the major actions and how to use them.

To test a frame action without leaving the main Timeline, choose Control⊏> Enable Simple Frame Actions. Then run your animation.

For a lovely example of a frame action, open bounce.fla from the Ch10 folder of the CD-ROM (see Figure 10-2). To see how the movie works, choose Control⊏>Test Movie. Then close the window. Now double-click the last frame of Layer 1, the one with the *a* in it, and then click the Actions tab of the Frame Properties dialog box that opens. This action simply tells Flash to go to frame 1 and play; in other words, it loops the movie over and over again, creating the bouncing effect. *(The* bounce.fla *file is courtesy of Jeremy Wachtel, Vice President of Project Management at Macquarium Intelligent Communications.)*

Figure 10-2:
The bouncing marble from Macquarium.

Adding Actions to Buttons

A common way to add interactivity is to create a button. The viewer clicks the button and something happens (or stops happening). Usually, you add text near or on the button, so that your viewers know what the button is for.

If you already work on a Web site, you're familiar with the concept of hyperlinks. If you know HTML — the language behind Web pages — you know that you can create hyperlinks by using the <HREF> tag. This tag links text or an image to another URL. When people click the text or the image, they are teleported to that URL. You can create Flash buttons that accomplish the same purpose, but with much greater flair.

Buttons can do more! They can start or stop animation, jump to different parts of a movie, and stop sounds, among other things.

The process of adding an action to a button is simple. The difficult part is deciding which actions to use. Later in this chapter, we review all the possible actions and how to use them. (See the end of Chapter 8 for an example of a button that links to a different Web page.)

To create a button with actions, follow these steps:

1. **Create the button and place an instance of the button on the Stage.**

   See Chapter 8 if you need help with creating buttons.

2. **With the instance selected, choose Window⇨Actions to open the Object Actions window, shown in Figure 10-3.**

   The Object Actions window is the same as the Frame Actions window but it applies to buttons and movie clips instead of frames.

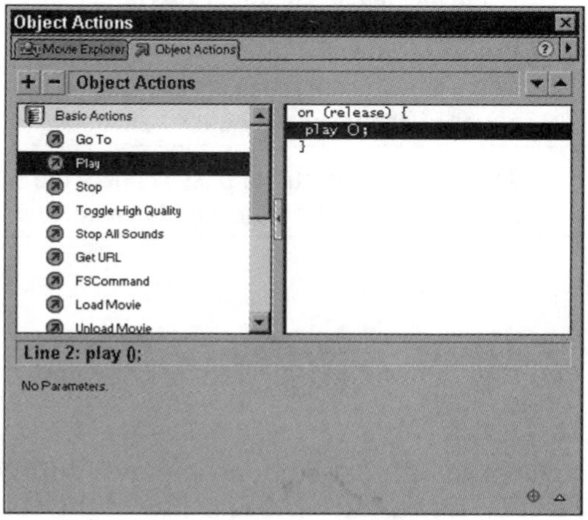

Figure 10-3:
In this example, a Play action has been added to the button.

3. **Click Basic Actions and double-click an action from the list.**

4. **If you want to change the default On (Release) statement, click to select it and choose a different option at the bottom of the window.**

   If the Parameters area is not displayed at the bottom of the window, click the triangular arrow in the bottom-right corner of the window.

   See Table 10-1 for more information on the statements you can use to define when a button action goes into effect.

5. **If the action requires parameters, type the required information at the bottom of the window.**

   Some of the most common actions and their parameters are listed later in this chapter in the "Using Actions" section. You can continue to add additional actions by selecting the action and repeating Steps 4 and 5.

6. **Click the Close box of the Object Actions window.**

Table 10-1	Button Action Statements
Statement	*When the Action Occurs*
Press	When the user clicks the button
Release	When the user releases the button of the mouse
Release Outside	When the user moves the mouse outside of the hit area and releases the mouse button
Key Press	When the key you specify next to the Key Press checkbox is pressed
Roll Over	When the mouse cursor passes over the hit area of the button, without clicking
Roll Out	When the mouse cursor passes out of the hit area of the button, without clicking
Drag Over	When mouse cursor passes over the hit area of the button, with the mouse button held down
Drag Out	When the mouse cursor passes out of the hit area of the button, with the mouse button held down

Adding an Action to a Movie Clip

With Flash 5, you can now add an action to a movie clip instance. Previously, actions were only on frames or in buttons. Actions in movie clips work within the Timeline of the movie clip, not on the main Timeline of the entire movie. Therefore, you can create movie clips that are interactive within themselves.

You add an action to a movie clip in the same way you add one to a button; both are objects to which you can add an action. To create a movie clip with actions, follow these steps:

1. **Create the movie clip and place an instance of the movie clip on the Stage.**

   Chapter 8 explains how to create movie clips if you need a refresher.

2. **With the instance selected, choose Window⇨Actions to open the Object Actions window.**

3. **Click Basic Actions and double-click an action from the list.**

   Flash automatically inserts an OnClipEvent statement, using the default Load event.

4. **If you want to change the default OnClipEvent (Load) statement, select it and choose a different option at the bottom of the window.**

   If the Parameters area is not displayed at the bottom of the window, click the triangular arrow in the bottom-right corner of the window.

   See Table 10-2 for a list of the events available for OnClipEvent.

5. **If the action requires parameters, type the required information at the bottom of the window.**

   You can continue to add additional actions by repeating Steps 4 and 5.

6. **Click the Close box of the Object Actions window.**

Table 10-2	Movie Clip Action Statements
Statement	*When the Action Occurs*
Load	As soon as the movie clip loads into memory, that is, pretty much at the beginning of the movie
EnterFrame	As the movie clip enters each frame
Unload	In the first frame after the movie clip is removed from the Timeline
Mouse down	When the (left) mouse button is clicked
Mouse up	When the (left) mouse button is released
Mouse move	When the mouse is moved (anywhere on the screen)
Key down	When any key is pressed
Key up	When any key is released
Data	When data is received from either a loadVariables or loadMovie action

Using Actions

Before you can create actions, you need to know which actions are available. In this chapter, we explain only the basic actions. For more information about advanced actions and programming in ActionScript, choose Help⇨ ActionScript Reference. Then refer to the preceding sections for instructions on inserting actions into frames, movie clips, and buttons.

The following sections describe the most common actions.

GoTo

GoTo tells your movie to go to a different frame. To define the frame, insert the action and click the Type drop-down list at the bottom of the Frame or Object Actions window and choose one of the options. You can define the frame in several ways:

- ✔ **Frame Number:** Defines the frame by its number on the timeline. In the Frame text box, type the number of the frame.

- ✔ **Frame Label:** Defines the frame by a label you have given it. Using a label is preferable if you may move frames to a different location on the Timeline, thereby changing their number. If you move a frame with a label, the label follows the frame. (Create a label by typing it in the Label text box of the Frame panel.)

- ✔ **Expression:** If you've written some ActionScript to calculate a frame number, you can use the ActionScript expression to specify the frame.

- ✔ **Next Frame:** Goes to the next frame.

- ✔ **Previous Frame:** Goes to the previous frame.

What do you want to happen after your movie goes to the desired frame? GoTo has two variations:

- ✔ **GoTo and Stop:** The movie goes to the specified frame and stops playing. You may want to do this if you want to wait for the user to press a button at that frame's location.

- ✔ **GoTo and Play:** The movie goes to the specified frame and plays. Use this when you want to jump to a new area of the movie and play the animation there. This is commonly used to loop a movie. On the last frame, you insert an action that goes to the first frame and plays the movie over again. GoTo and Play is also used in preloaders that play while a bigger movie is loading. (See Chapter 12 for more information.)

GoTo and Play is the default. To create a GoTo and Stop action, uncheck the GoTo and Play check box at the bottom of the Frame/Object Actions window. (If the Parameters area is not displayed at the bottom of the window, click the triangular arrow in the bottom-right corner of the window.)

Play

The Play action tells a movie or a movie clip to start playing. You can use this action to play a movie clip when a button is pressed or at any point you specify in the Timeline. For the Play action to work, the following things must be take place so that Flash knows what to play:

✔ The movie clip must be present on the Timeline (just drag it from the Library).

✔ The movie clip must have an instance name.

✔ You use the Tell Target action (described later, in the "Tell Target" section) to tell Flash what to play.

Stop

Stop stops a movie or movie clip from playing. (Did you guess?) One important use is at the end of a movie clip, because otherwise movie clips automatically loop. You can also put a Stop action on a button so that users can stop an introduction and get to the rest of your site. For a tidy ending to a movie, Flash users often place a Stop action at the end.

Look for Jay M. Johnson YE2k.fla in the Ch10 folder of the CD-ROM. In Frame 470, you see a Stop action. Because the music continues after that frame, the Stop action neatly stops everything at the point where the movie displays some buttons for you to press. Choose Control⇨Test Movie to see how it works. *(Thanks to Jay M. Johnson for this Flash movie.)*

Toggle High Quality

This action allows you to give your viewers control over the graphic quality of the movie. You can create a button with this action to switch display quality between high and low.

Stop All Sounds

The Stop All Sounds action simply stops all sounds from playing.

Get URL

The Get URL action is the Flash equivalent to a hyperlink in HTML, the language used to code Web pages. Get URL is often used on buttons, so when you click the button, you jump to another Web page. You need to supply the URL so Flash knows where to send your viewers.

From the Windows drop-down list, choose from the following options:

- ✔ **Self:** Opens the new Web page in the current window. Viewers can return to the previous window by using the Back button of their browsers.

- ✔ **Blank:** Opens a new window. Viewers can close this window (by clicking the Close box) to return to the previous window that is still displayed.

- ✔ **Parent:** If you have a movie within a nested frame, puts the new Web page in the parent of the nested frame (that is, one level above the nested frame).

- ✔ **Top:** If you're movie is in a frame within a window, this blows away all the frames and replaces them with the new Web page.

If you have ActionScript or some other programming that collects data and applies them to variables, you can specify what you want to do with the values of those variables. This is often used to send the data from a form that users fill in on the screen to a database or e-mail message. If you don't have any such programming, just leave the Variables setting at its default of Don't Send. If you do, you need to choose how you want to send the data:

- ✔ **Get:** Sends the variable values as part of the URL text. You are limited to the number of values you can send (to 1,024 characters).

- ✔ **Post:** Sends the variable values in a separate packet of data. You can send more variables and the data is somewhat more secure.

Look for Jay M. Johnson YE2k.fla in the Ch10 folder of the CD-ROM. Go to Frame 471, on the button 2 layer. Open the Actions window and click the button in the bottom-right of the screen that says, go to the official site Youth Evolution 2000 www.youthevolution2000.org. In the Actions window, you see the Get URL action that makes the button link users who click it to this other site. (Note that this site was for a conference in May 2000 and may no longer be active.)

FS Command

You can use the FS Command to control the Flash Player or other applications, like a browser. For example, the FS Command lets you execute JavaScript that you have written on the Web page. In the Command text box, type the name of the JavaScript command you have created. In the Arguments text box, add any arguments that your command requires or takes.

You need to add some code to the HTML page. For more information, see the FS Command in the ActionScript Reference Help.

Load Movie

Load Movie lets you load any Flash Player movie (SWF) that Flash can find. It can be another Flash Player movie residing in the same folder or somewhere else on the Web. You can use Load Movie to let users choose what they want to see next. This type of transition is smoother than using Get URL to load new Web pages.

You need to set the following parameters:

✔ **URL:** Type the URL. If the movie you're loading is in the same folder as the current movie, you can just type its name. If it's in a subfolder, for example, just type the path to the file, such as movies/mymovie.swf. But if the movie is elsewhere on the Web, type in the entire URL.

While you are testing your movie, you must place the SWF file in the same folder as the open movie and simply list the filename. Therefore, if you will use a different arrangement on the Web, be sure to change the reference to the file as necessary.

✔ **Location:** Choose Level and specify a level number if you want to maintain more than one open movie at a time.

- To replace the main (original) open movie (and any other loaded movies) with the new movie, specify level 0. This is like switching movies.

- To load a new movie without replacing the original movie (or any other loaded movie), specify a level number not used by any other movie. You can continue to load movies on different levels above the movie in level 0. The frame rate, background color, and movie size are determined by the movie in level 0.

- To replace a movie that is already loaded, use the level number of that movie.

✔ **Target:** Type the name of a movie clip that you want to replace by loading an SWF file. This lets you insert an external movie into a movie clip. Note that the SWF file will be placed in the same location as the movie clip, with the same rotation and scale.

As described in the section on the Get URL command, if you have ActionScript or some other programming, you can specify what you want to do with the values of those variables. Choose Don't Send, Get, or Post.

Unload Movie

Unload Movie unloads Flash Player movies that you have loaded by using the Load Movie command. You need to specify either Level or Target as well as the parameters explained in the previous section. Using this command helps to make sure that transitions are smooth and frees up your computer's memory sooner rather than later.

Tell Target

If you loaded movies by using Load Movie or you inserted movie clips onto your Timeline, you have more than one Timeline functioning at once. You can send secret messages from one Timeline to another by using the Tell Target command. In this way, one Timeline can control another. You use Tell Target in conjunction with another command. The Tell Target part tells Flash who you're talking to and the other command tells your target what to do.

Suppose that you have a main Timeline with an animation of a pastoral scene. Some flowers are waving about, and so on. Now you create two movie clips. One is a rabbit hopping over to a flower and away again. The other is a ladybug flying away from the flower and back again. You want the ladybug to fly away whenever the rabbit gets to the flower. Since the two movie clips are not the same length, you need the rabbit movie clip to tell the ladybug movie clip when to play. You can do this with Tell Target, Go To and Play, and Stop.

Here's another example. Suppose that you have some buttons on your main page. You want users to pass their mouse cursor over the button to display a description of where they will go if they click the button. You can create a movie clip for each button and use Tell Target to play the appropriate movie clip when the mouse cursor goes over the button. Here again, you use Go To and Play and Stop.

The Tell Target command requires only one parameter — the target. You can type in the target, but if the target is within the movie, you can make life easier by clicking the Insert a Target Path button in the bottom-right corner of the Frame/Object Actions window to open the Insert Target Path dialog box, as shown in Figure 10-4.

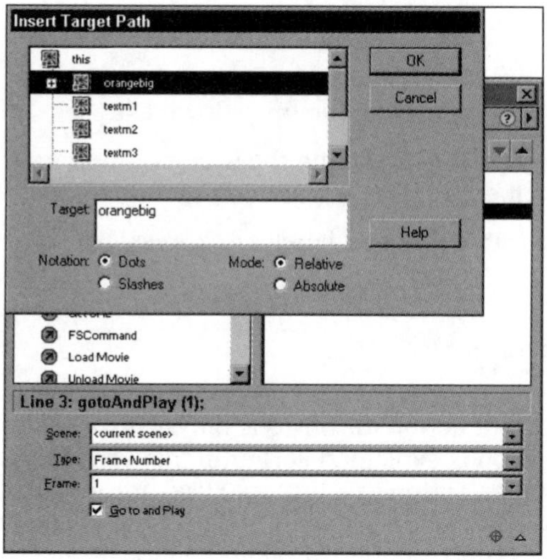

Figure 10-4: The Insert Target Path dialog box tries to make finding a target easier.

The other settings in this dialog box are as follows:

- ✔ **Notation:** The Flash 5 standard is to separate parts of the movie clip path with dots. You can also use the Flash 4 standard, which is slashes.

- ✔ **Mode:** Determines how the hierarchy of movie clips is displayed. Relative mode displays only instances of movie clips in the current frame of the current Timeline and any other movie clips within them. Flash uses the prefix *this* to refer to the current Timeline. Absolute mode displays every movie clip instance in the entire movie.

Choose a movie clip and click OK to insert it into the Tell Target command.

The best way to understand Tell Target is to look at an example. Look in the Ch10 folder for `HelpDesk-TellTarget.fla`. This movie displays movie clips when you pass the mouse cursor over a button.

Look in Chapter 14 for more information on working with Tell Target.

If Frame Is Loaded

The If Frame Is Loaded action checks if a specific frame is loaded into memory. The main use for this action is to create a preloader that plays a short movie while the main, larger movie is loading. You usually combine this action with the Go To and Play action. For more specific instructions and an example, see Chapter 12.

When you use the If Frame Is Loaded action, you need to tell Flash which frame you're talking about. Complete the following parameters at the bottom of the Frame Action panel:

> ✔ **Scene:** Define the scene containing the frame. If you have a scene, you Help⇨can choose the scene from the drop-down list.
>
> ✔ **Type:** Choose how you want to define the frame — by frame number, label, or ActionScript expression.
>
> ✔ **Frame:** Type in the frame number, label, or expression.

On Mouse Event

You use the On Mouse Event action for buttons only. The procedure for adding an action to a button is explained earlier in this chapter as well as in Chapter 8. When you add an action to a button, Flash automatically adds the On Mouse Event so that you can specify when the action will occur in relation to using the button — for example, passing the mouse cursor over it or clicking it.

You can, however, manually add the On Mouse Event if you wish. You would do this if you were adding your own Action Script and not choosing an action from the list of actions.

Examining Advanced Actions

Flash contains many more actions than the basic actions we cover in this chapter. Flash 5 added a number of new advanced actions, as well. For more information, choose Help⇨ActionScript Reference and Help⇨ActionScript Dictionary. In this section, we briefly explain a few of these advanced actions to give you an idea of some of the possibilities.

Comment

To help make your ActionScript clear when you look back at it a few months later, you should add comments that explain the purpose of the ActionScript. Use the Comment command for this purpose. This command inserts two slashes after which anything you type is ignored when running the animation.

Programming constructs

If you're familiar with programming, you will recognize several familiar commands, such as For and While, which let you process certain actions repeatedly while certain conditions you specify are true. The If and Else statements create conditional expressions.

Start and Stop Drag

Flash lets you create objects that your audience can drag around the screen. Draggable objects are used for games, slider bars, and other fun purposes. See Chapter 14 for details on creating your own draggable objects.

Set Property

The Set Property command lets you set the properties of objects. You can set some of the following properties:

- **Alpha:** You can control the transparency of a movie clip instance.
- **Height:** You can change the height of a movie clip instance in pixels.

- ✔ **High Quality:** You can control the level of antialiasing applied to the movie; that is, the smoothing effect applied to the display. You can choose from Best, High Quality, and Low.

- ✔ **Rotation:** You can rotate a movie clip clockwise by a specified number of degrees.

- ✔ **Visibility:** You can make movie clips disappear and appear! True means they are visible and false means they are invisible.

- ✔ **Width:** You can control the width of a movie clip instance in pixels.

- ✔ **X:** You can control the X coordinate, or the horizontal position of the movie clip instance.

- ✔ **Y:** You can control the Y coordinate, or the vertical position of the movie clip instance.

- ✔ **X Scale:** You can control the horizontal scale of a movie clip instance as a percentage of its original 100 percent.

- ✔ **Y Scale**: You can control the vertical scale of a movie clip instance as a percentage of its original 100 percent.

Expert mode

After you get really good at ActionScript, you can write it from scratch. In the Object or Frame Actions window, click the arrow in the top-right corner, and choose Expert Mode. This allows you to type to your heart's content your own ActionScript code in the Actions panel. You can switch back and forth between Normal and Expert modes whenever you want.

Chapter 11

Breaking the Sound Barrier

• •

In This Chapter

▶ Adding sounds to your movies

▶ Manipulating sounds

▶ Controlling sound properties

• •

Silent movies have been gone for a long time now. Why should your Flash movies be silent?

You can create music and sound effects that play continuously or are controlled by your animation Timeline. You can also add sounds to buttons to liven things up a little. You can edit sounds and control when they start and stop. But be careful — sound adds a lot of overhead to a movie, slowing down loading on a Web site. If you're careful about how you use sounds, you can get great results.

Play It Louder!

In order to add a sound to your Flash movie, you must first import the sound. You can import AIFF, WAV, or MP3 sounds. Flash places these sounds in your Library. (See Chapter 2 for more about the Library.)

Before importing a sound, you should check out its statistics. Sounds vary in sample rate — measured in kilohertz (kHz), bit resolution, and channels. These statistics are important because they affect both the quality and the size of the sound file. Of course, the length of the sound also affects its size. Here's what you need to know:

✔ **Sample rate:** The number of times an audio signal is sampled when it's recorded in digital form. Try not to use more than 22 kHz unless you want CD-quality music.

✔ **Bit resolution:** The number of bits used for each audio sample. 16-bit sound files are clearer with less background noise, but if you need to reduce file size, use 8-bit sound.

✔ **Channels:** Mono or stereo. In most cases, mono is fine for Flash files and uses half the amount of data.

Often, you need to take a sound as you find it, unless you have software that can manipulate sounds. Luckily, you can set the specs of sounds when you publish your movie to an SWF file. You'll generally get best results by starting with high-quality sounds and compressing during publishing. (See Chapter 13 for details on settings for publishing Flash files.)

If you're using Windows and you have a sound stored on your hard drive, you can get its stats by following these steps:

1. **Open Windows Explorer by clicking the Start button and choosing Programs⇨Windows Explorer.**

2. **Locate the sound file on your hard drive and right-click it to open a shortcut menu.**

3. **Choose Properties.**

4. **Click the Details tab and read the stats next to the Audio Format entry (see Figure 11-1).**

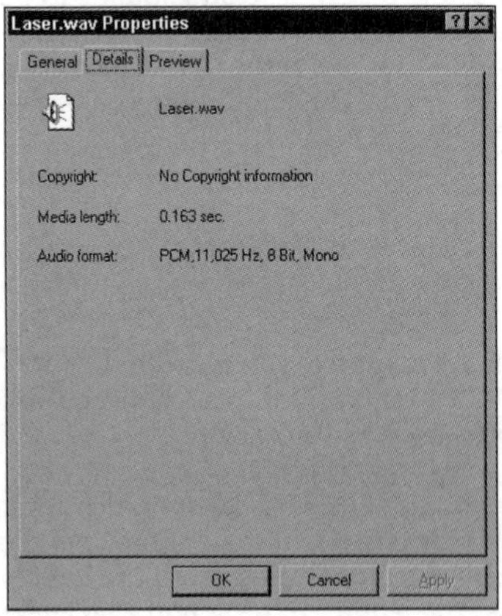

Laser.wav Properties ? ☒

General [Details] Preview

Laser.wav

Copyright: No Copyright information

Media length: 0.163 sec.

Audio format: PCM,11,025 Hz, 8 Bit, Mono

OK   Cancel   Apply

Figure 11-1:
This sound
file is 11
MHz (11,025
Hz), 8 bit,
and mono.

For both Mac and Windows, you can also check a sound's stats after you've imported the sound into Flash. The next section explains how to import a sound.

Importing sounds

Importing a sound is easy. To import a sound, follow these steps:

1. **Choose File⇨Import to open the Import dialog box.**
2. **Locate the sound you want to import.**
3. **Click Open (Windows) or Add (Mac); then click Import.**

Nothing seems to happen, but Flash has placed your sound in the Library. Choose Window⇨Library to check it out. To see the sound's stats, click the name of the sound in the Library window. Then click the Properties button at the bottom of the Library window.

The Flash libraries contain a number of sounds that you can use. Choose Window⇨Common Libraries⇨Sounds to see which sounds are available.

Placing sounds into a movie

After you import a sound into your movie, you need to place it and set its parameters. To place sounds in a movie, follow these steps:

1. **Create and name a new layer for the sound.**

   Click the plus sign at the bottom of the layer list to add a new layer. Each sound should have its own layer. Sounds are combined *(mixed)* when the movie is played.

2. **With the desired keyframe in the new layer selected, open the Library and drag the sound onto the Stage.**

   Flash places the sound on the active layer. Flash extends the sound until the next keyframe, if there is one.

3. **Choose Window⇨Panels⇨Sound to open the Sound panel (see Figure 11-2).**

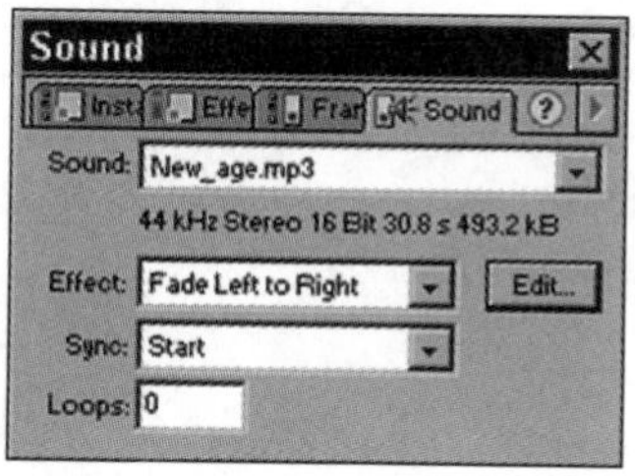

Figure 11-2:
The Sound
panel.

Sound

Inst Effe Fran Sound ?

Sound: New_age.mp3

44 kHz Stereo 16 Bit 30.8 s 493.2 kB

Effect: Fade Left to Right   Edit...

Sync: Start

Loops: 0

4. **From the Sound drop-down list, choose the sound you want to place in your movie.**

   If necessary, click the keyframe where the sound starts. The Sound drop-down list shows all sounds that you have imported. The sounds stats are listed below the name of the sound (kilohertz, channels, bits, duration, and file size).

5. **If desired, choose an effect from the Effect drop-down list.**

   These effects are fairly self-explanatory. For example, Left Channel plays the sound only from your left speaker. Fade In starts the sound softly and gradually brings it up to full volume. The default setting is None.

6. **Choose a synchronization option from the Sync drop-down list.**

   - **Event:** Plays the sound when its first keyframe plays and continues to play the sound until it's finished, even if the movie stops. This is the default setting.

   - **Start:** Plays the sound when its first keyframe plays. But if the keyframe is played again before the sound is finished, Flash starts the sound again. Use this setting for button sounds when you want the sound to play each time the button is passed over or clicked. (See Chapter 8 for more information on adding sounds to buttons.)

   - **Stop:** Stops the sound. (See Chapter 10 for details on the Stop All Sounds action.)

   - **Stream:** Synchronizes the sound with the animation. Flash shortens or lengthens the animation to match the length of the sound, skipping frames if necessary. The sound stops when Flash plays the last frame containing the soundwave. Use this option when you want to match the sound with a portion of the animation in your movie. You can insert an ending keyframe before placing the sound to control when the sound ends.

7. **In the Loop text box, type the number of loops if you want to repeat the sound.**

   You can figure how many loops you need to play a sound throughout an animation by knowing how many seconds the sound is, how many frames your animation is, and the frame rate. If your animation is 48 frames and the rate is 12 frames per second (the default), your animation is 4 seconds. If your sound is 2 seconds long, loop it twice to play it throughout your animation. Use a high number of loops if you don't want to do the math, just to make sure.

8. **If you want, you can manually edit the sound, as discussed in the "Editing Sounds" section later in this chapter.**

After you place the sound, press Enter or use the Controller to play your movie and hear the results.

Sounds can add significantly to file size and download time. You can place sounds in a Shared Library to reduce file size. See Chapter 2 for information on creating and accessing Shared Libraries.

Editing Sounds

After you place a sound, you can edit the sound to fine-tune the settings. You should delete unused or unwanted portions of a sound in order to reduce file size. You can also change the volume as the sound plays.

To edit a sound, choose Window⇨Panels⇨Sound to open the Sound panel; then click the Edit button to open the Edit Envelope dialog box (see Figure 11-3).

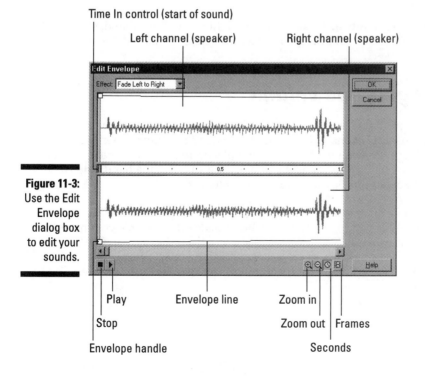

Figure 11-3:
Use the Edit
Envelope
dialog box
to edit your
sounds.

To see a specific section of a sound in more detail, click the Zoom In button. Zoom in when you want to edit small details of a sound.

 To see more of a sound's timeframe, click the Zoom Out button. Zoom out to edit the sound as a whole.

 You can display sounds in terms of seconds or frames. Click the Seconds button to show sounds in seconds. Click the Frames button to display sounds by frames.

Deleting parts of a sound

Between the left (top) and right (bottom) channel display is a narrow strip that controls the starting and ending points of a sound. By deleting the beginning and end of a sound, you can eliminate unused portions of the sound. Along this strip is a vertical bar at the beginning and the end of the sound. These bars control when the sound starts and ends. Use them to edit the sound as follows:

- **Time In control:** This bar, on the left edge of the sound, specifies the start of the sound. Drag it to the right to delete the beginning of the sound.
- **Time Out control:** This bar, on the right edge of the sound, specifies the end of the sound. Drag it to the left to delete the end of the sound.

Changing the volume

In both the left and right channel displays, Flash shows an *envelope line* to indicate the approximate direction of the sound's volume (refer to Figure 11-3). Where the volume changes, Flash places small squares called *envelope handles*. To change the sound's volume, drag an envelope handle up (to increase volume) or down (to decrease volume).

You can click an envelope line to add a new envelope handle. This new handle enables you to create a new direction for the sound's volume at the handle's location.

When you finish editing a sound, click OK to close the Edit Envelope dialog box.

Managing Sound

Sound can increase the size of your movie by such a great extent that you need to be very careful how you use it. You should make every effort to compress the sound. You can also lower the sampling rate; however, your sound's quality is reduced. Nevertheless, you should try out all the possibilities until you get the best results.

The *sampling rate* is the rate at which the computer measures sound and converts it into numerical data. The computer makes these sample measurements many thousands of times per second. A higher sampling rate provides more information about the sound and, therefore, better audo quality. But all those extra measurements make for a much bigger data file.

Flash offers two ways to control the properties of a sound:

✔ **Use the Publish Settings dialog box to specify properties for all the sounds in a movie.** If you only have one sound or a couple of similar sounds, it's easy to specify settings this way.

✔ **Use the Sound Properties dialog box to specify properties of specific sounds.** As long as you don't specifically override these properties when you publish, these settings stick. Use the Sound Properties dialog box when you want to specify different properties for each sound.

Because you specify the publish settings when you publish a movie, we discuss those settings in Chapter 13. Here we explain how to fine-tune your sound properties in the Sound Properties dialog box.

To open the Sound Properties dialog box, open the Library (choose Window➪Library) and double-click the icon of the sound you want to work with. Figure 11-4 shows the Sound Properties dialog box.

At the top of the dialog box, Flash displays statistics for the sound — its location, date, sample rate, channels, bits, duration, and file size. Use the Export Settings section to specify how you want to export the file. For each compression type, Flash displays the settings available for that type. As you choose settings, look at the bottom of the dialog box where Flash displays the new file size in kilobytes and in percent of original size. Here are the options available in the Compression drop-down list box:

✔ **Default:** Leaves the sound as is, with no compression.

✔ **ADPCM:** You can convert stereo to mono to cut down file size. Available sampling rates are 5, 11, 22, or 44 kHz. You can choose from 2, 3, 4, or 5 bits. Five bits results in the best sound; the Flash default is four bits.

✔ **MP3:** MP3 is available since Flash 4 and is a very efficient compression method. You can convert stereo to mono and choose a bit rate, measured in kilobits per second (Kbps). You can choose from 8 Kbps (poor quality) to 160 Kbps (near-CD quality). Generally, you want something between these two extremes. Try a bit rate between 20 and 84 Kbps for a good balance of file size and quality. You can also choose the quality — Fast, Medium, or Best. The Fast option optimizes the sound for faster download from your Web site, but with some quality compromise.

✔ **Raw:** You can convert stereo to mono and choose the same sampling rates as for ADPCM.

MP3 provides the best compression, letting you keep your quality as high as possible. (*Note:* Some users may still have the Flash 3 player, which doesn't support MP3.)

As you specify a group of settings, click the Test button to see the results. This handy button lets you hear how your sound file sounds with each setting.

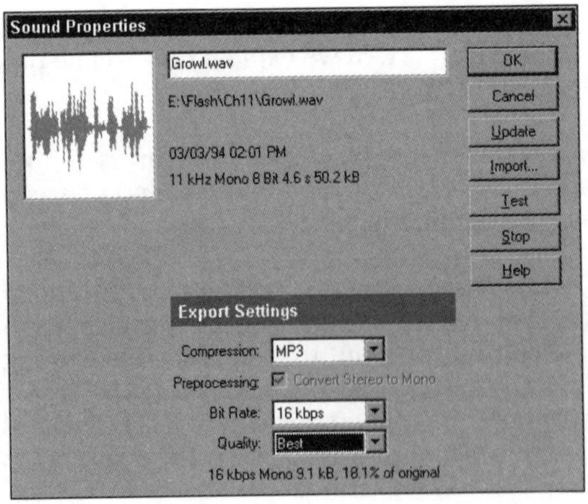

Figure 11-4:
Use the Sound Properties dialog box to set the properties of individual sounds, including their compression and quality.

The Sound Properties dialog box also lets you update the original sound after you modify it with sound editing software — click the Update button. You can also click Import to import a sound file. The Stop button stops playing a sound that you're previewing.

When you're done, click OK to finalize your settings and close the dialog box.

Part V
The Movie and the Web

The 5th Wave By Rich Tennant

"I can't really explain it, but everytime I animate someone swinging a golf club, a little divot of code comes up missing on the home page."

In this part . . .

The not-so-secret desire of every Flash movie animation is to appear under the bright lights on the Web. In this part, we show you how to make that happen. We explain how to put all the pieces together to create a way-cool Flash-only site. You see how to build a Web site that contains a complete navigational system so that viewers can get the information they need quickly. We cover three techniques for creating a complete site.

We also discuss the nitty-gritty of publishing your Flash movie to a Flash Player file, the only kind of Flash file a Web browser can display. Besides the Flash Player file, Flash can create the HTML code you need and the alternative images that you may want to use in case a viewer doesn't have the Flash Player. Flash makes it easy — just specify your settings and click Publish.

Chapter 12

Putting It All Together

• •

In This Chapter

▶ Offering your viewers a preloader

▶ Putting together an entire Web site with Flash

▶ Checking out your viewers' Flash Player version

▶ Analyzing your movies using the Movie Explorer

• •

*W*hen creating your Flash animation, you need to consider how you will integrate it with your entire Web site. Are you creating a small animation to insert onto an existing HTML site or do you want your entire site to be *Flashed*? In this chapter, we cover techniques for creating entire Web pages and sites using Flash.

We explain how to create a preloader that encourages your viewers to wait while your large Flash Player file loads. We cover the various techniques for making a Flash-only Web page and offer advice on testing for the Flash Player version that your viewers are using. Finally, we explain how to use the Movie Explorer to analyze your Flash movies.

Creating a Preloader

If you're very ambitious and create a huge Flash file, you may find that it takes an unacceptable amount of time to download to a viewer's browser. Your audience isn't going to wait forever.

In order to solve this problem, you should create a *preloader*. A preloader is a tiny movie that loads quickly and tells your viewers to wait. Often, all it says is loading. This movie contains ActionScript actions that determine when your main movie has loaded and then goes to that movie.

To create a simple preloader, follow these steps:

1. **Create two scenes, the second for your main movie and the first for the preloader.**

   The two scenes must be within the same movie. See Chapter 9 for the lowdown on creating and changing the order of scenes.

2. **Select the very last frame of your main movie.**

3. **Choose Window⇨Panels⇨Frame to open the Frame panel.**

4. **In the Label text box, type a label for this frame, such as** End.

5. **In the first scene (the preloader), create a small animation.**

6. **Click the first frame of your preloader scene and choose Window⇨Actions to open the Frame Actions window.**

7. **From the list of Basic Actions, double-click the If Frame Is Loaded action.**

   See Chapter 10 if you need a refresher on adding an action to a frame.

8. **At the bottom of the Frame Actions window, choose the main movie's scene in the Scene drop-down list (see Figure 12-1).**

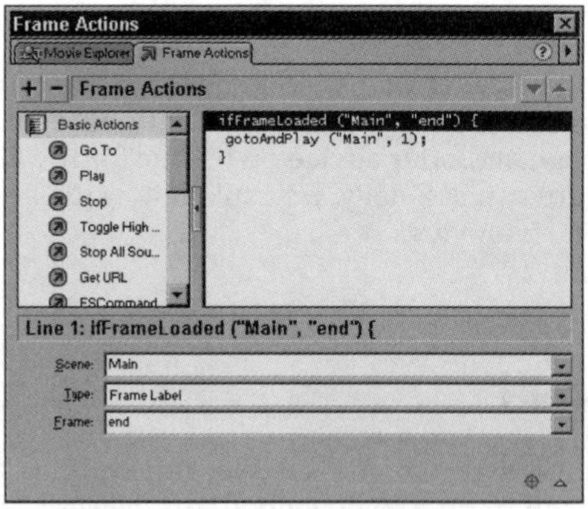

Figure 12-1: The bottom of the Frame Actions window for the If Frame Is Loaded action.

9. **From the Type drop-down list, choose Frame Label.**

10. **From the Frame drop-down list, choose the label you created in Step 4.**

11. **With the If Frame Is Loaded action selected, double-click the Go To action from the list of Basic Actions in the Frame Actions window.**

12. **At the bottom of the Frame Actions window, choose the main movie's scene in the Scene drop-down list, Frame Number in the Type drop-down list, and Frame 1 in the Frame drop-down list.**

13. **Ensure that the Go To and Play check box (at the bottom of the Frame Actions window) is checked.**

    Your ActionScript should look like Figure 12-2. The ActionScript specifies that if the last frame of the main movie is loaded, the playhead of the Timeline should go to the first frame of the main movie and play it.

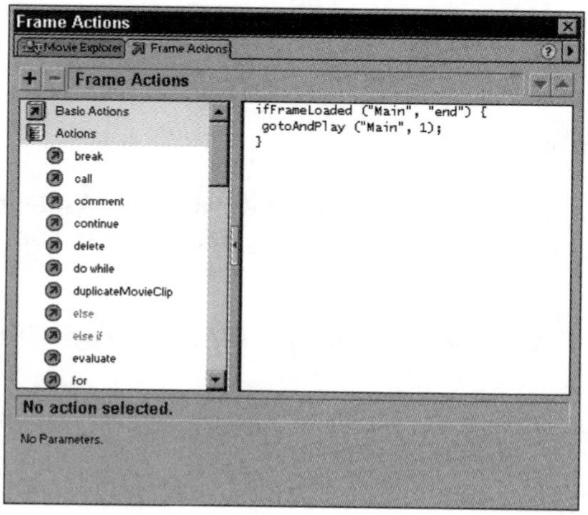

Figure 12-2:
Use this code in the first frame of your preloader.

14. **Click the last frame of your preloader scene.**

15. **In the Frame Actions window, double-click the GoTo action.**

16. **At the bottom of the window, set the Type to Frame Number and the Frame to 1.**

17. **Leave the scene at its default of <current scene> and ensure that Go To and Play is checked.**

    This ActionScript loops your preloader so that it plays over and over until your main movie is loaded.

You can test your preloader by choosing Control⇨Test Movie, but your main movie may load so quickly that you don't even see the preloader. Choose View⇨Show Streaming to see how your preloader works while your main movie loads, as explained in Chapter 13. You can also actually upload your file to a test page on your Web site to see how the preloader works. Make sure that your preloader is long enough for the eye to see. Remember that one frame displays for only a fraction of a second.

Creating an Entire Web Site with Flash

You can use Flash to create the complete user interface, along with all the graphics and text on your site. Typically, a fully Flashed site has the following structure:

- ✔ HTML page that tests for the Flash player and player version
- ✔ HTML file displaying a Flash movie that contains
  - • Preloader
  - • Intro
  - • Navigation page
- ✔ Other pages, if desired

The opening HTML page is the first thing your viewers see. Aside from your logo and anything else you want viewers to see, this page can contain three elements:

- ✔ Automatic or user-controlled download of the Flash player from Macromedia
- ✔ A button that leads viewers to an HTML site if they have a slow connection or don't want to download the Player (or ActionScript that takes them there automatically)
- ✔ A button that leads viewers to your Flash site (or ActionScript that takes them there automatically)

For information on creating an HTML page that tests for the Flash player, see the "Testing for the Flash Player" section later in this chapter.

To match a Flash movie in a Web page to the rest of the page, match the background colors of the movie (by choosing Modify⇨Movie) and the HTML page. (This technique doesn't work if your Web page uses an image for a background.) To set the background of the HTML page, edit the HTML file that Flash creates when you publish your movie. After determining the background color in hexadecimal code (by looking at the HTML code for the existing Web page), change the BGCOLOR tag in the HTML code in three places:

- ✔ In the background color where it says `<BODY bgcolor="#99CCFF">` (for example)
- ✔ In the OBJECT tag where it says `<PARAM NAME=bgcolor VALUE=#99CCFF>`
- ✔ In the EMBED code where it says `BGCOLOR=#99CCFF`

Once people get to your Flash page, you can do whatever you want. But many sites start with an intro, a preliminary movie that can either briefly explain what your site is for or just wow them.

Nevertheless, you want people to get to the main content of your site before too long. The main content section — often called the navigation section — usually contains buttons that people can choose to navigate through your site, get more information, or contact you.

You can create the navigation structure in three main ways:

✔ Attach Tell Target or Load Movie actions to the buttons to display the content of movie clips or Flash player movies (SWF files).

✔ Attach Get URL actions to the buttons to link to other HTML pages or movies on your site. You can, of course, create the HTML pages with Flash.

✔ Use the buttons to display information or graphics located on other parts of your Timeline by using the GoTo action.

The Tell Target and Load Movie actions are described in Chapter 10 with further information in Chapter 14. The Get URL action is explained in Chapters 8 (with regard to buttons) and 10. You can use combinations of these methods. For example, you can use Tell Target to display information when the mouse cursor is over a button, along with Get URL to link to another page when the button is clicked.

Look for HelpDesk-TellTarget.fla in the Ch12 folder of the CD-ROM for an example of buttons that use Tell Target to display information about the purpose of the buttons. Look for HelpDesk-LoadMovie.fla in the Ch12 folder for an example that accomplishes the same thing by using the Load Movie action. (This movie requires beginner.swf, tutorial.swf, and trouble.swf to be in the same folder as the movie. These files are also in the Ch12 folder of the CD-ROM.) For both movies, choose Control➪Test Movie to try them out.

Creating navigation with Get URL

When you attach a Get URL action to a button, the button links to another HTML page in the same way as a button on a regular, non-Flash HTML Web page does. For more information on the Get URL action, see Chapter 10. Also, Chapter 8 explains how to add an action to a button.

Using the Timeline to store Web content

In most cases, you use the Timeline to display frames in sequence — in other words, animation. But the Timeline can also store static frames. You can create anything on the Stage in those frames, and you can display what is in those frames whenever you want.

Suppose that you have several buttons on your main page. You want viewers to see a description of the kind of information they will see when they click the buttons. Perhaps moving the mouse over one button displays text stating something like, Information on our services. Another may say, How to contact us.

To create this informational text effect by using the Timeline, follow these steps:

1. **Place instances of your buttons on the first frame of the Timeline of your movie.**

2. **On each layer, about 20 or so frames after the first frame, add a keyframe containing a button.**

   These 20 or so frames leave enough room to store the static display frames on the Timeline. The buttons continue to be displayed throughout the movie until the ending keyframe. The more buttons you want to provide descriptions for, the further out your ending keyframe needs to be.

3. **Create a new layer for your static display and give it a name, such as** Descriptions.

4. **A few frames out (say on Frame 10) on the Descriptions layer, create a keyframe.**

   This starts a Timeline section for the static display of your first button.

5. **On Frame 15, create another keyframe.**

   This ends the first button's Timeline section.

6. **Select Frames 10 through 15 and open the Frame panel (choose Window⇨Panels⇨ Frame).**

7. **In the Label text box, type a label name.**

8. **On the Stage, create the graphics and words that you want to be displayed when a user passes the mouse cursor over your first button.**

   Place the graphics so that they don't cover your buttons when they appear.

9. **Repeat Steps 5 through 8 to create labels and displays for all your buttons, using subsequent sections of the Timeline until you reach the ending keyframe.**

10. **Select your first button.**

11. **Choose Window⇨Actions to open the Object Actions window.**

12. **From the list of Basic Actions, double-click Go To.**

13. **Click the first line of ActionScript, which by default says** on (Release).

14. **From the list of mouse events at the bottom of the Object Actions window, uncheck Release and check Roll Over.**

    The Roll Over event causes the action to occur when your viewer passes the mouse cursor over the button.

15. **Click the second line of ActionScript.**

    See Figure 12-3.

16. **At the bottom of the Object Actions window, uncheck Go to and Play to create a Go To and Stop action.**

17. **From the Type drop-down list, choose Frame Label.**

18. **From the Frame drop-down list, choose the first label that you created on your Timeline in Step 7.**

    Your ActionScript should look like Figure 12-3.

19. **Repeat Steps 9 through 14 for the rest of your buttons and their respective frame labels.**

20. **Create a new layer and call it** Actions.

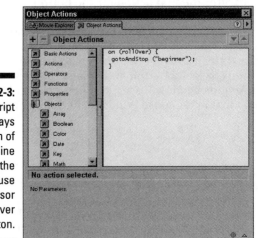

Figure 12-3:
ActionScript that displays a section of the Timeline when the mouse cursor passes over a button.

21. Place a Stop action on the first frame.

See Chapter 10 for instructions on how to add an action to a frame.

If you don't do this final step, your movie simply plays through all the frames, displaying your descriptions one after another. You only want viewers to see those frames when they pass their mouse over a button.

Choose Control⇨Test Movie to try it out! As you pass your mouse cursor over a button, the graphics and text on the appropriate frames appears. Figure 12-4 shows a Timeline with frames that are displayed when the mouse cursor passes over buttons.

Figure 12-4:
Use the Timeline to store material displayed for certain actions.

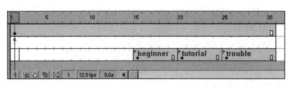

 If you want the display to disappear when users pass the cursor off a button, add a Go To and Stop action to the button instance that goes to Frame 1. Use a Roll Out event (instead of the Roll Over event you used first on the button). Place this second action right after the first action for the button.

 Look for HelpDesk-Timeline.fla in the Ch12 folder of the CD-ROM for an example of buttons that use the Timeline to display information about the purpose of the buttons. To test the move, choose Control⇨Test Movie. To see the ActionScript for the buttons, select a button and choose Window⇨ Actions to open the Object Actions window. To see the ActionScript for a frame, click a frame with an *a* in it and choose Window⇨Actions to open the Frame Actions window.

Testing for the Flash Player

Although most people have the Flash Player installed, you may still have some viewers with totally out-of-date browsers. For viewers that don't have the Flash Player, the Flash Player often downloads automatically as a result of the code that Flash places in the HTML file. If not, they may simply not be able to view your site. You can test for the presence of the Flash Player and, even more, you can test to see which version of the Flash Player they have. If you're using features that exist only in Flash 5, you want to make sure viewers have the Flash 5 player because people may still have the Flash 4 player installed (or an even earlier version).

You can test for the Flash Player in several ways; we describe two possibilities in the following sections.

Letting the user decide

Some sites let the viewer simply choose between a Flash site and a non-Flash site. The problem with this method is that many users have no idea what Flash is, let alone whether they have the Flash Player.

A better method to let users determine whether they have the Flash Player is to place a small Flash animation that is also a button on an initial HTML Web page. Instructions tell them to click the button if they can see the animation, which links them to the main portion of your Flash site. If they cannot see the animation, you can offer an image with a link (or linked text) to Macromedia's Flash Player download site and another link to an alternate HTML site. (See Chapter 8 for instructions on creating a Flash button.)

At the very least, you should offer users the opportunity to download the Flash Player. Do this with a link connecting them to the following URL:

```
http://www.macromedia.com/shockwave/download/
        index.cgi?P1_Prod_Version=ShockwaveFlash
```

Detecting the Flash Player version

A more sophisticated method is to automatically test for the version of the Flash Player. You can have one site for Flash 4 players, one for Flash 5 players, and a third HTML site for neither. Sounds complicated, no? But if you're very attached to effects that only exist in Flash 5, you may have no other choice.

Here's an ActionScript that you can place in the first frame of a movie. In this case, the ActionScript finds any Player greater than or equal to Version 4. (To be precise, this method can test for versions greater than 4.0r11. You cannot reliably use it to test for earlier versions. Also, it only works for users running Windows or the Mac OS, not Unix.)

```
1        ver = eval("$version");
2        if (ver.substring(4, 5) >= 4) {
3            gotoAndStop (10);
4        } else {
5            gotoAndStop (15);
6        }
```

Line 1 sets a variable called ver, but you can call it whatever you want. It then evaluates the version number of the player.

Line 2 evaluates the portion of the text string returned by the $version function that gives you the version number. (Other portions return the platform — such as Mac or Windows — revision number, and so on.) It then tests whether the version is greater than or equal to 4. You can change this. For example, in place of >=4, you can put ==5 (with two equal signs) to test whether your viewer has the Flash 5 Player.

Line 3 sends the movie to Frame 10 and stops. You can change this to anything you want. For example, you can use the Get URL action to send your viewer to another HTML page with your main Flash movie. You can also load a movie. (See Chapter 10 for an explanation of the Go To, Get URL, and Load Movie actions.)

Line 4 starts the alternative that happens if your test in Line 2 is not true (in this case, if the player version is not greater than or equal to 4).

Line 5 sends your viewer to Frame 15 and stops. Again, you can change this as explained for the code of Line 3.

To test this code, follow these steps (we assume that you have the Flash 5 player):

1. **Place the ActionScript just provided in your movie's first frame.**

   You can type it in by using Expert mode, or build it in Normal mode. (Chapter 10 explains how to place ActionScript in a frame.)

2. **Add a keyframe in Frame 10 and place some text there that says** Frame 10.

3. **Add a keyframe in Frame 15, and place some text that there that says** Frame 15.

4. **Choose File⇨Publish Preview⇨Default.**

   This creates an SWF Flash Player file from your movie.

   Because you have a Flash Player greater than or equal to Version 4, you should see Frame 10 on your screen.

5. **Close the browser window and change** >=4 **in Line 2 of the ActionScript to** ==6.

6. **Save your movie and go to Publish Preview again.**

   This time, you should see Frame 15 on your screen because the test in Line 2 was not true.

You can continue to play around with the ActionScript until you have something that works for you.

Creating alternate sites

However you direct viewers, you must create sites that they can see. Many Flash sites also include a complete set of non-Flash (HTML) pages for viewers who don't have the Flash player and don't want to bother downloading it.

If you use features unique to Flash 5, you can also create a Flash 4 site that uses only features available in Flash 4. Most people have the Flash 4 player. But don't forget how much time you spend updating your Web site now. Imagine updating three sites! Make sure that you think through the consequences of having so many alternatives.

Using Movie Explorer

The new Flash 5 Movie Explorer is a great tool for analyzing an entire movie. When you start creating complex relationships among several Timelines, you may find that it's hard to remember what you've done. Movie Explorer lays out the entire structure of your movie for you to see. Movie Explorer is also a great tool for troubleshooting problems that may arise. By visually displaying your movie's components, you can more easily find where the trouble lies.

Another use for Movie Explorer is to analyze other people's movies. When you open someone else's movie, you may wonder where the movie is. It may all be hidden in movie clips and actions that call other movies and movie clips. Movie Explorer can help you ferret out the magic behind the animation.

To open Movie Explorer, choose Window⇨Movie Explorer. Movie Explorer is shown in Figure 12-5.

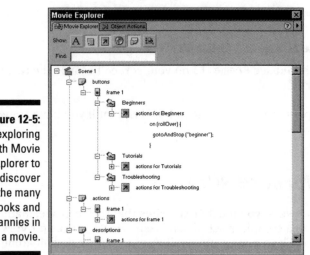

Figure 12-5:
Go exploring
with Movie
Explorer to
discover
the many
nooks and
crannies in
a movie.

You usually know what you're looking for when you open Movie Explorer. For example, you may be looking for ActionScript or movie clips. Use the buttons at the top of Movie Explorer to specify which movie elements are shown in the main window:

✔ **Show Text:** Displays all text objects in the movie.

✔ **Show Buttons, Movie Clips, and Graphics:** Displays a list of those objects.

✔ **Show ActionScript:** Lists all ActionScript in the movie.

✔ **Show Video, Sounds, and Bitmaps:** Lists those objects.

✔ **Show Frames:** Shows each frame that contains objects.

✔ **Customize Which Items to Show:** Opens the Movie Explorer Settings dialog box, where you can indicate which items you want to show by checking or unchecking them from a list. You can also choose to display Movie Elements (that is scenes), Symbol Definitions (a separate listing by symbol), or both. Click OK to close this dialog box.

Movie elements are shown in a hierarchical manner in Movie Explorer. For example, if a button has an action attached to it, you see a plus (+) sign (Windows) or a right-pointing triangle (Mac) next to the button. Click any plus sign (Windows) or right-pointing triangle (Mac) to expand the display, in this case to reveal the ActionScript for that button. Click any minus (–) sign (Windows) or down-pointing triangle (Mac) to collapse the display.

In the Find text box, you can type any expression to search the entire movie. Suppose that you want to know whether a movie contains the Tell Target action. Just type **tellTarget** in the Find text box, and Movie Explorer displays every instance containing that word.

The Find feature is not case sensitive, but it only finds whole words. Therefore, if the movie contains _tellTarget_ and you type **target**, you won't get any result at all. You also won't get anything if you type **tell target** (two words).

You can use Movie Explorer to select objects on the Stage or frames. Just click the item in Movie Explorer, and Flash selects the object or frame. (If you select a frame, Flash also includes the frames up to the next keyframe.) If you select a scene, Flash selects the first frame of the scene.

Movie Explorer contains an extensive menu that you can access either by clicking the right-pointing triangle at the top right of Movie Explorer or by right-clicking (Windows) or Control+clicking (Mac) inside the Movie Explorer window.

Some of the more useful features of this menu are as follows:

- **Find in Library:** Opens the Library (if it's not already open) and highlights the object that you previously selected in Movie Explorer.

- **Rename:** Lets you rename the selected object, such as a button instance.

- **Copy Text to Clipboard:** Copies text (selected in Movie Explorer) to the Clipboard (of course) so you can paste it into another application. You may want to use this feature to place text in a word processor for spell-checking. (How many Web pages have you seen with typos? We've seen way too many.)

- **Print:** Prints the entire contents of Movie Explorer. All items, whether collapsed or not, are printed.

If you have difficulty understanding one of the more advanced Flash movies on the CD-ROM, try opening Movie Explorer in the movie. Look for actions and movie clips. You may be surprised at what you can discover using this new feature.

Chapter 13

Publishing Your Flash Files

· ·

In This Chapter

▶ Reducing your movie's size for fast download

▶ Testing your Flash movies

▶ Publishing Flash movies to SWF, HTML, and other formats

▶ Making movies that play themselves

▶ Creating movie and image files

▶ Creating movies that viewers can print

· ·

*Y*our Flash movie is done. Now you need to publish it in its final form, most likely an SWF file that you can post on your Web site. In this chapter, we explain how to prepare a Flash movie for publishing and help you determine the ideal publish settings for your needs. You also have the option to publish to other graphic file formats (such as GIF, JPEG, QuickTime, AVI, and others) in case you want to create a non-Flash site or use your material in another program. We discuss these other file formats as well. We cover all the bases so you can get your animation up and running.

Note that although the letters SWF originally stood for Shockwave File, Macromedia no longer uses that term for Flash published movies, although the letters remain the same. So to follow Macromedia's usage, we refer to SWF files as Flash Player files.

Optimizing Movies for Speed

Throughout this book we offer suggestions for designing a Flash movie with speed in mind. Here we put them together so you can review your movie as a whole before you publish it.

Simplifying artwork

By simplifying the artwork in your movie, you can greatly reduce the size of a Flash movie, thereby increasing its speed. Here are the most important techniques:

✔ **Use symbols as much as possible:** You can turn any object or group of objects into a symbol. Backgrounds that continue for several frames should be turned into a symbol. Nest your symbols — for example, turn an object into a symbol and then use it in a movie clip or button. Remember that you can change the color of symbol instances — you don't need to create a new symbol. (Chapter 7 covers symbols in detail.)

✔ **Group objects whenever possible:** Groups are almost as efficient as symbols. (Chapter 4 explains how to create groups.)

✔ **Avoid bitmaps as much as possible:** If you must use bitmaps, use them only for still elements — don't animate them. (Chapter 3 explains how to import a bitmap and how to turn it into a vector graphic by tracing the bitmap.)

✔ **Optimize curves (choose Modify⇨Curves⇨Optimize):** Whenever possible, optimize curves to reduce the number of lines used to create a shape. (See Chapter 4 for further explanation.)

✔ **Use solid lines instead of dashed, dotted, and other line types when possible:** Try to avoid custom line widths. (Line types are explained in Chapter 3.)

✔ **Use the Pencil tool instead of the Brush tool whenever possible:** The Pencil tool uses fewer bytes in your movie.

✔ **Use the Web-safe color palette:** Avoid custom colors. (See Chapter 3 for the lowdown on colors.) Custom color definitions are kept with the Flash Player file.

✔ **Use solid fills instead of gradients:** Gradients are more complex and make the Flash Player file bigger.

Optimizing text

Text can also consume lots of bytes. Here's what you can do to reduce the byte bite:

✔ **Reduce the number of fonts and font styles (bold, italic) as much as possible:** Use simpler sans serif fonts if you can. You'll get the best results size-wise with the device fonts (sans, serif, and typewriter), although you may find these boring. Flash doesn't need to store the outlines of device fonts in the SWF file, so these take up fewer bytes. (See Chapter 5 for more on fonts.)

✔ **If you create text fields, limit the text and specify any restrictions you can in the Text Field Properties dialog box.** For example, limit text length and exclude unnecessary character outlines, such as numbers.

If you have a lot of text, consider which text really needs to be in the Flash file and which text can be created by using Hypertext Markup Language (HTML). For example, you can insert a Flash file on part of your Web page and add HTML-based text on the other part of the page.

Compressing sound

You can compress sounds to reduce file size. When you compress individual sounds in the Sound Properties dialog box, you can fine-tune settings for each individual sound in your movie. Later in this chapter, we review how to compress sound when you publish a Flash movie. Use the MP3 format whenever possible because it compresses well. If you need more information on compressing sounds, check out Chapter 11.

Here are some other ways you can reduce the size of your sound files:

✔ Adjust the sound's Time In and Time Out points to prevent silent areas from being stored in your SWF file.

✔ Reuse sounds by using different in and out points and by looping different parts of the same sound.

✔ Don't loop streaming sound.

See Chapter 11 for more information on editing and looping sound.

Animating efficiently

One of the most effective ways to reduce file size is to use tweens (see Chapter 9) whenever possible. Frame-by-frame animation creates larger files. Keeping animation localized in one area also helps. Small animations (animations where the objects don't move much) use less space than wide-area animations. Finally, place non-animated objects on different layers than animated objects.

Testing Movies

Before publishing your movie, you should test it. The first step is to simply play your animation, as explained in Chapter 9. But playing the animation on the Stage doesn't provide you with enough information to determine file size.

Movie clips and certain actions that interface with other movies (such as Load Movie) don't function from within your FLA file. To find those kinds of bugs, you have to test your movie in a browser. This section tells you how to test both ways.

Using the Test Movie command

After playing your animation, you want to use the Test Movie (or Test Scene) command. These commands provide estimates of downloading speed so you can find bottlenecks that pause your animation. You can also see the results of movie clips and all actions.

To test a movie or scene, follow these steps:

1. **Choose Control⇨Test Movie (or Test Scene).**

   Flash publishes your movie to an SWF file using the current settings in the Publish Settings dialog box (see the section, "Specify publish settings," later in this chapter) and opens a new window, as shown in Figure 13-1. You see your animation run. You can change the settings in the Publish Settings dialog box (File⇨Publish Settings) before using this command.

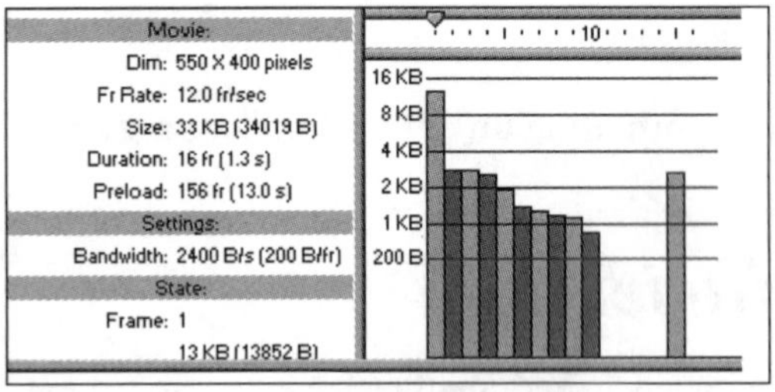

Figure 13-1:
Flash
displays
tools to
help you
analyze your
movie's
downloading
performance.

Movie:	
Dim: 550 X 400 pixels	
Fr Rate: 12.0 fr/sec	16 KB
Size: 33 KB (34019 B)	8 KB
Duration: 16 fr (1.3 s)	4 KB
Preload: 156 fr (13.0 s)	2 KB
Settings:	1 KB
Bandwidth: 2400 B/s (200 B/fr)	200 B
State:	
Frame: 1	
13 KB (13852 B)	

2. **Click the Debug menu and choose a downloading speed between 14.4 Kbps and 56 Kbps.**

   To specify your own settings, choose Customize and enter menu text to appear on the menu and the bit rate in bytes per second in the Customize Modem Settings dialog box. Click OK. Then open the Control menu again and choose your customized setting, which now appears on the menu.

3. **Choose View➪Bandwidth Profiler to see the graph showing download-ing performance.**

   The bandwidth profiler (shown by default) shows the byte size of each individual frame. Frames whose bars rise above the bottom red horizontal line cause loading delays.

4. **To see settings for any one frame, stop the movie by clicking the frame's bar.**

   To the left of the bandwidth profiler, Flash displays all the movie's statistics — dimensions, frame rate, file size, duration, and preload in frames and seconds. You also see the size of each individual frame.

5. **Choose View➪Streaming Graph to see how the Flash movie streams into a browser.**

6. **Choose View➪Frame by Frame Graph to see which frames contribute to delays. A frame whose bar extends above the red line may cause a bottleneck.**

   By default, Flash opens the SWF window in Streaming Graph mode.

7. **To close the SWF window, click its Close button.**

After you analyze your movie, you can go back and optimize it to eliminate delays. A short delay in the first frame is usually acceptable but significant delays during the movie result in jerky animation or pauses.

If you have a long movie divided into scenes, you can save time by using the Test Scene command.

Testing a movie in a browser

The final steps of testing a movie are publishing it and viewing it in a browser. For a quick view, you can use the Publish Preview command. Flash actually publishes your movie to an SWF file, creates the appropriate HTML file, and opens the HTML file in your default browser. Viewing your Flash Player file in a browser reveals how the browser will display the movie when you upload it to a Web site.

Flash uses the current settings in the Publish Settings dialog box to create the preview, including the types of file formats you have selected.

To preview your movie in a browser, follow these steps:

1. **Choose File➪Publish Settings to open the Publish Settings dialog box and choose the desired file formats and publish settings.**

   See the "Publishing Flash Movies" section in this chapter for more information on the Publish Settings dialog box.

2. **Choose File⇨Publish Preview and choose the desired format from the submenu.**

   Generally, you can use the first (default) HTML option, but if you have specified HTML settings, choose the second HTML option. Flash opens your browser and runs your movie.

3. **Close your browser to end the preview.**

As with any Web page material, you need to consider the following when testing a Flash Player file:

- ✔ **The browser your audience is using.** Preview your Flash Player file in Internet Explorer and Netscape Navigator, if possible. Ideally, you should try out at least one earlier version of each, too. Okay, so you probably won't, but don't say we didn't tell you.

- ✔ **The resolution of viewers' screens.** Test at least the following most common settings: 640 x 480, 800 x 600, and 1024 x 768. Remember that the amount of material that appears on the screen changes with the resolution. But if you preview at 640 x 480, you can be sure people with higher resolutions can see your entire movie.

- ✔ **The color settings of viewers' screens.** Common color settings range from 256 colors to 16 million. If you're using custom colors, some viewers may not see them accurately.

Professional Web site developers take this testing phase seriously. No matter how good an animation looks on your screen, if it doesn't translate well to a majority of viewers' screens, it's not a good animation.

Publishing Flash Movies

So you're finally ready to publish your Flash masterpiece. Don't be overwhelmed by all the options. Usually, you use only a few of them. Start by specifying the settings. Then publish the movie to create the SWF file viewed on a Web page.

After you specify the settings, you can click OK instead of publish if you want to go back to your Flash movie file and use Text Movie to see the results of your settings. You can try various settings until you're satisfied. Then click Publish to create the final SWF player file. Published files are always in the same folder as your FLA movie file; you can't choose another location. Of course, you can move the files afterward.

The Publish Settings dialog box lets you easily specify all your settings in one place. Then you click the Publish button and Flash creates the SWF player file according to your settings. Choose File⇨Publish Settings to open the Publish Settings dialog box, shown in Figure 13-2 with the Formats tab on top.

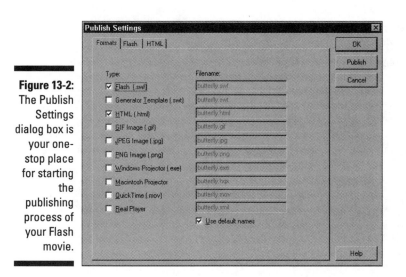

Figure 13-2:
The Publish Settings dialog box is your one-stop place for starting the publishing process of your Flash movie.

Flash automatically names the files it creates for you, using the Flash movie's name and adding the appropriate ending, such as .html and .swf. To specify your own names, uncheck the Use Default Names check box and type the names you want.

Most of the time, you only need the Flash (SWF) and HTML formats. But if you want other formats, check them on the Formats tab. When you check an additional format, the dialog box adds a new tab for that format (except for the Projector formats, which don't need one).

After you check the formats you want, click each tab to specify the settings for that format. The next few sections of this chapter explain each format, why you may want to use it, and how to specify the settings.

After you finish specifying all your settings, click Publish and Flash does your bidding, creating the files you need to put your great creation on the Web.

Publishing to SWF

The second tab of the Publish Settings dialog box is the Flash tab, which creates the Flash Player file, also called an SWF file. On this tab, shown in Figure 13-3, you specify settings that affect the SWF file.

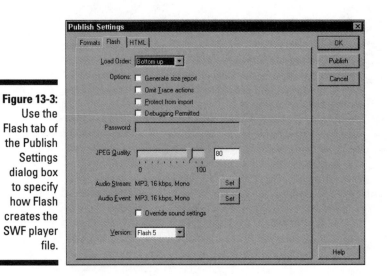

Figure 13-3:
Use the
Flash tab of
the Publish
Settings
dialog box
to specify
how Flash
creates the
SWF player
file.

Flash gives you the following options:

- ✔ **Load Order:** Specifies how Flash displays the first frame of the Flash movie. Bottom Up (the default) loads layers from the lowest layer upward. Top Down loads layers starting from the top layer and moving downward.

- ✔ **Generate Size Report:** Creates a TXT file (Windows) or SimpleText (Mac) file that you can use to troubleshoot problem areas. The report relates the various parts of your movie to the number of bytes they require in the SWF file.

- ✔ **Omit Trace Actions:** *Trace* is an action that displays information in a special window. Programmers use Trace to debug their ActionScript programming. Check this box to omit these codes from the SWF file.

- ✔ **Protect From Import:** Prevents the SWF files from being downloaded from the Web site and imported back into Flash. This feature isn't 100 percent safe, but it helps keep your work from being "borrowed."

- ✔ **Debugging Permitted:** Lets you use the Debugger to debug a Flash movie from another computer. If you permit debugging, you can add a password to protect the movie file. This is useful for ActionScript programmers, but beyond the scope of this book.

- ✔ **JPEG Quality:** Sets the compression (size) versus quality of bitmaps, if you have any in your movie. You can set the quality anywhere from 0 (lowest quality and highest compression) to 100 (highest quality and lowest compression).

✔ **Audio Stream:** Displays and sets the audio compression for stream sounds (that is, sounds that use the Stream Sync setting in the Sound panel). This setting applies if you haven't set the compression for individual sounds in the Sound Properties dialog box. Also, if you check Override Sound Settings in the Publish Settings dialog box, this setting overrides the setting in the Sound Properties dialog box. To change the current setting, click Set. The options are the same as in the Sound Properties dialog box. (See Chapter 11 for details on setting sound properties.)

✔ **Audio Event:** Displays and sets the audio compression for event sounds (as set on the Sound tab of the Frame Properties dialog box). Otherwise, the same as Audio Stream.

✔ **Override Sound Settings:** Check this box to override settings in the Sound Properties dialog box. Then the settings here apply to all sounds in your movie.

✔ **Version:** Allows you to save in previous version formats for backward compatibility. If, however, you have used features that don't exist in Flash 4, some parts of your movie may not work properly.

Publishing to HTML

Web pages are created using Hypertext Markup Language, also known as HTML. If you work on a Web site, you may write the HTML code from scratch or use an HTML editor. However, many people use a Web authoring program, such as Dreamweaver by Macromedia or FrontPage by Microsoft.

To place a Flash Player file on a Web page, you need the proper HTML code. Luckily, Flash creates this code for you, suitable for both Internet Explorer and Netscape Navigator browsers. The HTML code simply tells the browser to look for and display your Flash Player file. Of course, you can write the HTML code yourself, but why would you want to do that?

Understanding the HTML code for a movie

Figure 13-4 shows the default HTML code created for a Flash movie, displayed in Windows Notepad. (Mac users can view HTML code created by the Publish command with SimpleText.)

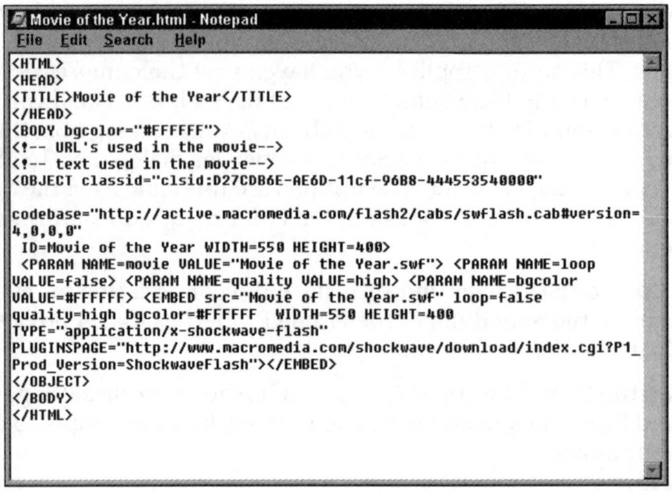


```
<HTML>
<HEAD>
<TITLE>Movie of the Year</TITLE>
</HEAD>
<BODY bgcolor="#FFFFFF">
<!-- URL's used in the movie-->
<!-- text used in the movie-->
<OBJECT classid="clsid:D27CDB6E-AE6D-11cf-96B8-444553540000"

codebase="http://active.macromedia.com/flash2/cabs/swflash.cab#version=
4,0,0,0"
 ID=Movie of the Year WIDTH=550 HEIGHT=400>
 <PARAM NAME=movie VALUE="Movie of the Year.swf"> <PARAM NAME=loop
VALUE=false> <PARAM NAME=quality VALUE=high> <PARAM NAME=bgcolor
VALUE=#FFFFFF> <EMBED src="Movie of the Year.swf" loop=false
quality=high bgcolor=#FFFFFF  WIDTH=550 HEIGHT=400
TYPE="application/x-shockwave-flash"
PLUGINSPAGE="http://www.macromedia.com/shockwave/download/index.cgi?P1_
Prod_Version=ShockwaveFlash"></EMBED>
</OBJECT>
</BODY>
</HTML>
```

Figure 13-4: Flash creates HTML code that looks like this when you publish a Movie to a player file.

If you know some HTML, this page will look familiar to you. It starts with the *tags* (codes) that all HTML documents contain, namely `<HTML>`, `<HEAD>`, `<TITLE>`, and `<BODY>`. Here's how to understand the rest of the codes, as much as is necessary:

- After the `<BODY>` tag, you see `bgcolor="#FFFFFF">`. This is the background color of the entire HTML page.
- After the comments (which start with !–), you see the `OBJECT` code. Microsoft Internet Explorer requires this tag to display your Flash player files. The `OBJECT` code includes the following:
  - Detailed codes (which are required to tell Internet Explorer how to display your player file).
  - Specification of the version of the Flash viewer to look for and where to download it if necessary.
  - The width and height of the display in the browser.
  - The name of the file (`VALUE="Movie of the Year.swf"`).
  - Parameter settings for looping, quality, and background color. You set background color by choosing Modify⇨Movie in Flash and choosing a background color in the Movie Properties dialog box. (See Chapter 2 for details on using this dialog box.)

✔ The EMBED code is for Netscape Navigator and accomplishes the same thing as the OBJECT code. Within this code you see the following:

  • The name of the player file.

  • Parameters for looping, quality, and background color. (See the preceding comments for the OBJECT code.)

  • The width and height of the display in the browser.

  • The type of file, that is, a Flash player file, called shockwave-flash in the HTML code.

  • Where to go to download the Flash player if necessary.

✔ Finally you see the closing <EMBED> and <OBJECT> tags as well as the tags that end every HTML document, </BODY> AND </HTML>.

If you want to use the HTML document as is, you can. But if you want to place your Flash player file in an existing HTML file, as you would for a Flash button, for example, you need to insert the <EMBED> and <OBJECT> codes into the desired location of your existing file. This is easy — copy the HTML code starting from <OBJECT through </OBJECT>, thus omitting the tags that are already on your existing HTML page. Then paste this code into your existing HTML document where you want your Flash player file to display on your page.

Generally, the HTML <OBJECT> and <EMBED> tags created by the Flash publishing process reference the SWF file by simply mentioning the filename. In that case, the SWF file must be in the same folder on your Web site's server as your Web page's HTML file. If you usually keep images in a subfolder and want to place your SWF file in that subfolder, change the references for *both* the <OBJECT> and <EMBED> tags to add the path to the subfolder. If you already do this for other images, the process is the same for the SWF file. For example, if you keep your images in a subfolder called images and the current code refers to tulip.swf, change the reference for both the <OBJECT> and <EMBED> tags to images/tulip.swf.

Specifying HTML settings

To create the HTML file, you need to specify the HTML settings from the HTML tab of the Publish Settings dialog box, as shown in Figure 13-5.

Templates

The first setting is to choose a template. The template determines the format and contents of the HTML file. To keep matters simple, choose the default, Flash Only. Table 13-1 explains the other template options. For more information, see Chapter 12.

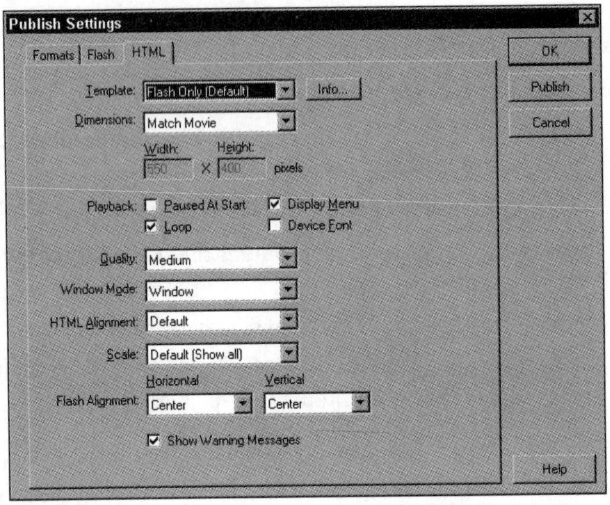

Figure 13-5:
Use the
HTML tab of
the Publish
Settings
dialog box
to specify
how Flash
creates the
HTML code
for your
player file.

Table 13-1	HTML Template Options
Option	**Comments**
Flash Only (Default)	Creates an HTML file as described in the previous section, with `<OBJECT>` and `<EMBED>` tags.
Ad 3 Banner	Adds VBScript to detect the Flash 3 player. On the Formats tab of the Publish Settings dialog box, also choose GIF, JPEG, or PNG. This image is displays if the Flash 3 player isn't available.
Ad 4 Banner	Adds VBScript to detect the Flash 4 player. On the Flash tab, specify Version 4 of Flash. Otherwise, the same as Ad 3 Banner.
Ad 5 Banner	Adds VBScript to detect the Flash 5 player. On the Flash tab, specify Version 5 of Flash. Otherwise, the same as Ad 3 Banner.
Ad Any Banner	Adds VBScript to detect the Flash 3, 4, or 5 player. Otherwise, the same as Ad 3 Banner.
Flash with FSCommand	Use when you have added an FSCommand action to your movie to interface with JavaScript. The HTML file also includes the `<OBJECT>` and `<EMBED>` commands.
Generator Ad Any Banner	Like Ad Any Banner. Use when you will integrate Flash with Generator. Requires Generator 2 on the server. See Note below.

Option	Comments
Generator Image Output	Displays an image. Use when you will integrate Flash with Generator. Requires Generator 2 on the server. On the Formats tab of the Publish Settings dialog box, also choose GIF, JPEG, or PNG. See Note below.
Generator Only	Creates an HTML file with the `<OBJECT>` and `<EMBED>` tags. Use when you will integrate Flash with Generator. Requires Generator 2 on the server. See Note below.
Generator QuickTime	Creates an `<EMBED>` tag to display a QuickTime Flash movie. Use when you will integrate Flash with Generator. Requires Generator 2 on the server. (See the Note at the end of this table.)
Image Map	(If you don't know what an image map is, don't worry about this option.) Instead of displaying an SWF player file, uses a GIF, JPEC, or PNG image (which you need to choose from the Formats tab) as an image map coded in your HTML page. You need to use the `<IMG>` tag with the USEMAP attribute. In your Flash movie, create a frame label of #map to specify which frame should be the map image.
Java Player	Use the Flash Java Player instead of the Flash player. Includes the required `<APPLET>` tags. On the Flash tab of the Publish Settings dialog box, you must specify Version 2 of Flash. You need to upload the Java class files to your Web server. You can find these in the Players subfolder of the folder containing the Flash program (generally Flash 5\Players).
Quick Time	Creates an `<EMBED>` tag to display a QuickTime Flash movie based on your Flash movie. You need to check QuickTime on the Formats tab. A QuickTime Flash movie plays only with QuickTime 4 or higher. QuickTime 4 can recognize only Flash 3 features.
User Choice	Includes Flash 5 viewer detection and a JavaScript cookie so that the viewer can choose between viewing the Flash player file or an image (GIF or JPEG). On the Formats tab, choose SWF and either GIF or JPEG.

Note: *Generator 2, another Macromedia product, comes in two flavors. Developer Edition updates Macromedia Flash Web sites automatically, providing real-time information in graphical format. Enterprise Edition creates personalized visual Web sites. You can create Flash movies for use with Generator. For more information, go to* www.macromedia.com/software/generator.

Dimensions

The Dimensions options control the size allotted to your Flash player movie on your Web page. You have three options:

- ✔ **Match Movie:** Matches the width and height that you set in the Movie Properties dialog box (choose Modify➪Movie).

- ✔ **Pixels:** Lets you specify, in pixels, the Width and Height. Type the desired values in the text boxes.

- ✔ **Percent:** Lets you specify the area used by the Flash player movie as a percent of the browser window size. The 100% setting is ideal for pages that are designed to take up the entire page. Type the desired values in the text boxes.

Playback

The Playback section determines the values of parameters in the HTML code. You have four options:

- ✔ **Paused at Start** creates a PLAY parameter whose value is FALSE. The viewer must start the movie by clicking a button in the movie — the button's instance needs to have a Play action in it. Alternatively, viewers can right-click (Windows) or Control+click (Mac) the movie and choose Play from the shortcut menu, but they may not be aware of this. By default, this check box is not checked, so movies start to play automatically.

- ✔ **Loop** creates a LOOP parameter whose value is TRUE. The movie repeats over and over. By default, this check box is checked, so make sure to uncheck it if you don't want to loop your movie!

- ✔ **Display Menu** creates a MENU parameter set to TRUE. This enables viewers to right-click (Windows) or Control+click (Mac) the movie and choose from a menu. The menu options are Zoom In/Out, 100%, Show All, High Quality, Play, Loop, Rewind, Forward, and Back. Without this option, About Flash Player is the only item on the shortcut menu. By default, Display Menu is checked.

- ✔ **Device Font** applies to Windows playback only. When checked, the HTML file includes a DEVICE FONT parameter set to true and Flash substitutes *anti-aliased* (smoothly curved) system fonts for fonts not available on the viewer's system. By default, this item is not checked.

Quality

The Quality section determines the QUALITY parameter in the <OBJECT> and <EMBED> tags of the HTML code. Quality refers to the level of anti-aliasing, which means the smoothing of the artwork so it doesn't have jagged edges. Of course, the lower the quality, the faster the playback. Usually, you want to find a middle ground between quality and speed. You have six options:

✔ **Low** doesn't use any anti-aliasing.

✔ **Autolow** starts at low quality but switches to high quality if the viewer's computer, as detected by the Flash player, can handle it.

✔ **Autohigh** starts at high quality but switches to low quality if the viewer's computer can't handle the playback demand. This option should provide good results on all computers.

✔ **Medium** applies some anti-aliasing but doesn't smooth bitmaps. This option is a good middle ground between low and high.

✔ **High** always uses anti-aliasing for vector art. Bitmaps are smoothed only if static, not in a tween. This is the default setting.

✔ **Best** always uses anti-aliasing, including for animated bitmaps.

Window Mode

Window Mode specifies how the player movie's window interacts with the rest of the page. It sets the WMODE parameter of the `<OBJECT>` tag and only applies to Internet Explorer 4.0 and higher. The Window setting plays your movie in its own window. The Opaque setting creates an opaque background. The purpose is to have other elements pass behind the movie. The Transparent setting makes the Flash background color transparent so that other elements on your Web page show through. The latter setting can slow down playback.

HTML Alignment

The HTML Alignment setting specifies the ALIGN attribute and specifies how the player movie is aligned within the browser window. You have five options:

✔ **Default** centers the Flash movie. If the browser window is smaller than the movie, this option crops the edges of the movie.

✔ **Left** aligns the movie along the left side of the browser window. If the browser window is too small, this option crops the other sides of the movie.

✔ **Right** aligns the movie along the right side of the browser window. If the browser window is too small, this option crops the other sides of the movie.

✔ **Top** aligns the movie along the top of the browser window. If the browser window is too small, this option crops the other sides of the movie.

✔ **Bottom** aligns the movie along the bottom of the browser window. If the browser window is too small, this option crops the other sides of the movie.

Scale

The Scale setting defines how the movie is placed within the boundaries when (and only when) you set a width and height different from the movie's original size, using the Pixels or Percent options in the Dimensions section of the Publish Settings dialog box. You have three options:

- ✔ **Default (Show All)** displays the entire movie without distortion but may create borders on both sides of the movie.

- ✔ **No Border** scales the movie to fill the dimensions without distortion but may crop portions of the movie.

- ✔ **Exact Fit** fits the movie to the dimensions, distorting the movie if necessary.

Flash Alignment

Flash Alignment determines how the movie fits within the movie window (as opposed to the browser window). It works together with the Scale and Dimensions settings. In other words, it determines how the Flash movie fits within the dimensions you have specified. For the Horizontal setting, you can choose Left, Center or Right. For the Vertical setting, you can choose Top, Center, or Bottom.

At the bottom of the Publish Settings dialog box is the Show Warning Messages check box, checked by default. When checked, you see warning messages during the publishing process. Nevertheless, the publishing process continues, but you know that you may have made an error. For example, if you have chosen a template that requires a GIF or JPEG image, but have not checked either format on the Formats tab, you will see a warning message.

After you choose your settings, click OK to return to your movie or Publish to publish it.

Publishing to Other Formats

As we explain in the previous section, you can choose an HTML template that requires other formats or you can use other formats to create still images or create QuickTime movies. Although you have many options, after you try a few out, you'll generally find a satisfactory solution that doesn't require too much fiddling.

Creating GIF graphic files

Create a GIF graphic when you want to give viewers without the Flash player an alternative image or for any reason you like. You can also create animated GIFs. To specify the settings, check GIF Image on the Formats tab and then click the GIF tab, as shown in Figure 13-6.

You can also create static GIF images by choosing File⇨Export Image, as explained in the section, "Exporting Movies and Images," later in this chapter.

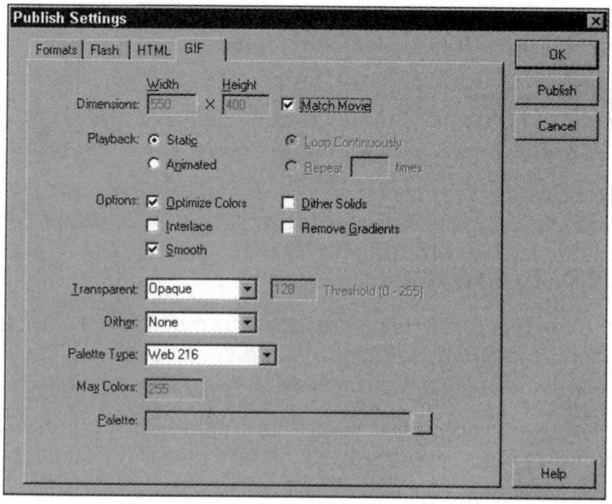

Figure 13-6:
The GIF tab
of the
Publish
Settings
dialog box.

On the GIF tab, you can specify the following settings:

- ✓ **Dimensions:** Check Match Movie to match the settings in the Movie Properties dialog box (choose Modify⇨Movie). Uncheck Match Movie to specify a different Width and Height. If you change the Width and Height, you need to calculate proportional measurements to avoid distorting the image.

- ✓ **Playback:** This section determines whether you create a static or an animated GIF:

  - • **Static** creates a single still image GIF. By default, Flash uses the first frame. To specify a different frame, create a frame label of #Static on the frame you want to use. (To create a label, click the frame and choose Window⇨Panels⇨Frame. Type a label name in the Label text box.)

- **Animated** creates an animated GIF. If you choose this option, choose either Loop Continuously or Repeat, entering the number of times you want to repeat the GIF. To save only some of your frames, create a frame label of #First on the first frame you want to save and #Last on the last frame.

✔ **Options** specifies how the GIF appears:

- **Optimize Colors** removes unused colors from the file's color table, in order to reduce the size of the file.

- **Interlace** causes a static GIF to load in incremental resolutions, so the image first appears fuzzy, and then successively sharper. Some people like this option because viewers may be able to click the image before it fully downloads, reducing their waiting time.

- **Smooth** antialiases (smoothes) the artwork. Text usually looks better (and file size is larger) but occasionally you may get an undesirable "halo" effect. In that case, turn off smoothing.

- **Dither Solids** does just that — it dithers solid colors as well as gradients and images. *Dithering* is a way to approximate colors not available in the color palette by using a range of similar colors. See the Dither option that follows.

- **Remove Gradients** turns gradients into solids. Gradients may not look good in a Web-safe color table. Nevertheless, Flash uses the first color in the gradient, which may not be the color you want.

✔ **Transparent** determines how your movie's background and colors with alpha (transparency) settings are translated into the GIF format. You have three options:

- **Opaque** makes the background of the movie opaque.

- **Transparent** makes the background of the movie transparent.

- **Alpha** lets you set a threshold below which all colors are transparent. You can specify any number between 0 to 255. A value of 128 is equivalent to an alpha setting of 50%. Any colors whose alpha setting is below the number you set disappear because they become transparent.

✔ **Dither** enables dithering, defined in the previous Options/Dither Solids item. Dithering helps to create more accurate-looking colors but increases file size. Choose one of the three options:

- **None** to disable dithering

- **Ordered** provides a medium amount of dithering and a corresponding medium increase in file size.

- **Diffusion** provides the best quality dithering and increases file size the most. It only works with the Web 216 color palette. (See Chapter 3 for a description of color palettes.)

✔ **Palette Type** determines the color palette for the GIF image. (See Chapter 3 for a discussion of colors in Flash.) The GIF file format can't have more than 256 colors. You have four options:

- **Web 216** uses the standard 216-color palette that includes only Web-safe colors (those that look good on all Web browers). You can usually get good results for Flash artwork without increasing file size.

- **Adaptive** creates a unique color table for your GIF, based on the actual colors present. You get more accurate color, although these colors may not be Web safe. Also, file size may be larger. Use this option if accurate representation of colors is most important, as in a photographic bitmap image. You can use the Max Colors text box to specify how many colors you want in the table. The default is 255. Use fewer colors to reduce file size.

- **Web Snap Adaptive** works like the Adaptive option but optimizes the color palette for the Web. Colors close to the 216 Web-safe colors are turned into one of the colors in that palette. Other colors function like the Adaptive option. As with the Adaptive option, you can specify the number of colors in the palette in the Max Colors text box.

- **Custom** lets you specify a palette in the ACT format. Click the ellipsis (...) button to browse for a color palette file. (Chapter 3's section on colors explains how to create a color palette and save it in ACT format.)

After you specify your settings, click OK to return to your movie or click Publish to publish the GIF file as well as the other formats you chose.

Creating JPEG graphic files

JPEG files can display many more colors than GIF files and therefore produce more realistic photos and other complex drawings. JPEG graphics are compressed to reduce file size. But they decompress when downloaded, using more memory.

To create a JPEG image, choose JPEG on the Formats tab. Flash then creates a JPEG tab in the Publish Settings dialog box, as shown in Figure 13-7.

Flash publishes the first frame of your movie unless you label a different frame with the label #Static. (To create a label, click the frame and choose Window⇨Panels⇨Frame. Type a label name in the Label text box.)

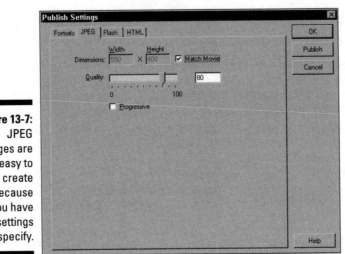

Figure 13-7:
JPEG
images are
easy to
create
because
you have
few settings
to specify.

You have the following options:

- ✔ **Dimensions:** By default, Flash matches the dimensions of the movie. Uncheck Match Movie to specify your own Width and Height.

- ✔ **Quality:** You can choose the quality by using the slider bar or the text box. A lower setting means lower image quality but a smaller file. A higher setting produces a better quality picture, but file size is larger. For your first effort, try the default of 80, and then adjust the setting based on the results.

- ✔ **Progressive:** Displays the image in increments of greater resolution. This option is equivalent to using the Interlaced option for GIF files, as explained in the previous section.

After you're done, click OK to return to your movie or click Publish to publish the JPEG and other formats you specified.

Creating PNG graphic files

PNG files can display more colors than GIF files and support transparency. They offer some of the advantages of both GIFs and JPEGs, but not all browsers support them completely.

To create a PNG image, choose PNG on the Formats tab. Flash creates a PNG tab in the Publish Settings dialog box, as shown in Figure 13-8.

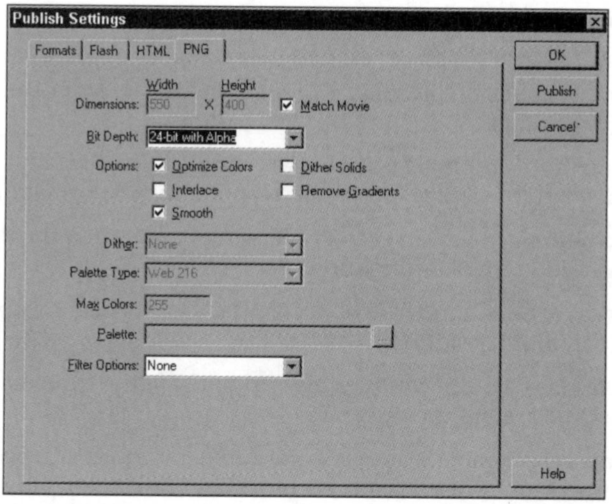

Figure 13-8:
Use the
PNG tab to
create PNG
images.

Flash publishes the first frame of your movie unless you label a different
frame with the label #Static. (To create a label, click the frame, choose
Window➪Panels➪Frame and type a label name in the Label text box.)

You have the following options:

- **Dimension:** By default, Flash matches the dimensions of the movie.
  Uncheck Match Movie to specify your own Width and Height.

- **Bit Depth:** Controls the number of bits per pixel, which in turn means
  how many colors the image contains. You can choose 8-bit for 256 colors
  (like a GIF), 24-bit for 16.7 million colors, or 24-bit with Alpha, which
  allows for transparency. When you choose 24-bit with Alpha, the movie
  background becomes transparent.

- **Options:** See the Options settings for GIF images explained previously.

- **Dither:** See the Dither settings for GIF images explained previously. This
  option applies only if you choose an 8-bit depth.

- **Palette Type:** See the Palette Type settings for GIF images explained previously. This option applies only if you choose an 8-bit depth.

- **Max Colors:** See the Palette Type settings for GIF images explained
  previously.

- **Palette:** See the Palette Type settings for GIF images explained
  previously.

✔ **Filter Options:** The PNG format filters an image line-by-line in order to compress it. You have five options:

- **None:** Applies no filtering. The resulting file is larger than with the other options.

- **Sub:** Filters adjoining pixel bytes (working horizontally). Works best when the image has repeated horizontal information.

- **Up:** Filters in a vertical direction. Works best when the image has repeated vertical information.

- **Average:** Uses a mixture of horizontal and vertical comparison. A good first try option.

- **Path:** Uses a more complex algorithm using the three nearest pixels to predict the next one.

- **Adaptive:** Creates a unique color table for your PNG, based on the actual colors present. You get more accurate color, although these colors may not be Web safe. File size may also be larger. Use this option if accurate representation of colors is most important, as in a photographic bitmap image.

After you specify your settings, click OK to return to your movie or click Publish to publish your PNG image and create the other files you have chosen.

Creating QuickTime movies

QuickTime is a format for digitized movies. QuickTime movies are played on the QuickTime Player. Flash lets you import, export, and publish QuickTime movies. (See Chapter 3 for instructions for importing QuickTime movies as well as other graphic images.) Exporting images and movies is covered in the section, "Exporting Movies and Images," later in this chapter.

You can import a QuickTime movie, add a Flash movie, and then publish the results as a Flash or QuickTime movie, thereby combining the two. (You can also import SWF player files directly into the QuickTime player of QuickTime 4 or later.) When Flash creates the QuickTime movie, it places the Flash movie in a separate Flash track within the QuickTime movie.

To publish a QuickTime movie from Flash, check QuickTime on the Formats tab of the Publish Settings dialog box and click the QuickTime tab that appears, as shown in Figure 13-9.

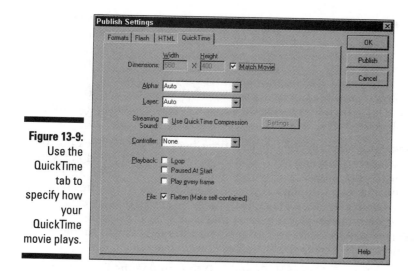

Figure 13-9:
Use the
QuickTime
tab to
specify how
your
QuickTime
movie plays.

Use these settings to configure your QuickTime movie:

✓ **Dimensions:** Match Movie sizes the QuickTime movie according to the size of your Flash movie. If you uncheck the Match Movie box, you can specify your own Width and Height.

✓ **Alpha:** Determines the transparency of the Flash track within the QuickTime movie. This setting makes sense only if you have combined QuickTime and Flash movies into one QuickTime movie. Use the Layer option, described next, in conjunction with this option. Auto, the default, makes the Flash track transparent if it's on top of other tracks, but opaque if it's on the bottom or the only content in the movie. Alpha-Transparent makes the Flash track transparent. You can see other content in tracks below the Flash track. Copy makes the Flash track opaque.

✓ **Layer:** Specifies how the Flash track is layered with QuickTime content. Auto places the Flash track in front of other tracks if Flash artwork appears on top of the QuickTime movie at any time. Otherwise, it places the Flash movie on the bottom layer. Top places the Flash track on top of other tracks. Use Top when you want your Flash movie to appear in front of the QuickTime movie. Bottom places the Flash track on the bottom. Use Bottom when you want your Flash movie to be a background to the QuickTime movie.

✓ **Streaming Sound:** Check Use QuickTime Compression to export all your streaming audio to a QuickTime sound track. Click Settings to specify how you want the audio compressed. (See Chapter 11 for a description of streaming sound.)

✔ **Controller:** A Controller is a control panel that lets you play back the movie. QuickTime has a controller similar to the Flash controller (described in Chapter 9). Choose None if you have created your own controller within your Flash movie to enable viewers to view the movie, or if you want your movie to play automatically. Standard displays QuickTime's controller. Choose QuickTime VR for a specialized controller for QuickTime VR movies that create panoramic and 3D viewing (called object) effects.

✔ **Playback:** Specifies how the movie plays. Check the Loop check box to replay the movie over and over. Check Paused At Start if you don't want the movie to play automatically when it opens. (If you choose a controller, the movie is automatically paused and the user uses the controller to start the movie.) Check Play Every Frame to display every frame, even if it means slowing down playback. (Otherwise, the QuickTime movie skips frames as necessary to maintain the timing.) This option also silences the QuickTime audio track.

✔ **File:** Check Flatten (Make Self-Contained) to combine the Flash movie with other content into one QuickTime movie. If not checked, Flash creates a QuickTime movie that references the Flash SWF file and any other QuickTime content that you may have previously imported into your Flash movie. File size is smaller, but you need to make sure that these related files are available in the same folder when played back on a Web site. If you don't check Flatten, be sure to check SWF on the Formats tab of the Publish Settings dialog box.

After you specify your settings, click OK to return to your movie or click Publish to publish your QuickTime movie and the other file formats you chose.

Creating Self-Playing Movies

You can also create *projectors* in the Publish Settings dialog box. A projector is a self-playing Flash movie that doesn't require the Flash Player. You can use a projector for a Flash movie that you want to place on a CD-ROM or even a floppy disk.

You can create a Windows or a Mac version from either platform. But if you create a Mac version in Windows, you need to use a file translator such as BinHex so that the Mac Finder recognizes it as an application.

To create a projector, follow these steps:

1. **Choose File⇨Publish Settings.**

   The Publish Settings dialog box opens.

2. **On the Formats tab, check Windows Projector, Macintosh Projector, or both.**

3. **Click Publish.**

4. **Click OK or Cancel to exist the Publish Settings dialog box.**

For Windows, Flash creates an EXE file. For the Mac, Flash creates a compressed BinHex file (HQX).

Placing a Flash movie in a
PowerPoint 2000 presentation

You can place a Flash movie in a PowerPoint presentation for awesome animation impossible with PowerPoint alone. Follow these steps:

1. **Create your Flash movie and publish it to an SWF file.**

2. **Move the SWF file to the desired location, perhaps the folder containing your PowerPoint presentation.**

   Write down the location; you'll need it later.

3. **In PowerPoint, display the slide where you want to place the Flash movie.**

4. **Choose View⇨Toolbars⇨Control Toolbox.**

5. **Click the Hammer button (More Controls).**

6. **Choose Shockwave Flash Object from the menu.**

7. **Drag a box across the PowerPoint slide to get the desired size and location.**

   Don't cover the entire slide. PowerPoint doesn't recognize your mouse click on top of the Flash movie. You need a little piece of your slide showing so you can click to the next slide.

8. **Right-click the box you just created and choose Properties.**

9. **In the Properties window, click the top line, Custom; then click the ellipsis (...) at the right.**

10. **In the Property Pages dialog box that opens, type the location of the SWF file that you wrote down earlier.**

11. **Set the other parameters.**

   For example, set Quality to Best, Scale to Show All, and Window to Window. Click Embed Movie if you want to make sure it's always included with the PowerPoint presentation.

12. **Click OK.**

13. **Click the close box to close the Properties window.**

14. **Switch to Slide Show view to view the movie.**

   If you movie didn't appear in Normal (or Slide) view, it will appear when you return to Normal view after running the slide show.

If the Flash movie doesn't play, open the Properties window again and look at the Playing property. If it says False, click Playing. Then click the down arrow and change the Playing property to True.

Tip: To make the Flash movie blend into your presentation, match the Flash movie background to the background of your Presentation template.

Don't forget to test your movie after you place it on a CD-ROM or floppy disk. Try it out with a variety of processor speeds if possible.

Using Publish Preview

If you want to specify Publish Settings, see the results, and then go back to tweak your settings, you can use Publish Preview instead of Publish. Publish Preview creates the files specified in the Publish Settings dialog box, just as the Publish command does. The only difference is the Publish Preview automatically displays the requested file, usually the SWF file. The value is simply saving the steps of manually opening your files in your browser — helpful when you're doing lots of tweaking and going back and forth between your publish settings and your browser several times to see what works best.

To use Publish Preview, follow these steps:

1. **Specify your settings using the Publish Settings dialog box (as explained earlier in this chapter) and click OK.**

2. **Choose File⇨Publish Preview.**

3. **From the Publish Preview submenu, choose the file format you want to preview.**

4. **When you're done, close the window or browser.**

Posting your movie to your Web site

After you finish publishing your movie, post it on your Web site or place it on a CD-ROM or other media. Refer to the "Understanding the HTML code for a movie" section, earlier in this chapter, for instructions on modifying the HTML code if you want to place your SWF file on an existing page or place your SWF file in a subfolder. Then upload both the HTML and the SWF file. If you also created other image files or a QuickTime movie, you need to upload them as well.

Open your browser and load the page containing your Flash movie. Hopefully, it works perfectly and looks great! If not, check out the HTML code, check your publish settings, and make sure the necessary files are in the proper location on your Web site's server.

Exporting Movies and Images

In addition to publishing, Flash lets you export QuickTime movies and image files. Export a Flash file when you want to use it in another application. For example, you may want to export a frame as a GIF file and insert it into a word processing document. Use Export Movie to export to a QuickTime movie or to create a still image of every frame. You can also use Export Movie to export to an SWF file. This method is a shortcut compared to publishing if you already have the HTML code you need and just want to update an SWF file.

To export a movie or image, follow these steps:

1. **To export to an image, select the frame you want to export.**

2. **Choose File⇨Export Image or File⇨Export Movie.**

3. **In the dialog box, navigate to the desired location and type a name for your image or movie.**

4. **Choose a type of file from the Save As Type drop-down list box.**

5. **Click Save.**

6. **Depending on the format you choose, a dialog box may appear. If so, specify the settings and click OK.**

   These settings are similar to or the same as described previously in this chapter for publishing movies and images.

Table 13-2 lists the types of files you can export.

Table 13-2			Export File Types
File Type	*Windows*	*Mac*	*Comments*
Encapsulated PostScript (.EPS)	X	X	Vector format used in Adobe Illustrator and recognized by many other applications.
Drawing Exchange Format (.DXF)	X	X	This format causes you to lose fills when importing into AutoCAD.
Windows Bitmap (.BMP)	X		Raster (bitmap) format. Many applications recognize it. Offers variable bit-depths and transparency support. File size is large.

(continued)

Table 13-2 *(continued)*

File Type	Windows	Mac	Comments
Metafile (.EMF/.WMF)	X		Vector format supported by many applications. Creates smaller files than EPS.
FutureSplash Player (.SPL)	X	X	The original version of Flash before Macromedia bought it.
Graphics Interchange File (.GIF)	X	X	Raster format, limited to 256 colors.
Joint Photographic Experts Group (.JPEG/.JPG)	X	X	Raster format, supports 24-bit color.
QuickTime (.MOV)	X	X	QuickTime 4 format movie.
QuickTime Video (Macintosh)		X	On Macs only, uses the QuickTime 3 format, bitmapping all content.
Picture (PICT)		X	Raster format that can be used with all Mac and many PC applications. Variable bit-depths. Transparency support.
Portable Network Graphic (.PNG)	X	X	Raster format that supports variable bit-depth and transparency.
Video for Windows (.AVI)	X		Raster video format. Files can get large.
Windows Audio (.WAV)	X		Exports just the sound.

After you export a movie or image, you can then import it into the desired application for further editing or display.

Creating Printable Movies

Suppose, for example, that you want your Web site viewers to be able to print out a form on your Web site that you created in Flash. Or perhaps you want them to print out your contact information, so that your Web page can become your business card. Flash Player's printing features enable your viewers to print out receipts, information sheets, coupons, or whatever helps you do business on the Web. You can specify certain frames in a movie, including the main Timeline, a button, or a movie clip, to be printable from the Flash Player shortcut menu. Viewers right-click (Windows) or Control+click (Mac) to access the Print command.

Your viewers need instructions on how to print, so place some text somewhere telling them what to do.

Of course, viewers can use their browser's Print command to print. The result, however, isn't nearly so controllable. When we tried it, our browser printed the first frame only, which was useless in our example. The browser also added the URL, the name of the movie, the date, and the page number.

By default, the Flash Player's shortcut menu lets viewers print the entire movie, frame by frame. This is fairly useless for most purposes. But by specifying which frames are printed and the print area, you can use the Player's Print command to make specific information or forms available to your viewers.

Preparing your movie for printing

If you want a nice clean result, you need a nice clean frame. The Flash Player prints all objects on all layers of the movie. If you want to create a form, for example, put it in its own frame and make sure objects on other layers don't continue into that frame.

Alternatively, you can specify the print area so that you include only the area you want printed, excluding other objects on the Stage in the frame. But if you specify a small area, this area becomes the entire page size when printing, so the objects in that small area are enlarged to take up the entire printed page. You can control the layout by changing the dimension, scale, and alignment HTML settings (on the HTML tab of the Publish Settings dialog box).

Make sure that everything you want to print is on the Stage. For example, if you want to print from a movie clip, it must be on the Stage and have an instance name.

You can make a movie clip invisible by setting its visible property to false. (Use the Actions panel.) This capability enables you instruct viewers to print a form that they don't see on the screen.

You can exclude text that instructs users how to print from the printable area.

Specifying printable frames

To specify which frame or frames you want to print when your viewers choose Print from the Flash Player shortcut menu, follow these steps:

1. **With the movie open, choose Window⇨Panels⇨Frame to open the Frame panel.**

   The shortcut is Ctrl+F (Windows) or ⌘+F (Mac).

2. **Select the frame in the Timeline that you want printed.**

3. **In the Frame panel, type #p in the Label text box, as shown in Figure 13-10.**

For each additional frame that you want to specify for printing, select the frame and label it #p.

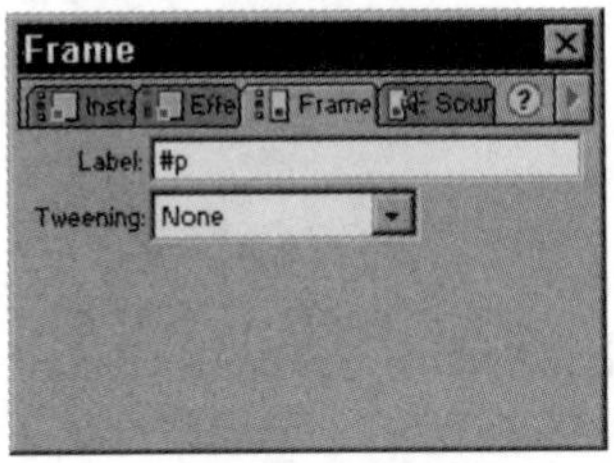

Figure 13-10:
Use the
Frame panel
to label
frames for
printing.

Frame
Inst Effe Frame Sour
Label: #p
Tweening: None

Specifying the print area

Unless you specify the print area, the Flash Player prints the entire Stage. If you have loaded other movies, the Flash Player uses their Stage size. You may, however, want to specify a different area. As mentioned earlier, you may want to include instructions on how to print, but you may not want the instructions to be printed. You can exclude other objects on the Stage as well.

Choosing a very small print area results in an output of very big objects. The Flash Player sizes up your objects to take up the entire printed page.

Usually, you create an object, such as a rectangle to specify the print area. If you don't mind having a rectangle around your printed material, you can simply place the rectangle in the same frame. If you don't want the rectangle to print, however, follow these steps to specify the print area:

To specify the print area, follow these steps:

1. **If it's necessary to organize your objects, create a new layer for the rectangle.**

   You can use any shape, but remember that printer paper is rectangular. Give it a name such as Print Area.

2. **Select the frame you want to print, clicking the new layer.**

3. **Create the rectangle around the objects you want to be printed.**

   You may have to experiment with different size rectangles. See the instructions in the section, "Printing movies from the Flash player," later in this chapter, to test the printing of your movie.

   Use the No Fill feature for the rectangle so you can see the material you want to print.

4. **Select the rectangle and choose Edit⇨Cut to cut it to the Clipboard.**

5. **Click the frame after the printable frame, on the new layer.**

   Using the next frame is just a way of keeping the printing area rectangle close to the frame you have specified for printing. You could use any frame without a #p label.

6. **Choose Edit⇨Paste in Place.**

   You now have a rectangle of the right size, but in its own frame.

7. **With the frame containing the rectangle selected, choose Window⇨Panels⇨Frame to open the Frame panel.**

8. **In the Label text box, type #b to signify that the shape in this frame will be used as the boundary for the print area.**

You can have only one #b label in a Timeline.

You can place a Print action in a frame. A Print action offers options that are unavailable when you use the procedure we just explained. You can print frames in other movie clips as well as on the main Timeline. You can also specify vector or bitmap printing. Vector printing is clearer, but you lose transparency. For more information on creating actions, see Chapter 10.

Turning off the Print command

If you don't want your viewers to be able to print your movie from the Flash Player, you can disable the Print command on the Flash Player's shortcut menu.

Viewers can still print frames by using the browser Print command, but they may not get anything useful.

To turn off the printing command, follow these steps:

1. **Choose Window➪Panels➪Frame to open the Frame panel.**

2. **Select the first keyframe in the main Timeline.**

3. **In the Label text box of the Frame panel, type !#p.**

   This frame label disables the Print command for the entire movie.

As explained earlier in this chapter, in the "Specifying HTML settings" section, you can uncheck the Display Menu check box on the HTML tab of the Publish Settings dialog box to remove all the Flash player shortcut menu commands.

Printing movies from the Flash Player

Before uploading your printable movie to your Web site, you should test the printing function. To do so, use the Publish Settings dialog box to specify the publish settings you want, as explained throughout this chapter. Then choose File➪Publish Preview➪Default. Your browser opens and you see your movie play.

To test print your movie, right-click (Windows) or Control+click (Mac) in the browser. In the Flash Player shortcut menu, choose Print.

Choose the print range to select which frames to print, or choose All. In Windows, you can also choose Selection to print the current frame. If only one frame has been made printable, the Pages option appears dimmed. Any option you choose prints the frame you have specified for printing. Click OK (Windows) or Print (Mac) to print.

After you upload your movie onto your Web site, viewers use the same procedure to print your movie.

Place text on your page giving your viewers instructions on how to print your movie. Many viewers don't even know that the shortcut menu exists.

Chapter 14

Frequently Asked Questions

*I*n this chapter, we answer some frequently asked questions about Flash while explaining how to create some very cool effects and streamline the process of creating Flash movies.

Drag and Drop

You can create draggable movie clips to use for games, drag 'n' drop interfaces, or slider bars. Although creating draggable movie clips is an advanced function, it's too much fun to leave out of this book. The secret is to create a button inside a movie clip and to attach the actions to the button.

To create a draggable movie clip, follow these steps:

1. **Choose Insert⇨New Symbol to create a new symbol.**

2. **Name your new symbol, click the movie clip behavior, and click OK.**

3. **On the Stage, create an object that you want to be draggable.**

4. **With the object selected, choose Insert⇨Convert to Symbol to open the Symbol Properties dialog box.**

5. **Name the symbol, click the button behavior, and click OK.**

   You now have a button inside a movie.

6. **Choose Window⇨Actions to open the Object Actions window.**

   Any actions you add now are placed inside the button.

7. **Open the Actions list (not the Basic Actions list) and double-click startDrag.**

   The startDrag action appears in the right side of the window.

8. **Click the first statement on the right side of the panel; at the bottom of the Object Actions window, uncheck Release and check Press.**

   Flash substitutes the on (press) action for the on (release) action. Choosing Press makes the drag function work when you press the mouse button.

9. **Click the third line of ActionScript (containing just the bracket).**

10. **From the Actions listing, double-click stopDrag.**

    Flash adds the stopDrag statement on the right side of the Object Actions window and automatically assigns this the On Release event. This is what you want — now when you release the mouse button, the drag effect stops. You can see the ActionScript in Figure 14-1.

11. **Click the Close button to close the Object Actions window.**

12. **Choose Edit⇨Edit Movie to return to the main Timeline.**

13. **Press Delete to delete the symbol you created in Step 3.**

    Don't worry, the symbol is in the Library.

14. **Drag the movie clip you created from the Library to the Stage.**

    To open the Library, choose Window⇨Library.

15. **Choose Control⇨Test Movie and then click and drag your movie clip.**

    It follows your mouse!

Figure 14-1:
ActionScript
for a simple
drag-and-
drop object.

```
on (press) {
  startDrag ("");
}
on (release) {
  stopDrag ();
}
```

You can constrain the movement of the movie clip to certain areas. For example, in a slider bar, you don't want the movie clip going all over the page, only along the bar. See startDrag in the ActionScript Dictionary.

Creating a custom cursor

You can use drag and drop to create a custom cursor, just for fun. This cursor appears on your Flash Web page as your viewer moves the mouse around.

To create a custom cursor, follow these steps:

1. **Create a graphic symbol in the shape you want to use for the cursor.**

   It can contain more than one shape, but don't make it too complicated.

2. **Choose Insert⇨New Symbol to create a new symbol; then assign the movie clip behavior and name the symbol. Click OK.**

3. **Open the Library (choose Window⇨ Library) and drag the graphic symbol onto the Stage.**

4. **To center the symbol, cut the symbol and paste it back onto the Stage.**

   As explained in Chapter 4, cutting and pasting centers an object on the display. If you haven't moved the display (for example, by dragging either scrollbar), the symbol is now in the center of the Stage.

5. **Create some animation.**

   A rotating shape is good. You don't want your cursor flying all over the place. Or you can just leave it still, like your usual cursor is, but with a more interesting shape. (See Chapter 9 for all the details on creating animation.)

6. **Choose Edit⇨Edit Movie to return to the main movie Timeline.**

   The movie clip is now in the Library.

7. **Drag the movie clip from the library to any-where on the Stage.**

8. **Choose Window⇨Actions to open the Object Actions window.**

9. **From the list of action types on the left side, click Objects and then click Mouse.**

10. **Double-click Hide from the Mouse options.**

11. **From the list of action types on the left side, click Actions. Double-click startDrag.**

12. **At the bottom of the Object Actions window, check the Lock Mouse to Center check box.**

    Your ActionScript looks like this:

    ```
    onClipEvent (load) {
        Mouse.hide();
        startDrag ("", true);
    }
    ```

13. **Choose Control⇨Test Movie to use your new cursor.**

Enjoy your cursor!

Tip: Put your cursor on the top layer of the Timeline so that it moves in front of buttons and other objects that you may want to use with it.

Look for `drag and drop tree.fla` in the Ch14 folder of the CD-ROM. Open the movie and choose Control⇨Test Movie. Drag the decorations onto the tree. Have fun! Also look for `draganddrop_ex.fla` in the same folder of the CD-ROM. This example includes some more complex ActionScript. *(Thanks to Craig Swann of Crash!Media at* `www.crashmedia.com` *for this file.)*

Motion Tween Troubleshooting

For motion tweening to work, you need to make sure that several pieces are in place. (Review Chapter 9 for the basic instructions on motion tweening.)

Motion tweening problems can arise from any number of sources, a few of which follow:

- ✔ Make sure that you've created a symbol, a group, or text. Imported bitmaps also qualify. If you've created a symbol, you can tween either the symbol itself (if you're not planning on reusing it) or one of its instances. Motion tweening just doesn't work on graphics that you haven't converted to symbols.

- ✔ If you have a dashed line instead of a solid line indicating your motion tween on the Timeline, you didn't properly create an ending keyframe. Undo the steps that created the tween, create an ending keyframe, and try again.

- ✔ If you're having trouble changing the length of the tween by dragging on one of the keyframes, that keyframe wasn't included when you created the motion tween. Select the offending keyframe by itself (press Control for Windows or ⌘ for Mac as you select, if necessary), and choose Motion from the Tweening drop-down list of the Frame panel.

- ✔ If you can't seem to remember the steps, use our memory jogger:

Funny	First keyframe — create it
Objects	Object — create it or drag it from the Library
Love	Last keyframe — create it
Moving	Move the object
So	Select all the frames for the tween
Tween	Tweening — Choose Motion from the Tweening drop-down list

- ✔ If you can't figure out why your motion tweening isn't working, you may have some action or setting that you don't even remember. Movies can get very complex and comprehending all the relationships and interconnections can be difficult. Try copying the object you're animating onto the Clipboard and pasting it into a new, "clean" movie. You can copy and paste frames as well. In the new movie you should be able to analyze the situation more clearly.

✔ If the animation worked previously, try undoing your last several actions. You can also try removing any recently created objects or ActionScript. If you can revert to the time your animation worked, you can start again from there.

✔ Only the simplest ActionScript and button behaviors work on the Stage. If you're trying to run your animation by using the Controller or pressing Enter, try Control⇨Test Movie instead. If your movie has more than one scene, try Control⇨Test Scene to try to isolate the problem to one scene.

✔ If you have more than one object on a layer, place each object on its own layer. (See Chapter 6 for a discussion of working with layers.) Animate only one object on a layer.

Synchronizing Sound with Motion

Suppose that you want certain parts of your animation synchronized with specific sounds. For example, each time a ball bounces you want it to make a sound. Without specifically synchronizing the sounds, the sound and the animation may play at different speeds. A faster computer may play the animation faster, but doesn't adjust the length of the sound. (For basic information on adding sound to Flash, see Chapter 11.)

In order to synchronize animation with the sound, you need to use a stream sound. When you add the sound file to a frame, choose Stream from the Sync drop-down list of the Sound panel. Then adjust the keyframes so that the animation and the sound end at the same time.

To be more precise, you can synchronize your animation with specific parts of the sound. To accomplish this, choose Modify⇨Layer and choose 200% or 300% from the Layer Height drop-down list. You can also click the little button at the top-right corner of the Timeline and choose Medium or Large for the size of the frames from the option menu that appears. Now you can see the shape of your sound wave more clearly so that you can adjust the keyframes of your animation to match certain parts of the sound.

One way to pinpoint which frame to use for placing an animation event is to drag the playhead (the red rectangle) just above the Timeline. This technique lets you control the speed of the animation. You can drag left or right until you find the exact frame that you want to work with. You can then move a keyframe to that frame, for example, to move an animation event to a frame containing a specific portion of your sound.

New ActionScript Format

Flash 5 ActionScript has evolved to contain features and syntax that closely resemble JavaScript, a programming language often used for Web pages. Many of the old features have been retained to maintain compatibility with previous versions of Flash. In addition, ActionScript omits some of JavaScript's features where they are irrelevant or can cause conflicts with previous versions of Flash.

ActionScript now uses, by default, a dot syntax. Dots (periods) separate objects from their properties or the actions you're applying to the objects (called *methods*). Another use for dots is to show the path to a movie clip or movie. Earlier versions of ActionScript used a slash syntax (which you can still use in Flash 5) to separate the parts of an expression. The new syntax also uses curly braces ({ and }) to separate complete statements from each other.

When specifying a target for the Tell Target or Load Movie action, you can choose to use either slash or dot syntax in the Insert Target Path dialog box. (See Chapter 10 for information on using this dialog box.)

Many Flash users prefer the dot syntax because it's more compatible with the new JavaScript style of ActionScript. If you're already familiar with JavaScript, you should become comfortable with the dot syntax quickly.

The Best Bitmap Formats

The quick answer to the question of the best bitmap formats is that there isn't any best *bitmap* format. The best formats to import into Flash are vector formats because they're smaller, scale perfectly, and load more quickly.

Okay, sometimes you just *have* to use a bitmap. Maybe you need to put your boss's photograph into the animation or a photo of the product you sell. Maybe you want an effect you can only create in Photoshop. What do you use?

You may not have a choice of format. If your Information Systems department hands you a logo in JPEG format, you probably have to use it.

A trick for changing a file's format is to open an existing bitmap file in an image editing program. Most let you save that file in another format.

Other times, you can choose your format. For example, when you scan a photo, most scanner software lets you choose from among several formats. A digital camera may also let you choose the format. Of course, if you create the bitmap in an image-editing program, you can choose from any format the program supports. (See Chapter 3 for instructions on importing bitmap images. *Hint:* Choose File⇨Import.)

Here are some commonly used bitmap formats:

✔ The GIF file format, which generally displays well in a browser, can't have more than 256 colors. Use a GIF format for simple drawings that have a limited color palette.

✔ JPEG files can display many more colors than GIF files and therefore produce more realistic photos and other complex drawings. Although JPEG graphics can be highly compressed to reduce file size, they lose some fidelity as a result. Also, when Flash recompresses the file during export or publishing, you may end up with an unfocused mess.

✔ BMP doesn't lose quality when compressed, but the BMP format results in larger file sizes.

✔ PNG is a nice compromise. It doesn't lose quality when compressed and allows many more colors than the GIF format (as well as providing the capability for transparency).

Your final result is the SWF file that you publish. Flash compresses bitmaps (as well as the entire movie) as the movie is exported to an SWF Flash Player file. Therefore, you need to think about the entire round trip journey that your bitmap is going to make. You may have to test varying bitmap formats and publish the movie for each to see the exact results.

When you export, you can set the JPEG quality on the SWF tab of the Publish Settings dialog box. You also set the overall quality on the HTML tab. For that quality setting, only the High and Best settings smooth (anti-alias) the bitmaps in the movie. (See Chapter 13 for more information about publishing your Flash movie.)

When you import a bitmap image into Flash, you can take the following steps to ensure good-looking results.

✔ Save your graphics in the highest quality possible. If you have a photograph, don't import it as a GIF file.

✔ Don't over-compress your original bitmaps, but don't import 100K files either. Find a happy medium. Try saving an image in several formats to see the difference in quality and size.

✔ Save the file in a larger size than you think you'll use. When your movie is displayed in a browser window, the entire movie is often scaled up to fit the browser window.

✔ Set the compression type and quality in the Bitmap Properties dialog box. After you import the image, open the Library (choose Window⇨ Library) and right-click (Windows) or Control+click (Mac) the image and choose Properties to open the Bitmap Properties dialog box, as shown in Figure 14-2.

Bitmap Properties

bug2-simple.jpg

E:\Flash\bug2-simple.jpg

Tuesday, February 15, 2000 8:24:58 PM
51 x 53 pixels at 32 bits per pixel

☑ Allow smoothing

Compression: Photo (JPEG) ▼

☑ Use imported JPEG data

OK

Cancel

Update

Import...

Test

Help

Figure 14-2: Use the Bitmap Properties box to fiddle with your bitmaps.

Rescaling a Movie's Size

You create a beautiful Flash movie that takes up the entire page. But then your boss says that you need to fit it into an existing HTML page, which translates into reducing the size of the whole thing by 25 percent. What do you do? Get a new boss, if possible.

Barring that, you can rescale the size of the movie by following these steps:

1. **Decide the amount of the reduction you need to achieve, such as 25 percent.**

2. **If you have any hidden layers, right-click (Windows) or Control+click (Mac) any layer and choose Show All.**

   This ensures that all layers are considered in the reduction.

 3. **Click the Edit Multiple Frames button (just below the Timeline).**

4. **Drag the onion skin markers to the beginning and ending frames of your animation.**

   See Chapter 9 if you need more information on how to use the onion skin markers.

5. **Choose Edit⇨Select All.**

6. **Choose Window⇨Panels⇨Info to open the Info panel.**

   You see the Width (W), Height (H), and X and Y coordinates.

7. **Multiply all the numbers in the Info panel by the reduction percentage.**

   Write down the results of your calculations, just to be safe.

8. **Click in the W (Width) text box and type the new number for the reduction percentage; then press Tab to move to the next box.**

9. **Repeat Step 8 for the H (Height), X, and Y text boxes.**

You're done! Flash scales your entire movie by the percentage you specified.

Good Authoring Practices

Every Flash user collects a number of techniques that make creating a Flash movie easier. The following items are a few ideas to help you get started.

- ✔ Save multiple versions of your movie by choosing File⇨Save As. If a problem arises, you can always go back to a previous version and start again.

- ✔ As soon as you have an overall structure, test your movie in both the Netscape Navigator and Internet Explorer browsers, at various resolutions, if possible. You can more easily fix problems early, before you develop a very complex situation. Use Control⇨Test Movie as soon as you develop your animation and continue to test in this way for each new significant change.

- ✔ Add comments (see Chapter 10) to your ActionScript so that you can figure out what you did when you go back to your movie after your vacation.

- ✔ Use consistent names for symbols. Many Flash users add the type of symbol after the name, so a button could be called Contact-btn and a movie clip could be called Intro-mc. When you start creating movie clips inside of buttons, you may get confused if you don't name your symbols intelligently.

- ✔ Use meaningful names for your instances. If you have three instances of a button symbol, you need to be able to distinguish which is which. You can name them by their purpose, such as E-mail, Services, and Clients.

- ✔ As you complete work on a layer, lock the layer to avoid making unwanted changes.

You're sure to discover other techniques as you become more experienced in Flash.

Creating 3-D in Flash

Actually, you can't create 3-D in Flash. Flash is decidedly a 2-D program. But, not to be deterred, Flash users have created many tricks to make you think you're seeing 3-D.

One simple approach is to rotate a 2-D object in what appears to be 3-D space. For example, you can draw a circle and scale it in one dimension so that it becomes progressively more of an oval until all you see is a straight line. Continue to expand it from the line through fatter and fatter ovals until you have a circle again. You've just apparently rotated the circle 180 degrees. Continue until you're finished. You can select a group of frames and copy them or reverse them. (See Chapter 9 for more details.) You can see a simple example in Figure 14-3.

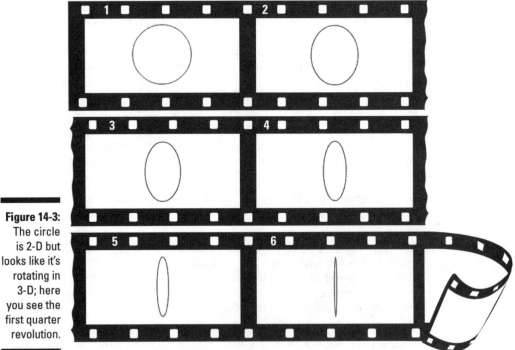

Figure 14-3:
The circle is 2-D but looks like it's rotating in 3-D; here you see the first quarter revolution.

REMEMBER

You can use shape tweening to create this 3-D effect. You can shape tween a circle into a line and back again to make it look like it's rotating.

Another common technique for simulating 3-D that you can try is to import an object from a 3-D program, such as 3D Studio Max, AutoCAD, or Cinema 4D.

In the following steps, we use AutoCAD as an example. To import an object from AutoCAD, follow these steps:

1. **Within AutoCAD, create the 3-D object, display the view that you want to start with, and choose File⇨Export.**

2. **Save the object as a WMF file (a vector format) and select the object when prompted.**

3. **Rotate the 3-D model slightly.**

   In AutoCAD 2000, you can use the 3-D Orbit command for this.

4. **Save this new view as a WMF file, consecutively numbered from the first file.**

   For example, if the first file is 3d1.wmf, name the second file 3d2.wmf.

5. **Repeat Steps 2 through 4 until you've rotated the model 360 degrees.**

6. **In Flash, choose File⇨Import and select the first WMF file that you created.**

7. **When Flash asks if you want to import all the files in the sequence, click Yes.**

   Flash imports all the files, placing them in consecutive keyframes. The WMF file imports with a border as well as the lines that make up the object.

8. **For each keyframe, do the following:**

   1. Click anywhere outside the objects, select just the border and press Delete.

   2. Select all the objects and choose Modify⇨Break Apart.

   3. Select the objects and choose Insert⇨Convert to Symbol.

You can now play your animation. Note that you lose any shading or materials you created in AutoCAD, so your model has a wire frame look. You can modify your 3-D object in Flash to create the appearance of solidity by using fills.

For an example of creating a simple 3-D animation using this technique, look in the Ch14 folder of the CD-ROM for 3d rotation.fla.

What if you don't have a 3-D program? Well, do you have Microsoft Word? Yes, folks, you can create 3-D objects in your lowly word processing program.

To create a 3-D object by using Microsoft Word, follow these steps:

1. **Open Microsoft Word, and in a new document, open the Drawing toolbar if it isn't already open by choosing View➪Toolbars➪Drawing.**

2. **On the Drawing toolbar, click the AutoShapes drop-down arrow and choose any shape you want.**

   You can even draw your own shape by using the Scribble tool (one of the options in the Lines submenu under AutoShapes).

3. **Click in your blank document to place the shape.**

   If you want, use the Fill Color tool to change the fill. Select the shape, and then from the Fill Color drop-down list choose Fill Effects and create a cool gradient on the Gradient tab.

4. **Click the 3-D button at the right end of the Drawing toolbar and choose a 3-D perspective that you like from the box that opens.**

   You may need to try out a couple of choices until you get the best effect.

5. **Click the 3-D button again and choose the 3-D Settings button at the bottom of the box to open the 3-D Settings toolbar.**

   Use the Tilt Left, Right, Up, or Down button to tilt the object until it looks perfectly flat, so that you don't see any of the 3-D effect. Keep the 3-D Settings toolbar open.

6. **Choose Edit➪Copy to copy the shape to the Clipboard.**

7. **Return to Flash and choose Insert➪New Symbol; specify a movie clip behavior for the symbol and then name it.**

8. **Click OK.**

9. **Choose Edit➪Paste to paste the shape into the first frame.**

10. **Go back to Word and decide which way you want your shape to rotate.**

    You can choose from up, down, left, or right.

11. **Select your 3-D shape in the Word document and click twice on Tilt Left (or Right or Up or Down) in the 3-D Settings toolbar.**

12. **Copy the shape to the Clipboard.**

13. **Go to Flash and create a keyframe in the next frame.**

14. **Paste the shape from the Clipboard.**

15. **Repeat Steps 11 through 14 until you're looking at your shape on edge.**

16. **Select all the frames except the first and the last and then choose Edit➪Copy Frames.**

17. **Click the first empty frame (the one after your last frame) and choose Edit⇨Paste Frames.**

    You now have the quarter revolution twice and need to modify the second set so that it becomes the second quarter revolution.

18. **Select all the frames that you've pasted and choose Modify⇨Frames⇨ Reverse.**

    If you play the animation now, it looks as if the shape is revolving one quarter and then back again.

19. **Select the first of the frames you pasted and choose Modify⇨ Arrange⇨Flip Horizontal (if you used Tilt Left or Right in Word) or Flip Vertical (if you choose Tilt Up or Down in Word).**

20. **Repeat Step 19 with the remaining frames that you've pasted.**

    You now have a half revolution.

21. **Select all but the first and last frames and then choose Edit⇨ Copy Frames.**

22. **Click the first empty frame after the last frame and choose Edit⇨ Paste Frames.**

23. **Select all the frames that you've pasted and choose Modify⇨ Frames⇨Reverse.**

You're done! Play your animation and watch your shape roll.

This method does have some disadvantages. First, all your images from Word are imported as bitmaps, not vector images. Second, you're animating frame by frame. As a result, your file is larger and downloads slower. If you use this method for just a small animation, however, it beats learning how to use a fancy 3-D program (and paying for it, too). Test the results and see if it works for you.

Look in the Ch14 folder for `rotating star.fla`, an example of using Word to create 3-D objects. The animation is in a movie clip, so choose Control⇨ Test Movie to see the results (or open the SWF file directly).

Referencing Objects for Tell Target

When you use Tell Target, you need to understand the methods Flash uses to refer to objects such as movie clips that have Timelines other than your main Timeline. Flash creates a hierarchy and uses a specific referral system so that you can be sure to tell your message to the right target.

If you're familiar with the hierarchical structure of folders and subfolders on a computer, you'll have no problem understanding how to refer to timelines in Flash.

In order to send a message to another object with a Timeline, that object must have been inserted or loaded by the time you reach the frame where you send the message. For example, if you have a frame action in Frame 20 to tell a movie clip to start playing, the movie clip must have been dragged onto the Stage on Frame 20 or before. In addition, you need to give the instance of the movie clip an instance name, using the Instance panel.

If you're adding the Tell Target ActionScript to the main Timeline and you want to refer to a movie clip inserted on the main Timeline, you can simply refer to the movie clip's instance name without any further ado. The easiest way to do so is to use the Insert Target Path dialog box. (See Chapter 10 for the full scoop.) Why not let Flash find your movie clip for you? Figure 14-4 shows this type of simple Tell Target reference. The name of the movie clip instance is Description1. (Flash can't always find your target so sometimes you have to type it in.)

Figure 14-4:
A simple
Tell Target
expression.

```
on (rollOver) {
  tellTarget ("Description1") {
    gotoAndStop (2);
  }
}
on (rollOut) {
  tellTarget ("Description1") {
    gotoAndStop (1);
  }
}
```

Suppose that you have a movie clip inside of a movie clip. Now you have two levels to deal with. Figure 14-5 shows this situation. As you can see, you refer first to the movie clip inserted on the main Timeline; then use a dot, and finally refer to the movie clip inserted inside the first movie clip. The Insert Target Path dialog box creates this syntax for you.

Figure 14-5:
A Tell Target
action
referring to
a movie clip
inside a
movie clip.

```
tellTarget ("cloud9.description9") {
  gotoAndStop (1);
}
```

You can also place a Tell Target action in a movie clip to tell the main Timeline what to do. This is sort of like your kids telling you what to do, because the main Timeline is the parent of the movie clip. Appropriately, the way to talk to the main Timeline is to use the expression _parent, as shown in Figure 14-6. Here you have a movie clip that plays some animation. At the end of the animation, it instructs the main Timeline to go to Frame 15 and play animation contained there.

Figure 14-6:
The upstart movie clip is telling its parent what to do.

```
tellTarget ("_parent") {
  gotoAndPlay (15);
}
```

What if you want one movie clip to tell another what to do? (For an example of why you use this type of structure, see the explanation of Tell Target in Chapter 10.) Flash lets siblings talk to each other as long as the siblings go through the parent. You can use _parent to represent the parent movie's timeline, then add a dot and the name of the other movie clip's instance name. If your movie clips are nested two layers down, you need to say _parent._parent. (That's like going through the grandparents.) Figure 14-7 shows an example of one movie clip telling another movie clip to play.

Figure 14-7:
One sibling movie clip invites the other to play.

```
tellTarget ("_parent.circle1") {
  gotoAndPlay (2);
}
```

In Flash 5, Macromedia recommends using the With action in place of Tell Target. You can use it to perform multiple actions on the same target. We find Tell Target simpler to explain, but you may want to check out the With action.

Making Drop-Down Menus

You can take your Web site to a whole new level by designing the entire site in Flash. As we describe in Chapter 12, you can use Flash to create, animate, and program for interactivity your navigation system, text, and graphics. For the ultimate in controlling the graphic look and feel of your site, you can also create drop-down menus (or pop-up or fly-out menus) in Flash.

You can create drop-down menus in Flash by using a variety of methods. The following general steps outline one method:

1. At Frame 1, create a main button that will become your main menu.

2. Add a stop action to this frame.

3. Add an action to this main button to go to some later spot on the Timeline, say Frame 10.

4. At Frame 10, display not only the main button, but also its submenu buttons.

   So when you press the main menu button at Frame 1, the Timeline play-head jumps to the main menu plus submenu buttons at Frame 10.

5. Add actions to the submenus buttons to do whatever you want each submenu to do.

6. At Frame 10, create a giant invisible button with a *hit* area that covers the entire Stage (except for the area containing your menu and sub-menus) and whose only property sends you back to Frame 1 when the mouse rolls over it.

   This way, if the mouse moves off the main menu and submenu area, you get sent back to Frame 1 where only the main menu button resides — and the submenu buttons disappear. (See Chapter 8 for the details on buttons.)

Now that we've reviewed the general steps for this one method of creating drop-down menus, the following steps walk you through the complete process. We warn you, this is quite a long exercise. We assume that you're starting with a new movie.

To create a drop-down menu, follow these steps:

1. **Choose Insert⇨Layer until you have four layers.**

2. **Double-click the top layer and name it** Actions.

3. **Name the second through fourth layers** Main Menu, Submenus, **and** Other Area, **in that order.**

4. **Click the first frame of the Actions layer and choose Window⇨Actions to open the Frame Actions window.**

5. **On the left side of the Frame Actions window, click Basic Actions and double-click the Stop action.**

   This assigns a Stop action to the frame.

6. **Click Frame 10 of the Actions layer and choose F6 to insert a keyframe there.**

7. **In the Frame Actions window, double-click the Stop action.**

8. **Add a keyframe in Frame 10 of the Main Menu layer.**

9. **Select Frame 1 of the Main Menu layer.**

10. **Choose Insert⇨New Symbol, choose the button behavior, name it** menubutton, **and click OK.**

11. **Draw the button however you want.**

    Instances of this button are used for both the main button and the fly-out submenu buttons. (For information on using Flash drawing tools, see Chapter 3.)

12. **Click the Over frame and choose F6 to insert a keyframe there.**

13. **Create the button for the Over state.**

    Often, this is just a modification of the Up state button. For example, you may want to change the fill color. (See Chapter 8 for button info.)

14. **Click the Down frame, choose F6 to insert a keyframe there, and create the button for the Down state.**

15. **Choose Edit⇨Edit Movie to go back to the scene's Timeline.**

16. **Choose Window⇨Library to open the Library.**

17. **Drag an instance of menubutton to the upper-left corner of the Stage.**

18. **Choose Window⇨Actions to open the Object Actions window and double-click the GoTo action.**

19. **At the bottom of the Object Action window, set the Frame Number to 10 in the Frame text box.**

20. **Select the first line of code and at the bottom of the Object Actions window, check Roll Over and uncheck Release.**

    As a result of this action, whenever you pass the mouse cursor over the main button, the playhead of the Timeline moves to Frame 10. You'll create the submenu buttons at Frame 10.

21. **Choose the Text tool and create a text block on the button that describes the button.**

    For information on using the Text tool, see Chapter 5.

22. **Save your work so far by choosing File⇨Save.**

23. **Click Frame 10 of the Submenu layer and press F6 to add a keyframe there.**

24. **Drag an instance of your button just beneath the first button.**

25. **Drag another instance of the button just below the last one.**

    You may want to use the Align panel to align and distribute the buttons evenly. (See Chapter 4 for details.)

26. **Add text to both submenu buttons describing their purpose, as shown in Figure 14-8.**

    Eventually, you'll want to add actions to these buttons so that they do something, such as adding a Get URL action or a Go To and Play action. We leave this to your own creativity.

Figure 14-8:
A main
menu
and two
submenu
buttons.

27. **Click Frame 10 of the Other Area layer and press F6 to create a keyframe there.**

28. **Choose the Rectangle tool and choose a new fill color that's easy to see and very different from the button fill color. Then draw a rectangle that's slighly larger than the Stage so that the rectable covers the entire stage.**

29. **Choose another bright, contrasting fill color and draw a rectangle enclosing all three buttons (the main menu and the two submenus).**

30. **Select the rectangle that you just created and press the Delete key.**

    Because Flash creates a cut out when you place an object on top of another object of a different color, this leaves the large rectangle covering everything except the menu items.

31. **Select the large rectangle and choose Insert⇨Convert to Symbol.**

32. **Choose Button as the symbol's behavior, name it, and click OK.**

33. **Choose Edit⇨Edit Symbols.**

34. **Click the Hit frame in the button Timeline and press F6 to insert a keyframe.**

35. **Click the Up frame in the button Timeline, select the large rectangle, and press Delete.**

36. **Choose Edit⇨Edit Movie.**

    The large rectangle is now shown as transparent blue.

37. **Click the big transparent blue shape and choose Window⇨Actions to open the Object Actions window.**

38. **On the left side of the Object Actions window, click Basic Actions and double-click the On Mouse Event action.**

39. **At the bottom of the Object Actions window, check the Roll Over event and uncheck Release.**

40. **On the left side of the Object Actions window, double-click the Go To action.**

    Leave the default that goes to Frame 1.

You just created a big button covering everything *except* the menu buttons. When you pass your mouse cursor anywhere except over the menu buttons, you are automatically over the big button, which then sends you back to Frame 1 where there are no submenus — you're hiding them. In other words, when you pass the cursor over the main menu button, the submenu buttons fly out but when you move the cursor anywhere else, they disappear. Choose Control⇨Test Movie to watch your drop-down menu in action.

Look in the Ch14 folder for `drop-down menu.fla`. Choose Control⇨Test Movie to see the drop-down action.

Part VI
The Part of Tens

The 5th Wave   By Rich Tennant

"Well, it's not quite done. I've animated the gurgling spit sink and the rotating Novocaine syringe, but I still have to add the high-speed whining drill audio track."

In this part . . .

In the famous *For Dummies* Part of Tens, we fill you in
on the top ten Web design tips so that your Flash Web
site looks great and draws crowds. We answer the ten
most-asked questions — or at least the ten questions we
most wanted to answer. Here you find some cool techniques
for creating drag-and-drop objects and simulating 3-D effects
in Flash. In the chapter on the ten best Flash resources, we
manage to give you dozens of Flash resources, such as the
many Flash resource Web sites, while convincing our publisher that there are only ten. Finally, to top off the book,
we give you our vote for ten great Flash Web sites. Surf all
ten and be amazed and inspired by the possibilities!

Chapter 15

Top Ten Web Design Tips

*T*he vast majority of Flash movies end up on Web sites. To help ensure that your Web site is as attractive and useful as possible, this chapter offers ten Web design tips. Some of these tips apply to all Web sites and others are specific to those sites using Flash movies.

Set Your Goal

A general principle of Web design is to know why you have a Web site. Write out one main goal and perhaps one or two secondary goals. For example, the main goal of your site may be to sell used music CDs. A secondary goal may be to provide viewers with music reviews so that they can decide which CDs they want to buy. Another secondary goal can be to attract viewers to your site (so they can buy your CDs). Avoid putting material on your site that doesn't help you reach your goal.

How does your Flash movie help you attain your Web site's goal? Perhaps your movie displays the covers of your most widely sold CDs and plays some of the music, giving viewers an instant understanding of your site's purpose. On the other hand, if your Flash movie just displays an animated logo, it may even distract viewers from the important features of your home page.

Keep Pages Clean and Clear

Unlike television, the Web is an interactive medium. Viewers need to understand the purpose of your site and how to navigate it. Clutter and complex structures are counterproductive. You can use Flash to create a simple, compelling navigational system. But you must be careful when mixing and matching HTML and Flash elements in order to avoid confusion. Let all your buttons look similar — don't create five different shapes and colors of Flash buttons just because you can.

By default, the Flash HTML file loops your files. Looped short animations tend to look like the animated GIFs we all know and hate . . . and ignore. Avoid looped animation unless you have a good reason for it, especially if it moves across the Web page in a banner. Viewers may assume it's advertising.

Don't Overwhelm Viewers with Color

Too many colors create a chaotic impression. While your Web site doesn't have to be dull, you don't want it to be overwhelming either. Of course, there's nothing wrong with full-color photographs or graphics, but use a maximum of three colors for the background, text, and navigational aids. Most of your Web content is probably text, which viewers expect to be mostly in one font and one color. Navigational aids, such as buttons and links, should be the same color throughout your site.

Use Fewer Than Four Fonts

To create a Web page design with maximum coherence and impact, you should probably restrict your page design to two or three fonts at most. It makes visual sense to use one font for the body of your text and one font for the headlines. You could perhaps use a third font for a logo or for some other special item, but this may look best if it has some kind of strong visual harmony with the other fonts you are using.

Use four fonts and people may start to think that you're designing a ransom note, not a Web page.

Be Consistent

Each page on your site should have the same logo. Certain links should go on each page (such as a link to your home page) and be in the same place on each page. If you have other links, such as Search, E-mail, and so on, these should also be consistent throughout your site.

Text color, fonts, hyperlinks, backgrounds, buttons, and so on should all be consistent to avoid confusion and error.

Your URLs and page headings should also have a consistent theme. URLs should be as simple as possible, and headings need to be complete and clear. Viewers often see headings out of context, such as in the results of a search engine or in your table of contents. For example, if you're selling used CDs, don't use *Jazz* at the top of one page and *Looking for some Classical Music?* at the top of another. Instead, put *Used Jazz CDs* on the first page and *Used Classical CDs* on the next. These headings are simple, complete, and consistent.

If you're combining HTML and Flash content, use consistent fonts and colors for both.

KISS

As you probably know, KISS stands for *Keep It Simple, Stupid.* Sketch out the map of your site and make sure the lines of navigation are short and simple. Don't use long explanations when a short one will do. Don't use lots of images when one will suffice.

Your Flash movies should also be as simple as possible. Animation goes by fast. If too many objects are moving at once, viewers don't know where to focus their attention.

Keep It Lean and Fast

Viewers don't like to wait for a page to download. Throughout this book we have discussed ways to make your Flash movies smaller so that they download faster. As we were considering Flash movies to include on the CD-ROM of this book, we skipped over many that had preload sequences that took too long.

The same applies to the rest of your Web site. Keep the graphic images as small as possible and use as few as possible.

While we were preparing this book, we looked at dozens of Web sites created by using Flash. About ten percent took so long to download (on our 56K modem) that we gave up and went elsewhere. Another ten percent had an intro animation that took so long that we got tired of waiting for the buttons and content of the site to appear. You don't want potential viewers to give up on your site because it takes too long to load.

Know Who's Watching and How

Many Web site hosts provide you with information on the browsers (including which version) and the resolutions used by your viewers. You may not be able to cater to everything out there, but you should try to create a Web site that the vast majority of people can see.

Many sites that use Flash offer a non-Flash alternative rather than force viewers without the Flash Player to download it. The non-Flash alternative has non-animated graphics in place of the Flash movie. Figure 15-1 shows a site that offers both options.

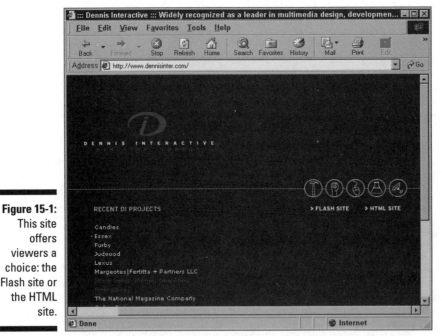

Figure 15-1: This site offers viewers a choice: the Flash site or the HTML site.

Thanks to Leslie Allen-Kickham for permission to display this Web site.

Remember that viewers on a screen with 640 x 480 resolution can see a lot less than viewers on screens with a higher resolution. Those with lower resolution may miss important parts of your Web page and Flash animation.

Support the Flash Player

As explained in Chapters 12 and 13, you can choose to publish an HTML file that detects whether the Flash Player is installed on the viewer's computer. If not, it displays an image file. (You need to publish to one of the image formats at the same time for this to work.)

The default HTML text doesn't check for the Flash player, but it includes the location to download the player. In some situations, the Flash Player will download automatically when not available or a window will pop up offering the viewer the chance to download it. Many sites include a button that says, `Can't see the animation? Download the Flash Player here,` or something to that effect. The button links to Macromedia's download center at `www.macromedia.com/shockwave/download/index.cgi?P1_Prod_Version=ShockwaveFlash.`

Many Web surfers have no idea how Web sites are created and have never heard of Flash. Therefore, giving viewers a choice of Flash and non-Flash sites may not be meaningful. (Of course, if you're a Web site designer and you think potential clients viewing your site may be savvier than most viewers, you may have no problem in this regard.) In most situations, it may be better to use the words *animated* and *non-animated.* Of course, feel free to use the word *Flash* along with some explanation. We want the world to know what Flash is, don't we?

Test, and Then Test Again

As described in Chapter 13, you need to test your Web site in both Netscape Navigator and Internet Explorer. Testing at various screen resolutions (680 x 480, 800 x 600, and 1024 x 768) is also extremely important. You should further test your Web site at various Internet connection speeds, such as 28.8 Kbs and 56 Kbs, as well as at faster speeds (DSL and cable modem connections). Test your Web site on a system that doesn't have the Flash player as well as one that does.

Finally, have a few friends review your site and navigate through it. Ask them to write down their impressions, moments of confusion, questions, and comments. (Of course, they can also write down profuse praise.) When you work on a Web site, you get so involved in it that you need someone objective and without your inside knowledge to provide a fresh perspective.

Chapter 16

Ten Best Flash Resources

*F*lash is such a flexible program that you never stop learning. And just when you think you've got it, out comes a new version! In this chapter, we point you to the many resources that you can turn to when you want to increase your knowledge about Flash.

Of course, we think that this book is a great resource on Flash. But you're already using this book and we admit that a lot more about Flash is out there, readily available to help you become a truly great Flash animator.

Do the Tutorials

Flash comes with two tutorials. One teaches you just the basics. You can find it by choosing Help⇨Lessons and going through each lesson in turn.

The second tutorial is more complex and is designed to give you a taste of the full capabilities of Flash. Choose Help⇨Using Flash. Then in the Using Flash table of contents, choose Tutorial. For easiest use, print out the tutorial so that you don't have to switch back and forth between the instructions and Flash on-screen.

Take a Course

Many colleges and universities offer courses in Flash. Sometimes these courses are part of a Web design or graphic art course or they may stand alone. To find these courses, call local education institutions and ask!

The advantage of a course led by a teacher is that you have a chance to ask questions — and receive answers. A teacher also guides the learning process and possibly even gives you lots of tips and hints!

Look on the Flash Web Page

Macromedia maintains a large resource on its Web site. Go to `www.macromedia.com/support/flash` where you can find learning tips, support, technical notes, news, and updates. Macromedia also has a great Gallery of great Flash Web sites. It's lots of fun to look at these sites and wish you could do that. Someday, you will! Go to `www.macromedia.com/software/flash/` and click the Showcase link.

You can try going to `www.flash.com`, but it just redirects you to `www.macromedia.com/software/flash/`.

Macromedia also runs Macromedia University, which offers courses in Flash and other Macromedia products. Go to `www.macromedia.com/university/` for more information.

Join a Flash Discussion Group

Macromedia maintains several Flash newsgroups where anyone can ask questions and get expert answers. The two main newsgroups are

- ✔ **Flash:** for technical issues relating to Flash and the Flash player. Go to `news://forums.macromedia.com/macromedia.flash`.
- ✔ **Flash Site Design:** for discussing techniques as well as technical issues. Go to `news://forums.macromedia.com/macromedia.flash.sitedesign`.

If you're not sure how to get into a newsgroup, you can go to `www.macromedia.com/support/flash/` and click the link for Online Forums. You must be set up to read newsgroups for this to work.

Several other excellent active discussion groups reside on Web sites. The best way to tell if a discussion group is active is to see how many messages have been posted in the last one or two days. You can also check out how many different people are participating. See the section, "Check out the Flash Resource Sites," later in this chapter.

You can also subscribe to a *listserv,* an ongoing discussion sent by e-mail. FLASHmacromedia-L is a listserv specifically for users who want to discuss Flash techniques. You can ask questions and get answers from the community of Flash users. To sign up, go to www.onelist.com/subscribe/ FLASHmacromedia. You can also send a blank e-mail to flashmacromedia-digest@onelist.com (to get the compiled format) or flashmacromedia-normal@onelist.com (to get every e-mail separately).

Join a User Group

A Flash user group is simply a group of Flash users in a local area. You may be able to find a user group near you. If not, you can start one! User groups get together periodically and discuss problems and their solutions. Sometimes they bring in speakers as well. Macromedia maintains a newsgroup on User Groups where you can post announcements about user groups. You can find it at news://forums.macromedia.com/macromedia.general.usergroups. You can also get to this newsgroup at www.macromedia.com/support/ flash/. Click the link for Online Forums and scroll down until you see the User Groups item.

At the same location, you can find newsgroups for various international locations.

Check Out the Flash Resource Sites

You'll find a huge Flash community on the Internet, so vast in fact, that you'll probably never be able to participate in all its offerings. These Web sites offer news, tutorials, discussion groups, tips, and links to other Flash resources.

Some of these sites are more up to date, lively, and complete than others. The quality of the tips and tutorials vary widely. Some specialize in tips for beginners, others for advanced users. The following is a brief review of all the ones we find useful, in alphabetical order.

www.artswebsite.com/coolstuff/flash.htm

This site includes lots of great examples and downloads from a Flash teacher. You also find tutorials on some great, popular effects (see Figure 16-1).

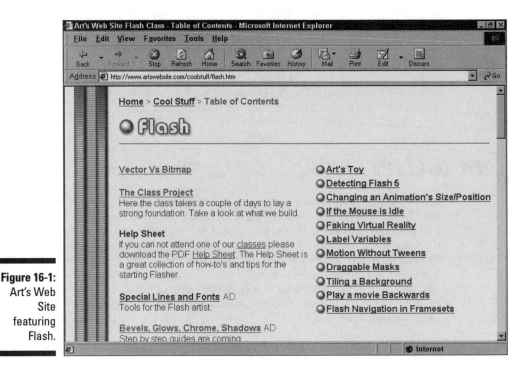

Figure 16-1:
Art's Web
Site
featuring
Flash.

www.bertoflash.nu

This is a cute site with lots of examples, including Flash 5 examples. You can ask for the source files, some of which are quite sophisticated.

www.designsbymark.com/flashtut/index.shtml

This site, shown in Figure 16-2, contains a great set of tutorials, free music downloads, a discussion group, and links. You'll also find material on Photoshop, general Web design, and other computer art topics.

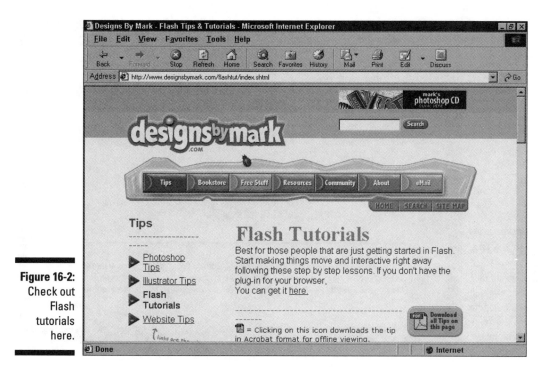

Figure 16-2:
Check out
Flash
tutorials
here.

www.enetserve.com/tutorials

Known as the Flash Academy, this site is associated with www.flasher.net (see Figure 16-3). It contains a good number of tutorials for which you can download source files. You also find links to other Flash and Web design sites here.

www.extremeflash.com

Look here for the following resources:

- ✔ Downloadable Flash movies
- ✔ Beginner, intermediate, and advanced tutorials
- ✔ Links
- ✔ Frequently asked questions
- ✔ Downloadable fonts and music

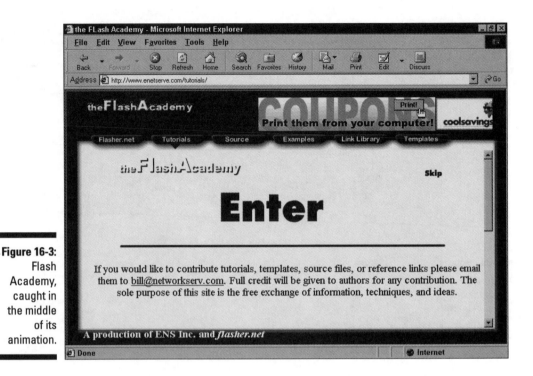

Figure 16-3:
Flash
Academy,
caught in
the middle
of its
animation.

www.flashaddict.com

You can find lots of tutorials, including source FLA files and a message board. Other features include links, news, and miscellaneous related items. You can also sign up for a newsletter. Tutorials come in several categories: beginners, intermediate, advanced, ActionScript, expert, gaming (creating games with Flash), text effects, other effects, and Flash apps (using Flash with other applications). You find plenty to keep you busy at this site.

www.flashfaq.net

This site is out of date but still has lots of great information, tutorials, downloads, FAQs, and links.

www.flashkit.com

Flash Kit is one of the largest sites and very up to date (see Figure 16-4). (We define up to date by having Flash 5 material within days after it shipped.) Lots of tutorials, an active discussion group (with Flash 5 topics, one for newbies, and many more), links, sounds, downloadable fonts, a job center — if you can think of it, you can find it here.

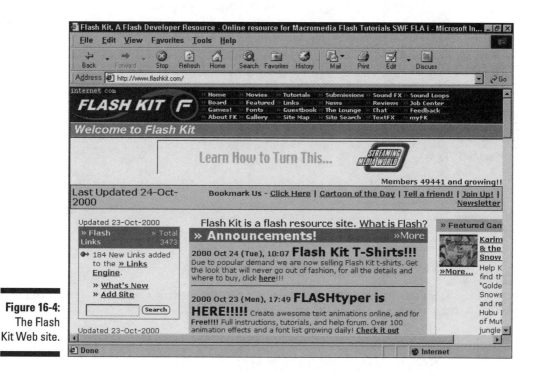

Figure 16-4: The Flash Kit Web site.

www.flashlite.net

FLASHlite, shown in Figure 16-5, is an up-to-date site with lots of Flash 5 information. You see lots of basic level tutorials to help you get up to speed. You can download the tutorials and source FLA files.

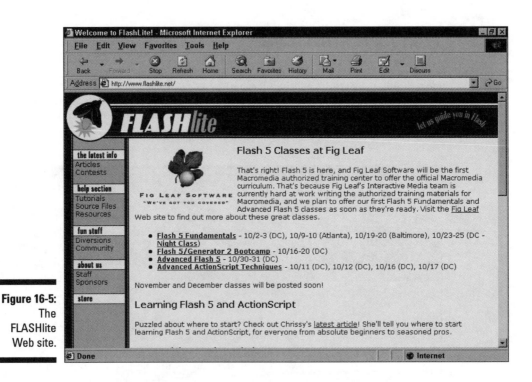

Figure 16-5:
The
FLASHlite
Web site.

www.flashmagazine.com

This site includes Flash 5 material, including lessons on ActionScript. You'll also find links, reviews, and articles.

www.flashmaster.nu

This is a comprehensive Flash resource site (see Figure 16-6) with more categories than most of the other sites. For example, it has a category on *site building* — creating an entire site with Flash. You'll also find the usual: tutorials, downloads, and FAQs. The interface is cool, too, but we didn't find any Flash 5 material here.

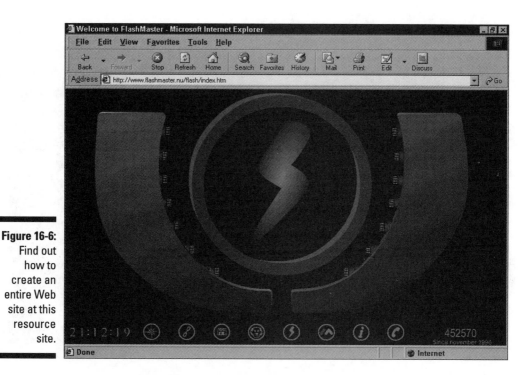

Figure 16-6:
Find out
how to
create an
entire Web
site at this
resource
site.

www.flashmove.com

For the most up to the minute news — they announced Flash 5 the day it shipped — check out this site, which features many links, tutorials with downloadable FLA files, a discussion group (forum), Flash 5 resources, and more (see Figure 16-7).

www.flashzone.com

Flashzone!, another multi-faceted site, includes news and articles, an active discussion group, and downloads of FLA files, tutorials, and links. The last time we looked, we didn't find any Flash 5 stuff. Even so, this site is worth a browse.

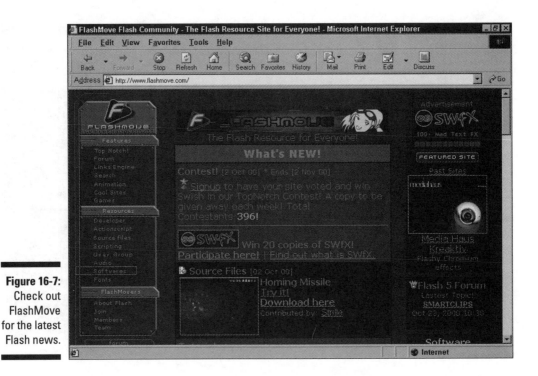

www.moock.org/webdesign/flash

Colin Moock is a master Flash designer and his Web site, shown in Figure 16-8, contains information on how to create many effects, mostly in the advanced category. You can download the FLA source file and generally you find lots to chew on here.

www.shockfusion.com

This site offers a series of discussion groups and resources for Flash developers.

www.thelinkz.com

This site has a well-developed set of links related to Flash. The links are organized by topics so that you can easily find what you want. For example, you can look for tutorials, educational resources, 3-D tools, 3-D resources, and so on.

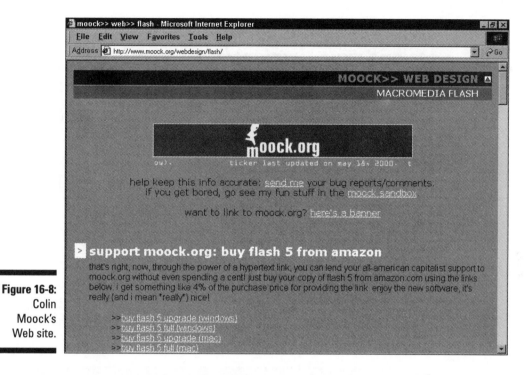

Figure 16-8:
Colin
Moock's
Web site.

www.turtleshell.com/guide/index.html

Turtleshell offers a number of simple tutorials for Flash that show you how to create popular effects. Tutorial categories include simple, advanced, effects, and actions. You'll also find links and downloads of FLA files with effects that you may want to use.

www.virtual-fx.net

This site features a very stylish interface and includes tutorials, downloads, links to newsgroups, a Flash gallery, and more. The tutorials, simple and clear, are based on Flash 3.

www.were-here.com/forum/ actionscript_project/start.html

At We're Here Forums, shown in Figure 16-9, you'll find a wealth of resources:

- A few dozen tutorials, including a Flash 5 ActionScript tutorial
- Articles
- FLA files downloads (over 200), including several from Flash 5
- An extensive forum (including two on Flash 5 and one for newbies)
- Links for music
- A career center
- Links to almost 400 Flash sites that you can look at (the Directory and Galleria)
- Links to other Flash resource sites

Overall, this is an active, up-to-date site. And on top of all the pluses, this site is *exceptionally* easy to navigate.

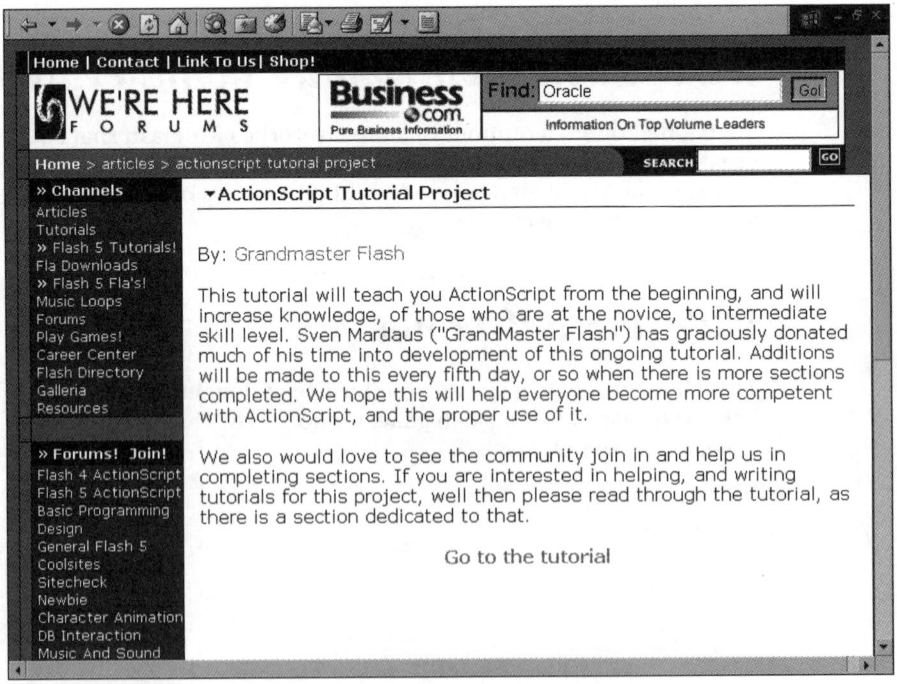

Figure 16-9: Find a wealth of information at We're Here Forums.

Check Out Sites That Use Flash

In Chapter 17, we list ten great sites that use Flash. Many of the resource sites have galleries of great sites, as does Macromedia. You can get many ideas by looking at what others do. Sometimes very simple sites are both beautiful and practical.

Our Sites

Check out the *Flash 5 for Dummies* page on the IDG Books Worldwide Web Site at `http://catalog.dummies.com/product.asp?isbn=0764507362`, as well as Ellen Finkelstein's site at `www.ellenfinkelstein.com`. This site contains tips and tutorials for beginners. We hope you find these sites helpful!

Collect Flash Movies

Many of the Flash resource Web sites let you download FLA movies. You can also trade movies with others you know who use Flash. Analyzing movies is a great way to see how effects are created. In Chapter 14, we explain how to use the Movie Explorer to ferret out all the hidden details of a movie.

Be sure to check out the Library of a movie — most of the secrets lie there. Select objects with the Actions frame open to see the actions attached to objects. You'll soon be on your way to adapting the techniques you see to your own projects.

Reuse Your Best Stuff

After you've created some great Flash movies, you can reuse your best stuff. Fade outs (changing transparency), glows (soft edges), and masks are simple effects that you can use again and again.

You can also reuse ActionScript on new objects. Once you get a technique down, you don't need to re-create the wheel.

If you've created an animated logo, you may be able to use that over and over. Certain simple animations can be created in new colors, using the same original symbols.

You can open the Library of any movie in your current movie. Choose File⇨ Open as Library and choose the Flash file that contains the library that you want to use.

Chapter 17

Ten Great Web Sites
That Use Flash

*I*t's almost absurd to try to choose the ten best Web sites that use Flash — there are so many good ones. In addition, by the time you read this book, who knows if these sites will still be around? Nevertheless, we wanted to give you a shortcut to finding top quality Flash sites so you could get ideas and see the possibilities.

How did we choose? Certainly, many wonderful sites we just missed. But we created a list of more than 100 sites and looked at them all. Our criteria were the following:

✔ **Beauty:** We wanted to show you sites that were beautiful examples of artistic Web design.

✔ **Practicality:** We chose only sites that seemed to have a real purpose.

✔ **Speed:** If we had to wait more than a minute for download on our 56K modem, we moved on. We rejected some very fascinating sites because of this restriction. But hey, more than a minute is way too long to keep your viewers waiting!

These sites are listed in no particular order — we list them in the order that we got to them. We looked for these sites during the Flash 5 beta period. Therefore, they were all in Flash 4. We rejected sites using the Flash 3 player on the assumption that they may not be using all the features available in Flash 4.

www.k2sports.com

A great preloader gets you quickly to the buttons so you can choose bikes, snowboards, skis, or skates. Try the bike button for a way cool cartoon. The site includes a Skip Intro button. Designed by Digital Sherpas at `www.digital-sherpas.com`.

www.crashmedia.com

This creator of Web sites has created a complex site for itself. The site, shown in Figure 17-1, includes the choice to download the necessary players and an alternate HTML site. The 3-D effects are effective as is the music and voice-over. Click Navigation to display the buttons. Click Clients and follow the directions to drag-and-drop the client buttons into the empty box. Definitely a flashy site.

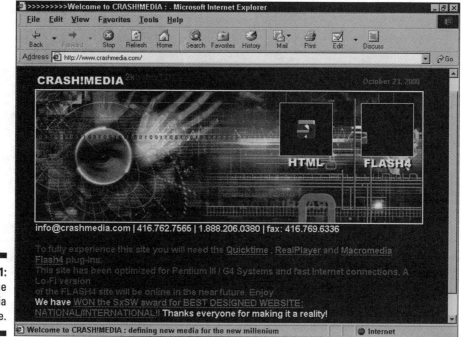

Figure 17-1:
The
Crash!media
Web site.

Thanks to Craig Swann for permission to display this Web site.

www.intellispace.com

IntelliSpace, the first managed optical IP network in the U.S., starts out by offering three options: to enter the site, to download the Flash player, or to go to the HTML site. When you enter the Flash site, shown in Figure 17-2, you see a very pretty (and quick loading) intro that relates to the company's business. There are Music On/Off and Skip Intro buttons. The navigation is clear and smooth.

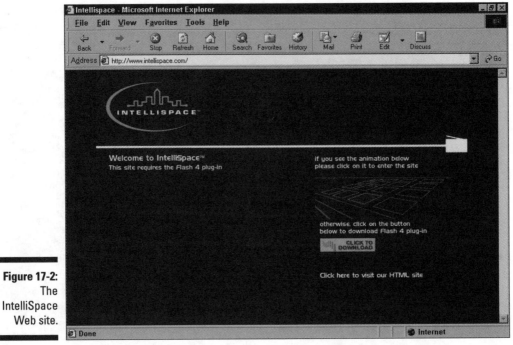

Figure 17-2:
The
IntelliSpace
Web site.

Thanks to Paul Brindak and Brian Hand of IntelliSpace for permission to display this Web site.

www.dennisinteractive.com

Dennis Interactive, a multimedia design company, offers an innovative site with unusual animation and button sounds (see Figure 17-3). Yet the site never loses its focus. The site offers a non-Flash alternative as well as an opportunity to download the Flash player.

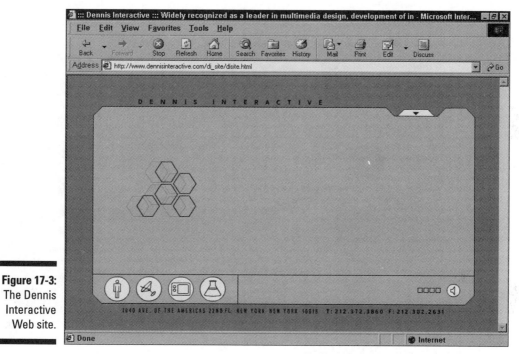

Figure 17-3:
The Dennis
Interactive
Web site.

Thanks to Leslie Allen-Kickham for permission to display this site.

www.areeba.com.au

Areeba offers a variety of Internet services and solutions for companies. Their site, shown in Figure 17-4, is beautiful, yet simple and easy to use. You always know how to get the information you need. They offer a non-Flash site as well.

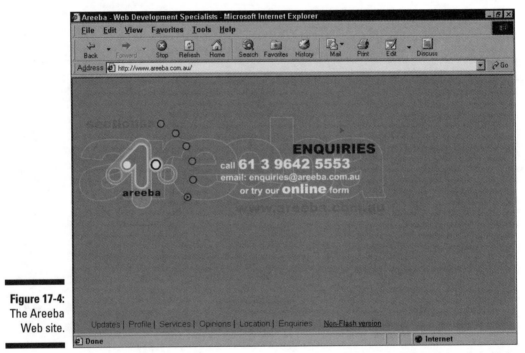

Figure 17-4:
The Areeba
Web site.

Thanks to Wayne Vickers of Areeba for permission to display this site.

http://4site.co.il

4site, a Web design and consulting company, offers a way-cool site for your inspection. The main page is a good example of an HTML page with Flash elements. Choose the American flag for the English site. (There are also French and Hebrew sites.) You then see a great example of typewriter text — text that appears letter by letter. Next is an entertaining sci-fi movie and you finally arrive at the site content. Quite spectacular. You can see the main HTML page in Figure 17-5.

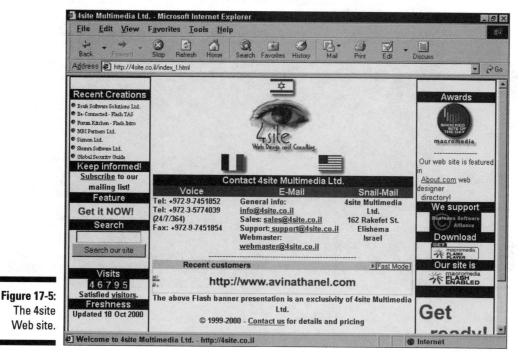

Figure 17-5:
The 4site
Web site.

Thanks to Moshe Doubior of 4site Multimedia Ltd. for permission to display this site.

www.hitachidigitaltv.co.uk/

This beautiful yet simple site, shown in Figure 17-6, is dedicated to explaining Hitachi Digital TV. You can download a screensaver based on the site that loads super-fast. The conception is totally appropriate for the product.

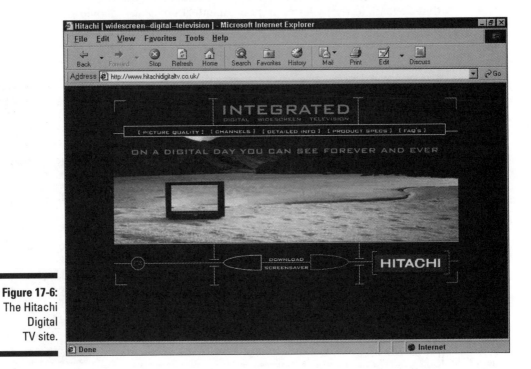

Figure 17-6:
The Hitachi Digital TV site.

www.davidgarystudios.com

Created in a super-futuristic style, this Web site is the home of Dreamwave Productions, Inc., specializing in high-end, interactive Web and CD-ROM applications. The site features the most unusual menu we've seen yet (see Figure 17-7).

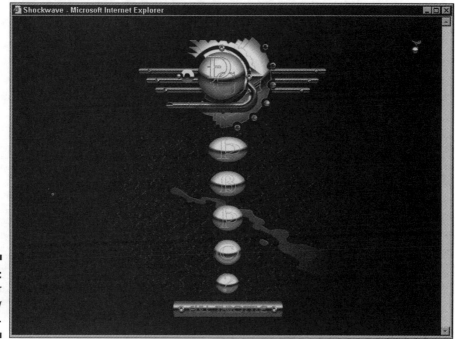

Figure 17-7: The site for David Gary Studios.

Thanks to David Gary Studios for permission to display this site.

www.telenet.co.uk

Click Site Introduction to see a great movie. This is the site of TeleNet Services, Ltd., a United Kingdom-based company specializing in Internet consultancy, design and e-commerce applications (see Figure 17-8). Explore all the menus — they're beautiful and easy to use.

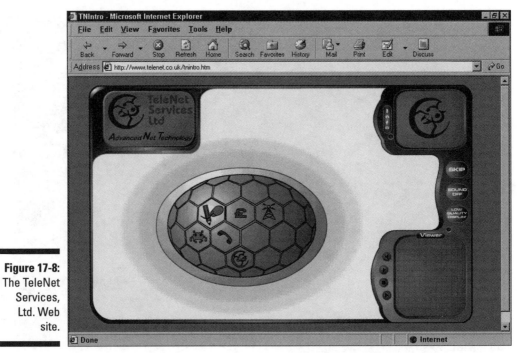

Figure 17-8:
The TeleNet Services, Ltd. Web site.

Thanks to Alastair Percival for permission to display this site. © TeleNet Services, Ltd. 1999.

www.rayoflight.net

Probably the most beautiful site we've ever seen. Ray of Light Productions/ Republik One, LLC offers a full range of design and Internet solutions for Web sites. An inspiring display. Have a peek at Figure 17-9, but go look at the real thing on the Internet.

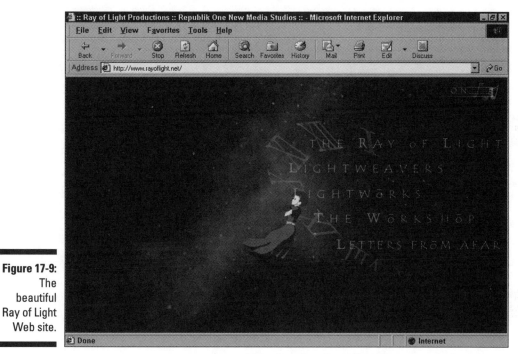

Figure 17-9:
The
beautiful
Ray of Light
Web site.

Thanks to Yasuto Suga of Republik One, LLC for permission to display this Web site.

Part VII
Appendixes

The 5th Wave   By Rich Tennant

"Well shoot — I know the animation's moving a might too fast, but <u>dang</u> if I can find a 'mosey' function anywhere in the toolbox!"

In this part . . .

*I*n the appendixes, we dump everything we couldn't fit elsewhere but thought too useful to forget. We explain how to install Flash (it's a snap) and customize your preferences. A new Flash 5 feature lets you create your own keyboard shortcuts — and we tell you how. One appendix shows you all the new Flash 5 panels and labels all those obscure buttons so that you know what they do. We offer a glossary of need-to-know terms and tell you what's on the CD-ROM. (Lots of stuff!)

Appendix A

What's Your Preference?

● ●

*I*nstalling Flash is pretty simple; nevertheless, sometimes a few pointers can help. After you're up and running, you may want to customize how Flash works. You can set quite a number of preferences. You can also create your own keyboard shortcuts.

Installing Flash

Installing Flash is a cinch, although you have a couple of options. Here's the lowdown on getting started.

You can install Flash four different ways:

- ✔ From a CD onto a PC
- ✔ By downloading it onto a PC
- ✔ From a CD onto a Mac
- ✔ By downloading it onto a Mac

We discuss these separately in the next four sections.

Installing Flash on a PC from a CD

So, you went out and bought "Flash in the Box" and you have a CD-ROM. To install Flash from the box, follow these steps:

1. **Exit all Windows programs.**

2. **Insert the CD-ROM.**

   In most cases, the setup program starts automatically. If not, choose Start⇨Run and click Browse. Then find and double-click Setup.exe on your CD-ROM drive. Click Run.

3. **Follow the instructions on the various screens that appear.**

   Unless you want to save space by not installing the lessons and samples, choose the Typical installation. Other than that, the most significant choice you have is where you install Flash. You can browse to change the location or accept the default, which is `C:\Program Files\ Macromedia\Flash 5.`

4. **After you follow the screen instructions, the setup program starts copying files; when completed, click Finish.**

5. **Read the ReadMe file offered on the last screen.**

   Although we guarantee that most of the stuff in the file is irrelevant to you, sometimes this file has just the weird detail that applies to your situation, so take the two minutes to read it.

Installing Flash by downloading it to your PC

If you like, you can download Flash directly from Macromedia's Web site. You can download the trial and pay for it within 30 days or you can pay for it first and then download it. Follow these steps:

1. **Go to** `www.macromedia.com/software/downloads/.`

2. **In the list of Macromedia products, find Flash and choose Try or Buy.**

3. **If you choose buy, follow the directions to pay for Flash. Either way, fill out the information requested by Macromedia.**

4. **Follow the instructions for downloading the installation file.**

   When you download the file, you choose the location on your hard drive. Remember this location.

5. **When the download is complete, double-click the installation file. Here's where you need to remember where you saved it.**

   The installation program guides you through the process of installing Flash.

6. **Unless you want to save space by not installing the lessons and samples, choose the Typical installation.**

   Other than that, the most significant choice you have is where you install Flash. You can browse to change the location or accept the default, which is `C:\Program Files\Macromedia\Flash 5.`

After you install Flash, you can play with it! If you download the trial version, you can buy it at any time by clicking Buy Now on the first screen when you open Flash.

Installing Flash on a Mac from a CD

If you bought Flash in a box, you have a CD that you can use to install Flash.

To install Flash from a CD, follow these steps:

1. **Insert the CD-ROM. Find and double-click the Flash 5 Installer icon.**

   A dialog box appears, asking you to select the applications you want to install: Flash 5 and/or Generator Authoring Extensions. (Generator is software that lets you create templates that can contain graphics, text, sound, and other content generated dynamically by a Web server.) You probably want to install only Flash 5 for now, which is the default setting.

2. **Click OK to choose the default setting.**

3. **When a window appears displaying a software license agreement, click the Accept button so that you can continue installation.**

4. **Unless you want to save space by not installing the lessons and samples, choose the Easy Install, which is the default.**

   Other than that, the most significant choice you have is where you install Flash. You can browse to change the location or accept the default location, which is on the startup disk drive.

5. **Click Install.**

   The installer program starts copying files. When it's done, you see the Macromedia Flash 5 folder displayed on your computer screen, containing the Flash 5 program, a few documents, and a bunch of other folders. One of the documents is the `ReadMe.html` file. You can view the contents of this file simply by double-clicking it. Although we guarantee that most of the stuff in the file is irrelevant to you, sometimes this file has just the weird detail that applies to your situation, so take the two minutes to read it.

Installing Flash by downloading it to your Mac

In this ultra-modern day and age, you can now buy Flash and install it on your computer without ever leaving your Web browser. To download Flash, follow these steps (or something like them, assuming Macromedia's Web site doesn't change too much):

1. **Go to** `www.macromedia.com/software/downloads/`.

2. **In the list of Macromedia products, find Flash and choose Try or Buy.**

3. **If you choose buy, follow the directions to pay for Flash. Either way, fill out the information requested by Macromedia.**

4. **Follow the instructions for downloading the installation file.**

5. **When the download is complete, double-click the installation file.**

    The installation program guides you through the process of installing Flash.

6. **Unless you want to save space by not installing the lessons and samples, choose the Easy installation.**

    Other than that, the most significant choice you have is where you install Flash. You can browse to change the location or accept the default, which is the startup disk drive.

After you install Flash, you can play with it! If you download the trial version, you can buy it at any time by clicking Buy Now on the first screen when you open Flash.

Setting Your Preferences

Flash offers a number of ways to customize how you work. Why not make Flash suit you?

The main location for settings preferences is the Preferences dialog box, shown in Figure A-1 with the General tab on top. To open the Preferences dialog box, choose Edit⇨Preferences.

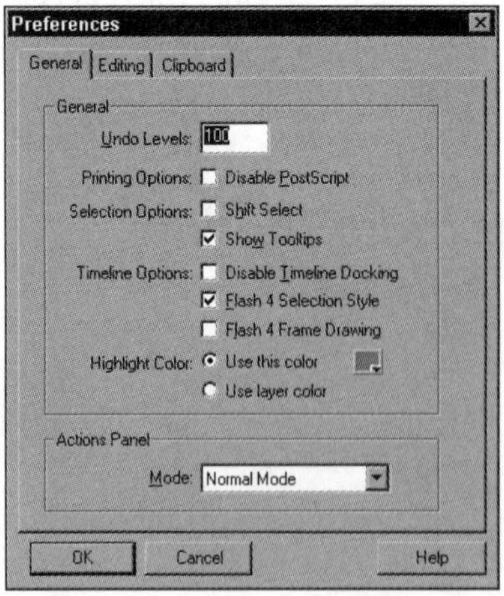

Figure A-1:
Use the
Preferences
dialog box
to bend
Flash to
your will.

The following sections describe how to use this dialog box.

General tab

On the General tab, you can set the following options:

- ✔ **Undo levels:** Set to 100 by default, you can enter any value from 0 to 300. The higher the value, the more memory Flash takes to remember all those steps. You may be surprised by how many commands you give in half an hour, so 100 is probably a good setting.

- ✔ **Printing Options — Disable PostScript:** For Windows only, checking this box disables PostScript output when you print to a PostScript printer. Check this box only if you have trouble printing to a PostScript printer. This option is unchecked by default.

- ✔ **Selection Options — Shift Select:** By default, this option is checked, which means that you have to press Shift to select more than one object (by clicking). If you don't, the first object is deselected. Unchecking this option means that you can click as many objects as you want to select them. This is an efficient way to work. If you select something by accident, press Shift to deselect it.

- ✔ **Show Tooltips:** By default, you see short explanations of Flash interface features (such as toolbars and buttons) when you pass your cursor over them. You can make the tooltips go away by unchecking this check box.

- ✔ **Timeline Options — Disable Timeline Docking:** Prevents the timeline from docking at the top of the window.

- ✔ **Timeline Options — Use Flash 4 Selection Style:** Lets you select one frame by clicking it. In Flash 5, clicking a frame selects the entire section between two keyframes and you use Ctrl+click (Windows) or ⌘+click (Mac) to select one frame.

- ✔ **Timeline Options — Flash 4 Frame Options:** Shows a hollow circle in blank keyframes. Flash 5 simply shows a dark vertical line on either side of the frame. Flash 4 shows a solid circle for all keyframes with content; Flash 5 shows a small open rectangle if the content is static.

- ✔ **Highlight Color:** Lets you specify the color of the box around selected symbols and groups. Click Use This Color and pick a color to specify your own color. Otherwise, you can choose Use Layer Color to use the layer's outline color.

- ✔ **Actions Panel:** Lets you choose the default for creating actions. You can use the Action panel's controls (Normal Mode) or type ActionScript from scratch (Expert Mode). You can change this at any time in the Actions Panel by clicking the arrow at the top-right corner of the panel to open the menu.

Editing tab

On the Editing tab, you can set the following items:

- **Pen tool — Show Pen Preview:** Displays a preview of the line or curve segment before you click the next point. Recommended!

- **Pen tool — Show Solid Points:** Checked by default. Uncheck this to show unfilled points at vertices.

- **Pen tool — Show Precise Cursors:** Displays a small crosshair instead of the pen-shaped cursor, for more precise placement of points.

The Drawing Settings are covered in Chapter 3.

Clipboard tab

The Clipboard tab enables you to set preferences for displaying, exporting, and importing certain objects. Here are your choices:

- **Bitmaps — Color Depth:** Specifies the color depth for bitmaps copied to the Clipboard. This setting applies to Windows only. You can choose to match the screen or set a color depth from 4-bit to 32-bit with alpha. You can use this setting to reduce the size of bitmaps that you paste into Flash from the Windows clipboard.

- **Bitmaps — Resolution:** Sets the resolution of bitmaps copied to the Clipboard. This setting applies to Windows only. Choose Screen to match your screen resolution or choose 72, 150, or 300. You can use this setting to reduce the size of bitmaps that you paste into Flash from the Windows clipboard.

- **Bitmaps — Size Limit:** This setting applies to Windows only. Lets you specify a size limit in kilobytes for the amount of RAM (memory) that is used for a bitmap on the Windows clipboard. If you have large images, you may need to increase this number, which is set to 250K by default.

- **Bitmaps — Smooth:** This setting applies to Windows only. This box, checked by default, applies anti-aliasing to bitmaps. Anti-aliasing smoothes the appearance of bitmaps so they don't appear so jagged. You can affect the smoothing of bitmaps during publishing as well by choosing the quality of the output. See the discussion of the HTML tab in Chapter 13.

- **Gradients:** This option applies to Windows only and lets you specify the quality of gradients that you *copy* to the Clipboard for use in other applications. Choose from none to best.

✔ **PICT Settings — Type:** This option applies to Mac only. Select Objects to maintain the vector format of objects copied to the Clipboard. Otherwise, select one of the bitmap formats.

✔ **PICT Settings — Resolution:** This option applies to Mac only. Select a resolution for objects copied to the Clipboard.

✔ **PICT Settings — Include Postscript:** Includes PostScript information with the graphic (on the Clipboard) for better output when printing the graphic on a PostScript printer. This option applies only to the Mac.

✔ **PICT Settings — Gradients:** Lets you specify the quality of gradients that you *copy* to the Clipboard for use in other applications. Choose from none to best. This option applies only to the Mac.

✔ **FreeHand Text:** By default, the Maintain Text as Blocks check box is checked so that text pasted from FreeHand can be edited in Flash.

When you finish setting your preferences, click OK.

Customizing Keyboard Shortcuts

A new feature of Flash 5 is that you can now set your own keyboard shortcuts. Opening the new panels in Flash 5 requires a trip to a submenu, so you'll want to create your own shortcuts for your favorites. You can create a shortcut for any menu item and change existing shortcuts as well. (See the Cheat Sheet at the front of this book for commonly used keyboard shortcuts.)

To create shortcuts, choose Edit⇨Keyboard Shortcuts to open the Keyboard Shortcuts dialog box, as shown in Figure A-2. (The figure shows the Windows version; the Mac version is nearly the same.)

You can't change the original set of shortcuts. Instead, create a duplicate set of shortcuts and modify the duplicate. Give the duplicate a new name, such as MyWay, and then use those shortcuts:

	To duplicate a shortcut set, click Duplicate Set at the top of the Keyboard Shortcuts dialog box.
	To rename a set of shortcuts, click Rename Set at the top of the Keyboard Shortcuts dialog box.
🗑	To delete a set of shortcuts, click Delete Set at the top of the Keyboard Shortcuts dialog box.

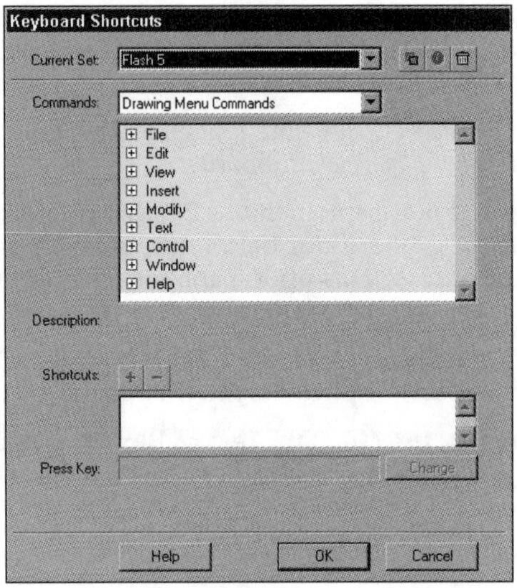

Figure A-2:
The
Keyboard
Shortcuts
dialog box
enables you
to bend
Flash to
your
individual
taste.

After you have a new set of shortcuts, choose the types of commands you want to change from the Commands drop-down list. You can change all three types of commands, but only one at a time:

- **Drawing Menu Commands** changes shortcuts for commands from the menu.

- **Drawing Tools** changes shortcuts for the tools in the Drawing toolbox.

- **Test Movie Menu Commands** changes shortcuts for commands from the menu that appears when you choose Control➪Test Movie.

For each type of command set, click the plus (+) sign (Windows) or the right-pointing arrow (Mac) on the list to display all the commands and their current shortcuts. Here's how to create a new shortcut:

1. **Select the command you want to customize.**

2. **Click the Add Shortcut button.**

   Flash adds a new shortcut named empty.

3. **Press the keyboard combination you want to use.**

   You must include Ctrl (Windows) or ⌘ (Mac). Flash tells you whether that combination is already assigned to another shortcut.

   - If you want to use that shortcut, click Change. Flash alerts you if the shortcut is already taken and lets you reassign the shortcut.

- If you don't want to use that shortcut, with the empty shortcut selected in the Shortcuts list, click Remove shortcut.

4. **Repeat Steps 2 and 3 to change as many shortcuts as you want.**

5. **Click OK when you finish changing shortcuts.**

Until you get used to your new shortcuts, create a list and tape it to the side of your monitor for easy reference.

Appendix B

The Toolbox and the Panels

· ·

*T*he toolbox has changed in Flash 5, and the panels are completely new. In this appendix, we help you discover these features in more detail. The panels, especially, have many unlabeled buttons and menus that hold hidden treasures, or at least hidden features, if you know where to look.

The Drawing Toolbox

The Drawing toolbox contains all of the drawing tools as well as many editing tools. Each drawing tool has its own *modifiers* that control how the drawing tool works. Here you see only one set of modifiers. See Chapter 3 for the full scoop.

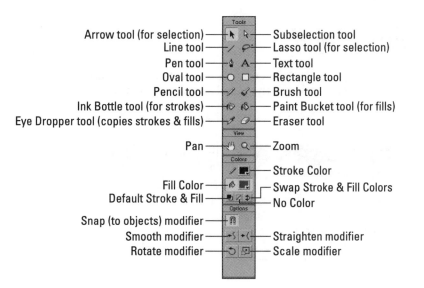

Arrow tool (for selection) — Subselection tool
Line tool — Lasso tool (for selection)
Pen tool — Text tool
Oval tool — Rectangle tool
Pencil tool — Brush tool
Ink Bottle tool (for strokes) — Paint Bucket tool (for fills)
Eye Dropper tool (copies strokes & fills) — Eraser tool
Pan — Zoom
Stroke Color
Fill Color — Swap Stroke & Fill Colors
Default Stroke & Fill — No Color
Snap (to objects) modifier
Smooth modifier — Straighten modifier
Rotate modifier — Scale modifier

The Info Panel

The Info panel lets you control the precise size and location of objects. (See Chapter 4 for more information on using this panel.) The X and Y measurements are relative to the top-left corner of the Stage.

Reference point of object
(click either the top-left corner or the middle)

Width of object | X (horizontal) location of object

Height of object

Y (vertical) location of object

The Fill Panel

The Fill panel lets you create fills — solid, linear gradient, radial gradient, and bitmap. Here you see the panel as it appears for a solid fill. (See Chapter 3 for lots more.)

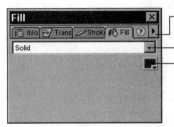

Option menu to add a new gradient to the color swatch list

Type of fill

Fill color

The Stroke Panel

The Stroke panel defines strokes, or lines. You can define the type of line — solid, dashed, dotted, and so on — as well as the width and the color. (See Chapter 3 for the full story.)

Option menu to create a custom line type

Preview window   Stroke color

Line type   Stroke width

The Mixer Panel

The Mixer panel is like an artist's palette. You can create your own colors for both strokes (lines) and fills.

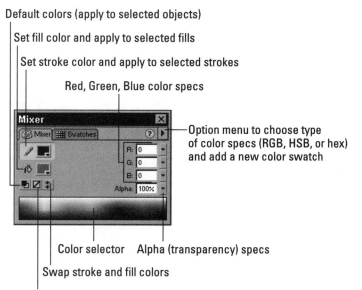

Default colors (apply to selected objects)

Set fill color and apply to selected fills

Set stroke color and apply to selected strokes

Red, Green, Blue color specs

Option menu to choose type of color specs (RGB, HSB, or hex) and add a new color swatch

Color selector   Alpha (transparency) specs

Swap stroke and fill colors

No fill or stroke (depending on which button is active)

The Transform Panel

Use the Transform panel to scale, rotate, and skew objects with precision. You scale by percent and you rotate and skew by degrees (increasing degrees going clockwise). To use the Copy and Apply Transform button: Select an object and specify any transform settings you want. Then click Copy and Apply Transform. Flash creates a new object with the new settings, on top of the old object. You can leave it there to create a composite object or immediately move it to a new location. (See Chapter 4 for more about this panel.)

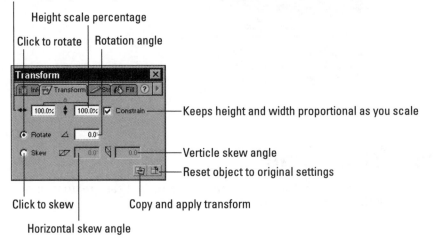

Width scale percentage

Height scale percentage

Click to rotate | Rotation angle

Keeps height and width proportional as you scale

Verticle skew angle

Reset object to original settings

Click to skew | Copy and apply transform

Horizontal skew angle

The Swatches Panel

You can use the Swatches panel to manage your colors. New colors and fills that you create appear here. (See Chapter 3 for more information.)

Option menu for managing swatches

Solid swatches

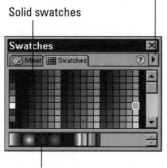

Gradient swatches

The Character Panel

You can tell that this panel has good character, so you can always trust what it says about your text objects.

Point size   Font color

Bold   Italic

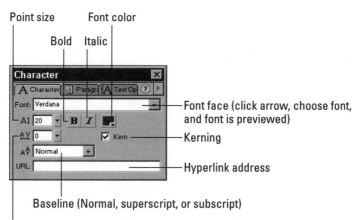

Font face (click arrow, choose font, and font is previewed)

Kerning

Hyperlink address

Baseline (Normal, superscript, or subscript)

Tracking (space between letters)

The Paragraph Panel

Use the Paragraph panel to set margins, indents, and line spacing. Boring, but sometimes useful.

Left margin

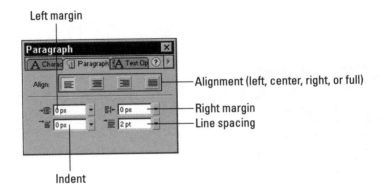

Alignment (left, center, right, or full)

Right margin

Line spacing

Indent

The Text Options Panel

The Text Options panel lets you format text for forms and dynamically update text (like the kind that shows the latest stock prices). You can also create variables to be sent to a database.

Choose Single Line or Multiline

Type of text

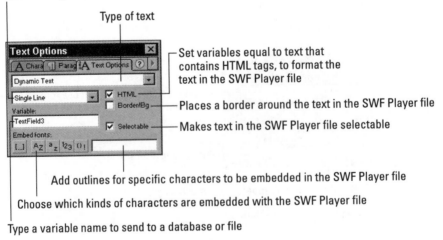

Set variables equal to text that contains HTML tags, to format the text in the SWF Player file

Places a border around the text in the SWF Player file

Makes text in the SWF Player file selectable

Add outlines for specific characters to be embedded in the SWF Player file

Choose which kinds of characters are embedded with the SWF Player file

Type a variable name to send to a database or file

The Instance Panel

The Instance panel controls symbol instances. You can change their type (movie clip, button, or graphic) and add properties appropriate for that symbol type. Remember that in order to target an instance using TellTarget, you must give an instance a name. (See Chapter 7 for more about this panel.)

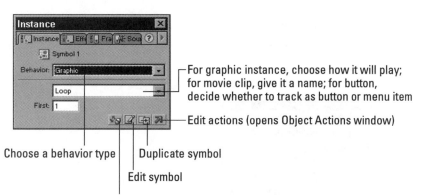

For graphic instance, choose how it will play; for movie clip, give it a name; for button, decide whether to track as button or menu item

Edit actions (opens Object Actions window)

Choose a behavior type   Duplicate symbol

Edit symbol

Swap symbols (turn one symbol into another)

The Clip Parameters Panel

You can assign variables with values to a movie clip to create a "smart" clip, a new feature for Flash 5. By adding ActionScript to the smart clip, you can create check boxes, pop-up menus, and more, which users can use to choose options. You define the parameters by choosing Define Clip Parameters on the Library Options menu and changing the values in the Clip Parameters panel. Here is a Frame variable with its value set to 1.

The Effect Panel

Use the Effect panel to change the color, brightness, and transparency of instances of symbols, without changing their parent symbols. The bottom part of the panel changes depending on which effect you choose. Here, the Tint effect is chosen. (See Chapter 7.)

Choose the type of effect you want to change on the instance

Percent of the chosen color to use

Choose a Tint (color)

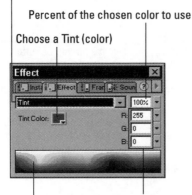

Define the color here using Red, Green, and Blue values

You can also choose a color here

The Frame Panel

The Frame panel is the place to create tweening and label frames. (Chapter 9 gives the lowdown on these topics.)

Create an acceleration or deceleration effect

Choose type of tweening

Give frame a label here

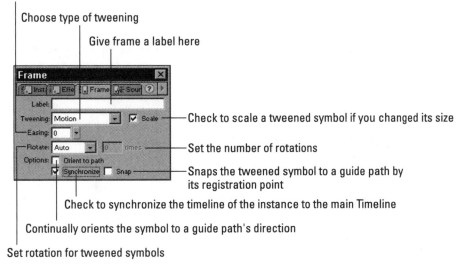

Check to scale a tweened symbol if you changed its size

Set the number of rotations

Snaps the tweened symbol to a guide path by its registration point

Check to synchronize the timeline of the instance to the main Timeline

Continually orients the symbol to a guide path's direction

Set rotation for tweened symbols

The Sound Panel

If sound's your thing, the Sound panel's your place. The Sound panel enables you to define the properties of sounds you insert into your movie. (See Chapter 11 for more details.)

The sound's stats

Choose the sound you have imported here

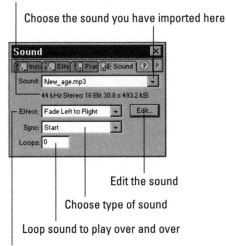

Edit the sound

Choose type of sound

Loop sound to play over and over

Add effects such as fading from left to right

The Scene Panel

The Scene panel is quite simple. Here you can move from one scene to another, change the order of scenes, as well as rename, add, and delete scenes.

Name and reorder scenes here

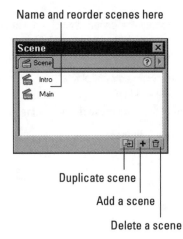

Duplicate scene

Add a scene

Delete a scene

Appendix C

What Those Obscure Terms Really Mean

● ●

absolute path: A complete description of the location of a file. On the Internet, this usually starts with `http://` and continues with the complete URL and filename (for example, `http://www.ellenfinkelstein.com/ index.html`). On a computer, an absolute path would start with the disk drive, such as C, and continue with the folder and filename.

action: An expression in ActionScript, the Flash scripting language, for controlling objects and creating interactivity in a movie (see Chapter 10).

ActionScript: The Flash scripting language. Uses a syntax similar to JavaScript for controlling objects and movies and creating interactivity in a movie.

ActiveX control: ActiveX controls are software building blocks that are often small enough to be downloaded over the Internet and that can provide extra functionality inside Windows applications. For example, one Flash ActiveX control enables you to play a Flash Player movie from within Microsoft Office documents.

adaptive color palette: A set (palette) of colors based on the actual colors in the image and used for accurate color representation. Flash can export GIF images with an adaptive color palette (see Chapter 13).

AIFF sound: A sound stored in the Audio Interchange File Format developed by Apple. Flash can import AIFF sounds (see Chapter 11).

alpha: Transparency. Flash can change the transparency of colors so that you can create see-through objects (see Chapter 3).

anchor point: A point that you specify when creating a Bezier curve or line segment with the Pen tool. An anchor point helps define the shape of the object (see Chapter 3).

antialiasing: A method of displaying objects so that they appear smoother. Aliasing is the jaggedness you get when you try to draw a diagonal line on the checkboard-like grid of the computer screen. Flash can antialias text, bitmaps, and shapes, both on the screen and when publishing movies.

authoring environment: The place where you create Flash movies (the Stage and the Timeline).

AVI: The Windows bitmap-based movie format. Flash can export to AVI format (see Chapter 13).

bit-depth: The number of binary digits (ones and zeros) of information per dot of color. A bit-depth of 8 gives you a palette of 2^8 colors (256 colors). A bit-depth of 24 (also called 24-bit color) gives you 2^{24} colors (more than 16 million), which is good for rendering photographic images.

bitmap: A type of graphic image made up of dots (see Chapter 2).

bit rate: A measurement of the quality of a sound, measured in kilobits per second — Kbps (see Chapter 11).

brightness: The lightness (or darkness) of an image (see Chapter 3).

button: Not the thing that holds your coat on. A button is an image that you click with your mouse. It often takes you to another page on the Web but can also display more information, start a Flash movie, and so on (see Chapter 8).

CGI script: A Computer Gateway Interface script. A computer program running on a Web server that can dynamically interact with a Web page. For example, software engineers use CGI scripts to enable users to search the database of an online bookseller for books by a specified author.

compression, sound: A method of reducing the size of sound files (see Chapters 11 and 13).

dithering: A method of combining existing colors in a color palette to approximate colors not in the palette. You can choose the dithering method when exporting a GIF file (see the GIF section in Chapter 13).

download: To copy software (such as an application or a document) from one computer (usually a computer somewhere out there on the World Wide Web) onto your computer.

Down state, button: The state of a button when you click it with your mouse (see Chapter 8).

easing, animation: A way of changing the pace of tweened motion animation so that the movement either speeds up or slows down throughout the time of the motion (see Chapter 9).

editable text: Text that users can change as they view your Flash movie on a Web site (see Chapter 10).

EMBED **parameter:** The HTML code required by Netscape Communicator/ Navigator to display a Flash player movie (see Chapter 13).

Expert mode: The view of the Action panel that lets you write ActionScript from scratch.

fill: An object that fills in a shape. You create fills with the brush and paint bucket tools. The oval and rectangle tools create fills and can also create strokes around the fills.

Flash Player file: The file with an extension of .swf that you create when you publish your Flash movie (which has an extension of .fla). You can only display an SWF file on a Web site.

frame: A representation of a small amount of time on the Timeline in an animation. By default, a frame represents $\frac{1}{12}$ of a second. Many frames displayed one after another create animation (see Chapter 9).

GIF: A compressed bitmap graphic file format often used on the Web. An animated GIF can display short animations. The GIF format is usually used for simple line art. The GIF format utilizes patented software code that makes its use politically objectionable in the view of some, which inspired the development of the nonpatented PNG file format (see Chapter 9).

gradient: A fill that varies in color. Flash can create linear gradients that create striped effects and radial gradients that create concentric effects (see Chapter 3).

group: A set of objects that function as one object for purposes of selection and editing (see Chapter 4).

guide layer: A layer that contains an object, usually a curved shape or series of line segments, which guides an animated object's motion. A bird flying in a circle is one example (see Chapter 9).

Hit state, button: The area of the movie that responds when the mouse clicks the button (see Chapter 8).

HTML: Hypertext Markup Language. The code most commonly used to create Web pages.

instance: A copy of a symbol that you can use on the Stage and for animation. You can change certain properties of instances without affecting the symbol (see Chapter 7).

interactivity: The ability of a Flash movie to respond to users. An example is clicking a button to turn off music (see Chapter 10).

interlacing: A way to display a GIF file as it loads so that the viewer sees the entire graphic but in increasingly clear values.

JPEG: A highly compressed, 24-bit bitmap graphic format. The JPEG format is usually used for photographs and other graphics with many colors.

kerning: A way to control the spacing between pairs of characters, such as A and V (see Chapter 5).

keyframe: A frame on the Timeline that contains a change in animation. For example, in order to create tweened animation, you need to create keyframes at the beginning and end of the tween (see Chapter 9).

layer: A level on the Stage that contains objects. Because objects on different layers cannot interact with each other, you use layers to organize objects. Different animations should always be on different layers (see Chapter 6).

Library: The storehouse for symbols, imported bitmaps, and sounds (see Chapter 2).

loop: To replay a movie over and over again. By default, movie clips loop. Also, the default setting when publishing a movie is to loop the movie (see Chapters 7 and 13).

mask: A special kind of layer that hides objects on layers below it. You can put a shape on a mask layer to reveal objects on lower layers within that shape (see Chapter 6).

motion path: A path, created with the line, pencil, or other tool, which defines the motion of an object in a motion tween. The motion path is on a guide layer (see Chapter 9).

motion tween: An animation that moves objects, created by defining the beginning and end points and letting Flash automatically fill in the in-between motion (see Chapter 9).

movie: A Flash file created in the authoring environment.

movie clip: Animation contained in a symbol. You can then place the symbol on the main Timeline so that you are playing a movie within the main movie (see Chapter 7).

Movie Explorer: The new Flash 5 feature for discovering all the components of a movie, including objects, layers, actions, and so on (see Chapter 12).

MP3: A highly compressed sound file format. Flash 5 can import MP3 files (see Chapter 11).

navigation: A set of buttons or hyperlinked text that enable the viewer of a Web site move through the various Web pages.

Normal mode: The view of the Action panel that lets you create ActionScript by selecting from a list of actions and parameters (see Chapter 10).

OBJECT parameter: The HTML code required by Internet Explorer to display a Flash player movie (see Chapter 13).

On Clip Event handler: A way to define what event, such as a frame loading, triggers the action in a movie clip (see Chapter 10).

On Mouse Event handler: A way to define what happens when the mouse interacts in different ways with a button, such as passing over it or clicking it (see Chapter 10).

Onion Skin mode: A method of viewing animation so that you see all the frames at once.

orient to path: A setting that rotates an object in a motion tween in the direction of its motion path. A bird turning as it flies is one example (see Chapter 9).

Over state, button: The state of a button when the mouse cursor passes over it (see Chapter 8).

palette: A set of colors that are available for use in drawing or publishing a graphic file.

panel: A new interface feature of Flash 5 that makes various settings available in tabbed windows.

PICT: A Macintosh graphic file format that can be either a bitmap or a vector file.

PNG: A bitmap graphic file format supported by both Windows and Macs that supports transparency.

pressure-sensitive tablet: A flat surface for drawing that is connected to a computer. The tablet usually comes with a stylus that looks like a pen. A pressure-sensitive tablet responds to the pressure you use with the stylus, to create variable-width lines, for example (see Chapter 3).

publish: To create a Flash Player file (SWF file) that can be viewed on a Web site (see Chapter 13).

relative path: A description of the location of a file, relative to another file, so that you don't have to describe the entire location. For example, if a file is in the same folder as the first file, you can just specify the filename, such as `index.html`.

RGB color: A method of defining a color according to the amount of red, green, and blue it contains (see Chapter 3).

sample rate: A means of controlling the fidelity and size of a sound file. Higher sample rates sound better but result in larger files (see Chapter 11).

scene: A division of a movie, used to help organize the movie into parts (see Chapter 9).

shape hint: A means of specifying how a shape tween changes shape (see Chapter 9).

shape tween: An animation in which one shape changes into another shape; you define the first and last shapes and Flash automatically fills in the intermediate shapes (see Chapter 9).

shared library: A library resting on a computer server that can be accessed by a Flash Player file (SWF file); used to make Player files smaller (see Chapter 2).

Stage: The rectangle in the middle of the Flash screen where you place objects for animation.

stroke: A line or outline. For example, a circle or rectangle can have an outline (see Chapter 3).

SWF: The filename extension for a Flash Player file. An SWF file can be displayed on a Web site. (A Flash FLA file cannot be displayed on a Web site.)

symbol: A named, saved object or set of objects. Symbols are stored in the Library and can be motion tweened. You can create instances of symbols and place them on the Stage (see Chapter 7).

synchronization, animation: A means to make sure that animation in a movie clip keeps pace with the number of frames it occupies in the main Timeline (see Chapter 9).

tablet, pressure-sensitive: See *pressure-sensitive tablet.*

tangent handle: A marker displayed when drawing with the Pen tool that determines the direction of a curve.

target: The object of an expression in ActionScript, specifically a Timeline. For example, if a movie clip tells the main movie what to do, the main movie's Timeline is the target.

template: A group of settings for the HTML code used to display a Flash Player file (SWF file). Flash offers a number of templates that you can use (see Chapter 13).

Timeline: A movie's set of frames along which the animation runs (see Chapter 9).

tween: See *Motion tween* and *Shape tween.*

type: Another word for *typography* or *text* (see Chapter 5).

upload: To copy software (such as an application or a document) from your computer to another computer (usually a computer somewhere out there on the World Wide Web).

variable: In ActionScript, a named holder for a value that you can retrieve for use in a script or a database.

vector: A definition of a distance and a direction. Vector graphics, such as those in Flash, are defined by equations, rather than the dots used in bitmap graphics (see Chapter 2).

WAV: A Windows sound format (see Chapter 11).

Web-safe color: A color that appears the same on all computer systems and in all browsers. There are 216 Web-safe colors, and they are defined by using a hexadecimal system (see Chapter 3).

Appendix D

What's on the CD-ROM

* *

*H*ere is some of the cool stuff that you'll find on the *Flash 5 For Dummies* CD-ROM:

- ✔ A collection of trial software from Macromedia, including Flash 5 (of course), Freehand 9, Generator 2, Fireworks 3.0, Dreamweaver 3.0, and a demo for ScreenTime for Flash, which lets you create screen savers from Flash movies.

- ✔ A library of geometric, whimsical, and artistic vector graphics ready to be instantly opened in any Flash movie.

- ✔ Over two dozen Flash movies that you can dissect and learn from.

System Requirements

Make sure that your computer meets the minimum system requirements in the following list. If your computer doesn't match up to these requirements, you may experience problems in using the contents of the CD:

- ✔ A PC with a 133 MHz Pentium or faster processor or a Mac OS computer with a Power PC processor.

- ✔ Microsoft Windows 95/98/2000, Windows NT 4.0 or later, or Mac OS system software 8.1 or later.

- ✔ At least 32MB of total RAM (Windows) or 32MB of free application RAM (Mac) installed on your computer. For best performance, we recommend at least 64MB of RAM installed.

- ✔ At least 204MB of hard drive space available to install all the software from this CD. (You need less space if you don't install every program.)

- ✔ A CD-ROM drive.

- ✔ A sound card for PCs. (Mac OS computers have built-in sound support.)

- ✔ A monitor capable of displaying at least 256 colors and 800 x 600 resolution or better.

- ✔ A modem with a speed of at least 14,400 bps.

Using the CD with Windows

Follow these steps to access the software on the book's CD:

1. **Insert the CD into your computer's CD-ROM drive.**

2. **Click Start⇨Run.**

3. **In the dialog box that appears, type** D:\START.HTM

   Replace *D* with the proper drive letter if your CD-ROM drive uses a different letter. (If you don't know the letter, see how your CD-ROM drive is listed under My Computer.)

   Your browser opens and the license agreement is displayed. If you do not have a browser, we include Microsoft Internet Explorer and Netscape Communicator on the CD.

4. **Read through the license agreement, nod your head, and then click the Accept button if you want to use the CD — after you click Accept, you'll jump to the Main Menu.**

5. **To navigate within the interface, click any topic of interest to take you to an explanation of the files on the CD and how to use or install them.**

6. **To install the software from the CD, click the software name.**

   You'll see two options — the option to run or open the file from the current location or the option to save the file to your hard drive. Choose to run or open the file from its current location, and the installation procedure will continue. After you are done with the interface, simply close your browser as usual.

Using the CD with the Mac OS

To install the items from the CD to your hard drive, follow these steps:

1. **Insert the CD into your computer's CD-ROM drive.**

   In a moment, an icon representing the CD you just inserted appears on your Mac desktop. The icon probably looks like a CD-ROM.

2. **Double-click the CD icon to show the CD's contents.**

3. **Double-click the Read Me First icon.**

   This text file contains information about the CD's programs and any last-minute instructions you need to know about installing the programs on the CD that we don't cover in this appendix.

4. **Click the Close box to close the Read Me document.**

5. **Open your browser.**

   In case you don't have a browser, we include the two most popular ones: Microsoft Internet Explorer and Netscape Communicator.

6. **Choose File⇨Open File (in Internet Explorer, or File⇨Open⇨Location in Navigator) and select the CD titled** Flash 5 For Dummies.

7. **Double-click the** Links.htm **file to see an explanation of all files and folders included on the CD; then click the Close box when you finish reviewing the file.**

8. **To open programs that come with installers, open the program's folder on the CD and double-click the icon** Install **or** Installer.

Software on the CD-ROM

The following sections tell you what software you'll find on the CD.

Dreamweaver 3.0

For Mac OS 8.1 or later and Windows 95, 98, or NT 4.0 or later. Trial version.

Dreamweaver is one of the premier Web site authoring programs. As a result, Flash and Dreamweaver make a great match. You can use Dreamweaver to create HTML pages and add your Flash Player files to them with ease. Visit Macromedia at www.macromedia.com/software/dreamweaver/.

Fireworks 3.0

For Mac OS 8.1 or later and Windows 95, 98, or NT (with Service Pack 3) or later. Trial version.

Fireworks is Macromedia's Web graphics creation program. Its features include both bitmap and vector graphic editing tools. Check out the Macromedia site at www.macromedia.com/software/fireworks/.

Flash 5

For Mac OS 8.1 or later and Windows 95, 98, or NT 4 or later. Trial version.

If you've gotten this far, you know all about Flash 5. For information and updates, go to www.macromedia.com/software/flash.

Freehand 9

For Mac OS 8.1 or later and Windows 95, 98, or NT 4 (with Service Pack 3) or later. Trial version.

For great vector graphics, Macromedia's Freehand is your tool. Because Freehand creates vector graphics, many Flash developers create graphics with Freehand and import them into Flash. Freehand's sophisticated drawing tools are used for print graphics as well as for the Web. For information and updates, visit `www.macromedia.com/software/freehand/`.

Generator 2 EE

For Windows 95, 98, or NT 4 (with Service Pack 5 or later) or later. Trial version.

Generator 2 Enterprise Edition lets you deliver continually changing content to a Web site. You can, for example, use it to create sites personalized for each viewer. For more information, go to the Macromedia Web site at `www.macromedia.com/software/generator/`.

Photoshop 5.5

For Windows 95, 98, NT 4, or later. Tryout version.

This popular and highly respected photo-manipulation program from Adobe Systems, Inc. is a must-have for any serious graphic designer and a great tool for developing Web graphics. To learn more, check out the Adobe Web site at `www.adobe.com`.

ScreenTime for Flash

For Mac OS 8.1 or later and Windows 95, 98, or NT 4 or later. Demo version.

ScreenTime for Flash lets you convert your Macromedia Flash movies into screen savers. The version on the CD-ROM is just a demo. For more information and updates, visit the Macsourcery site at `www.macsourcery.com/ScreenTime/screentime.html`.

Shockwave & Flash Player

For Mac OS 8.1 or later and Windows 95, 98, or NT 4 or later. Trial version.

The Shockwave Player is to Director 8 Shockwave Studio what the Flash Player is to Flash. Director 8 Shockwave Studio is a Macromedia program for combining graphics, sound, animation, text, and video to create streaming, interactive Web content. Director files are viewed with the Shockwave player. In the same way, Flash Player files are viewed with the Flash Player.

For more information on Director, go to www.macromedia.com/software/director/. For more information on the Shockwave Player, go to www.macromedia.com/software/ and look for the link to the Shockwave Player.

MindSpring Internet Access 4.0

For Windows 95/98/NT 4 or later and Mac. Commercial version.

If you don't have an Internet connection, the CD includes sign-on software for MindSpring, from MindSpring Enterprises, Inc., an Internet Service Provider (ISP) with award-winning customer support. (*Mac users:* The registration key for installing the Mac version of MindSpring is DUMY8579. Be sure to type it exactly as shown here, including capital letters.) You need a credit card to sign up with MindSpring. Go to www.mindspring.com for more information.

If you already have an Internet Service Provider, please note that the MindSpring Internet software makes changes to your computer's current Internet configuration and may replace your current settings. These changes may prevent you from being able to access the Internet through your current provider.

Microsoft Internet Explorer 5.5 Web browser

For Mac and Windows. Commercial product.

This is the popular, powerful Web browser from Microsoft that's packed with all the latest features for today's cybertravels. It's also free, which makes it a true bargain. This program is updated frequently, so check out the Microsoft Web site at www.microsoft.com.

Netscape Communicator 4.7

For Windows and Mac. Commercial version.

This free suite of programs from Netscape includes a full-featured browser (Navigator), e-mail program (Messenger), and an HTML editor (Composer). This program is updated frequently, so be sure to check out the Netscape site at home.netscape.com.

Your Own Personal Library

We've created over 50 vector graphics that you can use in your Flash movies. Some are geometric shapes that are hard to create in Flash. We added some "fun" shapes, some practical and others whimsical, such as our thought bubble and explosion. Finally, we included some artistic drawings of every-day objects. We hope you like them! (Please keep in mind that these files are provided for your personal use and are not to be sold or redistributed.)

All you see when you open the Flash file is a blank screen. To see the graphics, choose Window⇨Library. To use these shapes in another Flash file, choose File⇨Open as Library and choose Flash 5 for Dummies Library.fla.

An even better idea is to copy the FLA file from the CD-ROM to the Libraries subfolder of your Flash 5 folder. Then you can access this file at any time by choosing Window⇨Common Libraries.

Flash Movies Galore

Throughout the book, we refer you to the CD-ROM to look at Flash movies as examples of the features we are explaining. These movies are organized by chapter. They help you understand some of the more complex capabilities of Flash that are hard to explain or show in a figure. Some of these are real-world Flash movies that come from active Web sites. Others are examples we have created for you to isolate the Flash feature. Either way, we hope you can use these to further your understanding of Flash.

Note: Here are a few troubleshooting things to keep in mind when you use the Flash movie files provided on the CD:

- **Copy movie files to your hard drive.** Don't try choosing Control⇨Test Movie to test a movie directly from the CD. Copy the FLA file to your hard drive and then test the movie.

- **The Flash movie doesn't play.** Sometimes when you open a Flash movie, nothing happens when you try to play the animation. Choose Control⇨Test Movie to see the animation.

- **The fonts look different.** If some of the fonts required by the Flash files aren't available on your system, you may see less-than-satisfactory substitutions when you play the Flash Player files.

Resolving Your CD Problems

We tried our best to compile programs that work on most computers with the minimum system requirements. Alas, your computer may differ, and some programs may not work correctly for some reason.

The two likeliest problems are that you don't have enough memory (RAM) for the programs you want to use, or you have other programs running that are affecting installation or running of a program. If you get error messages like `Not enough memory` or `Setup cannot continue`, try one or more of these methods and then try using the software again:

- ✔ **Turn off any antivirus software that you have on your computer during the installation of the software:** Installers sometimes mimic virus activity and may make your computer incorrectly believe that a virus is infecting it. You'll undoubtedly want to turn your antivirus software back on when you're finished installing the software.

- ✔ **Close all running programs:** The more programs you run, the less memory is available to other programs. Installers also typically update files and programs. So if you keep other programs running, installation may not work correctly.

- ✔ **Have your local computer store add more RAM to your computer:** This step is, admittedly, drastic and somewhat expensive. But adding more memory can really help the speed of your computer and enable more programs to run at the same time.

If you still have trouble installing the items from the CD, please call the IDG Books Worldwide Customer Service phone number: 800-762-2974 (outside the U.S.: 317-572-3993).

Index

IDG Books Worldwide, Inc., End-User License Agreement

5. **Limited Warranty.**

   (a) IDGB warrants that the Software and Software Media are free from defects in materials and workmanship under normal use for a period of sixty (60) days from the date of purchase of this Book. If IDGB receives notification within the warranty period of defects in materials or workmanship, IDGB will replace the defective Software Media.

   (b) IDGB AND THE AUTHOR OF THE BOOK DISCLAIM ALL OTHER WARRANTIES, EXPRESS OR IMPLIED, INCLUDING WITHOUT LIMITATION IMPLIED WARRANTIES OF MERCHANTABILITY AND FITNESS FOR A PARTICULAR PURPOSE, WITH RESPECT TO THE SOFTWARE, THE PROGRAMS, THE SOURCE CODE CONTAINED THEREIN, AND/OR THE TECHNIQUES DESCRIBED IN THIS BOOK. IDGB DOES NOT WARRANT THAT THE FUNCTIONS CONTAINED IN THE SOFTWARE WILL MEET YOUR REQUIRE-MENTS OR THAT THE OPERATION OF THE SOFTWARE WILL BE ERROR FREE.

   (c) This limited warranty gives you specific legal rights, and you may have other rights that vary from jurisdiction to jurisdiction.

6. **Remedies.**

   (a) IDGB's entire liability and your exclusive remedy for defects in materials and workmanship shall be limited to replacement of the Software Media, which may be returned to IDGB with a copy of your receipt at the following address: Software Media Fulfillment Department, Attn.: *Flash 5 For Dummies,* IDG Books Worldwide, Inc., 10475 Crosspoint Blvd., Indianapolis, IN 46256, or call 800-762-2974. Please allow three to four weeks for delivery. This Limited Warranty is void if failure of the Software Media has resulted from accident, abuse, or misapplication. Any replacement Software Media will be warranted for the remainder of the original warranty period or thirty (30) days, whichever is longer.

   (b) In no event shall IDGB or the author be liable for any damages whatsoever (including without limitation damages for loss of business profits, business interruption, loss of business information, or any other pecuniary loss) arising from the use of or inability to use the Book or the Software, even if IDGB has been advised of the possibility of such damages.

   (c) Because some jurisdictions do not allow the exclusion or limitation of liability for consequential or incidental damages, the above limitation or exclusion may not apply to you.

7. **U.S. Government Restricted Rights.** Use, duplication, or disclosure of the Software by the U.S. Government is subject to restrictions stated in paragraph (c)(1)(ii) of the Rights in Technical Data and Computer Software clause of DFARS 252.227-7013, and in subparagraphs (a) through (d) of the Commercial Computer–Restricted Rights clause at FAR 52.227-19, and in similar clauses in the NASA FAR supplement, when applicable.

8. **General.** This Agreement constitutes the entire understanding of the parties and revokes and supersedes all prior agreements, oral or written, between them and may not be modified or amended except in a writing signed by both parties hereto that specifically refers to this Agreement. This Agreement shall take precedence over any other documents that may be in conflict herewith. If any one or more provisions contained in this Agreement are held by any court or tribunal to be invalid, illegal, or otherwise unenforceable, each and every other provision shall remain in full force and effect.

Installation Instructions

The *Flash 5 For Dummies* CD offers valuable information that you won't want to miss. The following sections tell you how to install the items from the CD.

Using the CD with Windows

To install the items to the hard drive on your Windows machine, follow these steps:

1. **Insert the CD into your computer's CD-ROM drive.**
2. **Click Start⇨Run.**
3. **In the dialog box that appears, type** D:\START.HTM.

   Your browser opens and displays the license agreement.
4. **Read through the license agreement, nod your head, and click the Accept button; the Main menu appears.**
5. **To navigate within the interface, click any topic of interest to take you to an explanation of the files on the CD and how to use or install them.**
6. **To install the software from the CD, click the software name and choose to run or open the file from its current location.**

Using the CD with the Mac OS

To install the items to the hard drive of your Mac, follow these steps:

1. **Insert the CD into your computer's CD-ROM drive and double-click the CD icon to display the CD's contents.**
2. **Double-click the Read Me First icon; read the file and close the window.**
3. **Open your browser.**
4. **Choose File⇨Open File (or File⇨Open⇨Location in Netscape) and select the CD titled** Flash 5 For Dummies.
5. **Double-click the** Links.htm **file to see an explanation of all files and folders included on the CD; then close the window.**
6. **To open programs that come with installers, open the program's folder on the CD and double-click the** Install **or** Installer **icon.**

For more complete information, see Appendix D, "What's on the CD-Rom."

Discover Dummies Online!

The Dummies Web Site is your fun and friendly online resource for the latest information about *For Dummies* books and your favorite topics. The Web site is the place to communicate with us, exchange ideas with other *For Dummies* readers, chat with authors, and have fun!

Ten Fun and Useful Things You Can Do at www.dummies.com

1. Win free *For Dummies* books and more!
2. Register your book and be entered in a prize drawing.
3. Meet your favorite authors through the IDG Books Worldwide Author Chat Series.
4. Exchange helpful information with other *For Dummies* readers.
5. Discover other great *For Dummies* books you must have!
6. Purchase Dummieswear® exclusively from our Web site.
7. Buy *For Dummies* books online.
8. Talk to us. Make comments, ask questions, get answers!
9. Download free software.
10. Find additional useful resources from authors.

Link directly to these ten fun and useful things at
http://www.dummies.com/10useful

For other technology titles from IDG Books Worldwide, go to
www.idgbooks.com

Not on the Web yet? It's easy to get started with *Dummies 101*®: *The Internet For Windows*® *98* or *The Internet For Dummies*® at local retailers everywhere.

Find other *For Dummies* books on these topics:
Business • Career • Databases • Food & Beverage • Games • Gardening • Graphics • Hardware
Health & Fitness • Internet and the World Wide Web • Networking • Office Suites
Operating Systems • Personal Finance • Pets • Programming • Recreation • Sports
Spreadsheets • Teacher Resources • Test Prep • Word Processing

IDG BOOKS WORLDWIDE. BOOK REGISTRATION

We want to hear from you!

Visit **http://my2cents.dummies.com** to register this book and tell us how you liked it!

- Get entered in our monthly prize giveaway.

- Give us feedback about this book — tell us what you like best, what you like least, or maybe what you'd like to ask the author and us to change!

- Let us know any other *For Dummies*® topics that interest you.

Your feedback helps us determine what books to publish, tells us what coverage to add as we revise our books, and lets us know whether we're meeting your needs as a *For Dummies* reader. You're our most valuable resource, and what you have to say is important to us!

 on the Web yet? It's easy to get started with *Dummies 101®: The
et For Windows® 98* or *The Internet For Dummies®* at local retailers
 here.

 know what you think by sending us
 he following address:

 Book Registration

 Blvd.
 6256

BESTSELLING BOOK SERIES

roup, Inc.
istered